Resolutions of a Pastor

Resolutions of a Pastor

A Biblical, Theological, and Personal Vision for Ministry

MICHAEL E. POHLMAN

Foreword by Tom J. Nettles

WIPF & STOCK · Eugene, Oregon

RESOLUTIONS OF A PASTOR
A Biblical, Theological, and Personal Vision for Ministry

Copyright © 2025 Michael E. Pohlman. All rights reserved. Except for brief quotations in critical publications or reviews, no part of this book may be reproduced in any manner without prior written permission from the publisher. Write: Permissions, Wipf and Stock Publishers, 199 W. 8th Ave., Suite 3, Eugene, OR 97401.

Wipf & Stock
An Imprint of Wipf and Stock Publishers
199 W. 8th Ave., Suite 3
Eugene, OR 97401

www.wipfandstock.com

PAPERBACK ISBN: 978-1-7252-9191-1
HARDCOVER ISBN: 978-1-7252-9192-8
EBOOK ISBN: 978-1-7252-9193-5

VERSION NUMBER 031025

A version of chapter 10 originally appeared in *Healthy and Wealthy? A Biblical-Theological Response to the Prosperity Gospel*. Edited by Robert L. Plummer. Dallas: Fontes, 2022. Used by permission.

Appendix C, A Minister's Prayer, is reproduced with permission from Banner of Truth Trust (UK).

Scripture quotations are from The Holy Bible, English Standard Version (ESV), © 2001 by Crossway, a publishing ministry of Good News Publishers. Used by permission. All rights reserved.

To my students past, present, and future.
May God make you resolute pastors.

And to the saints of Providence Baptist Church.
May these resolutions bear fruit among us.

"But he considered again that he had no armor for his back; and therefore thought that to turn the back to him might give him the greater advantage with ease to pierce him with his darts. Therefore he resolved to venture and stand his ground; for, thought he, had I no more in mine eye than the saving of my life, it would be the best way to stand."

—Christian, as he prepared to meet Apollyon
in Bunyan's *Pilgrim's Progress*

Contents

Foreword by Tom J. Nettles | ix
Preface | xiii
Introduction | xv

1. God | 1
2. Scripture | 19
3. Gospel | 32
4. Humanity | 46
5. Church | 62
6. Doctrine | 75
7. Prayer | 91
8. Preaching | 104
9. Godliness | 122
10. Suffering | 140
11. Eternity | 155
12. Slowness | 169

Epilogue: The Courage to Be a Pastor | 178

APPENDIX A: Paul's Vision for Ministry and Us:
An Exposition of Colossians 1:24–29 | 183

APPENDIX B: An Excerpt from the Second Helvetic Confession (1566) | 195

APPENDIX C: A Minister's Prayer | 197

Bibliography | 199
Index | 205

Foreword

Tom J. Nettles

Back in the day of hymn-singing, we sang with gusto a Palmer Hartsough hymn entitled "I Am Resolved." It contained some simple assertions born of mature contemplation as to what was lasting and of eternal value in Christian pilgrimage—"I am resolved no longer to linger, charmed by the world's delight; things that are higher, things that are nobler, these have allured my sight. . . . Taught by the Bible, led by the Spirit, we'll walk the heavenly way." Resolution constitutes an excellent way of highlighting things of substantial value for the purpose of continuing inculcation into life. To make a resolution is to raise to the level of consciousness and determination a path for practice, a method for meditation, and a way to convey continuing conviction to the soul, that is, the affections, the will, and the judgment.

Michael Pohlman has isolated a dozen prominent biblical ideas that should shape the personal life, and thus, the ministerial calling and function, of God's preachers. *Resolutions of a Pastor* is a deadly serious book pointing its readers—hopefully a few thousand pastors—to the task of watching oneself and one's doctrine, for in so doing he will save himself and his hearers. Ministerial faithfulness does not develop by whims or casual engagement with changing theories of leadership but through clear, well-formed, consciously-formed convictional intentions—resolutions—that express the biblical revelation concerning the pastoral office. These biblically-induced principles contain no room for fluff, for indecisive wandering, for procrastination, for "me time," for man-centered speculation, or for spiritual cowardice. The Savior who calls us to take up the cross, endure suffering for the short time of this life is "the true One, He is the just One,

Foreword

He hath the words of life . . . Heed what he sayeth, do what He willeth, He is the living way."

Pohlman does not invite us to consider any idiosyncratic ideas sparkling with the coruscations of personal imagination and original experimentation. He invites us into the doctrinal wisdom of centuries of sober, learned, faithful, sound Christian reflection on the pastoral implications of each category of thought. Theologians ancient and modern, pertinent confessional syntheses, pastors, and biblically-grounded, ministerially-minded contemporary writers join a choir of testimony to the heavenly calling of scripturally defined pastoral convictions. Singing in unison or in rich harmonious chords are Luther, Calvin, Bunyan, Owen, Mastricht, Edwards, Spurgeon, Hodge, Warfield, Packer, Piper, Trueman, Wells, Horton, the Westminster documents, the Belgic Confession, the Heidelberg Catechism, the Second London Confession, the Canons of Dort, and others. Those whom Pohlman consults have resigned any claim to write or speak outside the revealed propositions of Scripture or to question the ever-abiding relevance of the pastoral calling and task.

While humbly consulting the abiding profundity of writers fettered to the Word of God, Pohlman does not omit his personal stewardship of biblical exposition of that same Word. Finally, he makes sure that each resolution has firm grounding in clearly stated exposition of pertinent passages. His biblical work shows faithfulness to the resolutions he commends (e.g., "Resolved to pastor according to the sufficiency of Scripture," "Resolved to be gospel-driven in ministry," "Resolved to know and love the church," "Resolved to teach sound doctrine," "Resolved to promote personal and corporate prayer," and "Resolved to preach the word"). Six other resolutions, equally important and germane to faithful full-orbed ministry provide the context of his expositional argument as foundational to the historical sources consulted.

In a most tasteful and relevant way, the author draws from personal experience to illustrate the context and impact of the theological reasoning behind each resolution. Conversion, education, professional life, marriage, pride, failure, suffering, preaching, and teaching provide instances of congruent illustration for a variety of implications relevant to the resolutions. This gives existential authenticity to each point with no surrender of the objective biblical and doctrinal argument concerning each point. To live one's life before the face of God, governed by Scripture, formed by the gospel, and thrust into the world for the sake of image-bearers and the biblical maturity of the church, challenges a person at the core of his being. Learning rightly to handle the Word of truth in the task of doctrinal development, saturating one's life with unceasing prayer for the sake of effective, God-honoring, Bible-illuminating, sinner-confronting preaching, brings forth the sincere prayer of lament, "Who is sufficient for these things?" Then to do this ministry, maintaining these convictions in the personal pursuit of godliness, willingness to suffer with Christ to be conformed to his image, with the present relevance and abiding motivation of the expectation of Christ's return in time and rule in eternity—to this the preacher must be resolved. To these biblical doctrines and principles a minister should aspire while realizing that the purpose of God calls for long-haul perseverance, progress by small degrees, and faith in the certain but often invisible operations of divine grace.

These resolutions constitute a representative and coherent summary of the requirements of biblical ministry. The church is prompted to examine the principles endemic to a man's perception of his internal call and to compare that testimony with observable evidence for the legitimacy of an external call. Long term faithfulness and spiritual usefulness arise from such resolve as is discussed here when deeply ingrained in the conscience by God's Spirit operating according to revealed truth. Modern doctrinal vapidity, flamboyant fame-driven ministry, capitulation to various cultural pressures, the fiery darts of the evil one, and the deceitfulness of indwelling sin are all ready to wage war against such pure, spiritual, biblical resolutions as are discussed here. Without resolve, however, the battle is lost before being engaged. With such resolution, by the power of truth and the persevering power and purpose of the Holy Spirit, "you may be able to stand in the evil day, and having done all, to stand" (Eph5:13b NKJV). "I am resolved to enter the kingdom, leaving the paths of sin; friends may oppose me, foes may beset me, still will I enter in."

Preface

This book has been a labor of love. But it has also been written with a deep sense of urgency given the state of the pastorate in America, and the times in which we live. Being a pastor has always been hard. I believe it is only getting harder.

There have been many books written in recent years decrying the weak state of the church to withstand, let alone confront, the increasing hostility toward Christianity in America and around the world. While there are many reasons for the compromised nature of the church in our day, I'm convinced the main reason has to do with pastors. Indeed, as the shepherds go so goes the church. Therefore, my contribution to help strengthen the church is to strengthen her pastors.

Writing a book is made far easier with the support of others who believe in your work. I am grateful to my colleagues at The Southern Baptist Theological Seminary for their encouragement and example of true pastor-theologians. Preeminent among them is Dr. Tom Nettles. He is a true scholar and churchman. His example of a lifetime of faithful gospel ministry is worthy of emulation. I wanted someone to write the foreword who embodies the vision for ministry I commend. Dr. Nettles is that man. I am humbled by, and deeply appreciative for, his willingness to be associated with my work.

Many of these ideas have been refined in the classroom over the last decade of teaching. In addition to lecture writing, I have benefited greatly from the questions and feedback from my students at Southern Seminary and Boyce College. Their engagement with much of this content has crystalized my thinking and deepened my convictions. The churches I've had the privilege to serve as a pastor have given me the invaluable experience and trust of shepherding real people so that this book is not mere theory. I am deeply grateful to Wipf & Stock for championing this project from

Preface

the beginning, and for managing editor Matthew Wimer's encouragement and patience throughout. This book is better than it would have been otherwise given the expert editorial work of Cheyenne Haste. And last but certainly not least, my wife Anna and children have been a constant stream of encouragement as they've joyfully supported their husband and father in countless ways for the sake of getting these resolutions in print. May their sacrifice bear much fruit.

Michael E. Pohlman
Louisville, Kentucky
December 2024

Introduction

Why Another Book on Pastoral Ministry?

THE EMINENT HISTORIAN, E. Brooks Holifield, considers Christian clergy in America as a prominent group of people exercising authority over vast sections of the population:

> Over the long course of American history, from the seventeenth century to the twenty-first, few occupational groups have been more prominent in the national culture than the Christian clergy. For the first 150 years of the colonial period, they had significant authority both in the local cultures of the villages and towns and in the broader realms of authorship, education, and institutional leadership. By the early eighteenth century, they were issuing laments and warnings about the decline of their influence, but their anxieties proved to be premature. Though now they occupy merely one niche in the manifold array of professional groups, the clergy still speak with authority to millions of Americans, and they oversee congregations encompassing 60 percent of the population.[1]

Understanding American clergy as an "occupational group" with the potential to influence such a large percentage of the population, it is not unreasonable to commend another book on pastoral ministry. Indeed, it is warranted given the opportunity pastors have to either help or hurt the millions of people they lead.

As a professor in a Protestant seminary dedicated to training the current and next generation of pastors, I am deeply concerned about the

---

1. Holifield, *God's Ambassadors*, 1.

Introduction

current state of clergy in America.² Too often today we hear of another fallen pastor and the collateral damage done to the congregation as a result of his fall. In our day, when high profile pastors are uncritically embracing trendy leadership philosophies from the world or ideologies not grounded in Scripture, it is perhaps more important than ever to present a biblical-theological vision for pastoral ministry. The stakes are too high and the cost too great to settle for anything less. As the unfortunate headlines of pastoral malpractice continue to mount, pastors need to be equipped with the timeless vision for ministry God holds out in his Word.³

With the promise of numerical growth, pastors are annually bombarded with new leadership techniques and paradigms for ministry. Many of these are influenced more by secular business philosophy, pragmatic thinking, and homespun advice than the Bible.⁴ The church is left spiritually impoverished and ill-equipped to face the challenges of secularization for want of a biblical-theological vision for ministry. And even as there are several books available today that seek to cast a theological vision for ministry, the vast majority of contemporary pastoral ministry books are more "how-to" manuals than works designed to teach pastors how to think theologically, and then act out of those theological convictions. This book fills a gap in the literature by being exegetically vigorous and obviously informed by biblical, historical, and systematic theology. The result is a robust work of pastoral theology able to meet the ministry challenges of the twenty-first century.⁵

---

2. For the purposes of this book, I limit my discussion of clergy to pastors in the Protestant tradition.

3. In this sense, I aim to do for pastoral theology what Roger Scruton did for the political philosophy known as conservatism: "It is nevertheless necessary to emphasize that this work is an exercise in doctrine; it attempts not to prove a political vision, but to express it. The aim is to find the concepts and beliefs with which to articulate in modern terms an outlook that is too sober and serious to be merely modern." See Scruton, *The Meaning of Conservatism*, vii–viii. Indeed, my vision for pastoral ministry is "too sober and serious" to be merely contemporary. As it is an expression of biblical truth, it is not bound by a period or an era, but timeless.

4. See, for example, Bolsinger, *Canoeing the Mountains*; Brenneman, *Homespun Gospel*; Groeschel, *It*; Hornsby, *The Attractional Church*; Powell, Mulder, and Griffin, *Growing Young*; Rainer and Rainer, *The Millennials*; Rainer, *Autopsy of a Deceased Church*; Sayers, *Facing Leviathan*; Scroggins, *How to Lead in a World of Distraction*; Stanley, *Deep and Wide*; Comer, *The Ruthless Elimination of Hurry*.

5. The shift in the American church away from a biblical-theological vision for pastoral ministry to a more programmatic one was accelerated with the popularity of Rick Warren's *Purpose Driven Church* (1995). That said, it is encouraging to see scholarship

Introduction

In a different era, but with a similar concern, the English Puritan Richard Baxter called his fellow clergy to reform. He dared to become their "monitor." In doing so, Baxter understood the risk to his reputation as many of his peers would consider him arrogant and immodest for airing his concerns in plain English. Thankfully, Baxter counted his reputation less important than the glory of God, the welfare of the church, and the salvation of people:

> But it is the mere necessity of the souls of men, and my desire of their salvation, and of the prosperity of the Church, which forceth me to this arrogance and immodesty, if so it must be called. For who, that hath a tongue, can be silent, when it is for the honour of God, the welfare of his Church, and the everlasting happiness of so many souls?[6]

This book is my effort toward a reformed pastor today.

The Glory of the Pastorate

In his classic work on pastoral ministry, Charles Bridges sought to capture the glory of the office:

> This is a great and excellent thing, for men to be set over the Church, that they may represent the person of the Son of God. The dignity however of the sacred office belongs to a kingdom "not of this world." It is distinguished therefore, not by the passing glitter of this world's vanity, but by eternal results, productive, even in their present influence, of the most solid and enduring happiness. For surely it is the highest dignity, if not the greatest happiness, that human nature is capable of here in this vale below, to have the soul so far enlightened as to become the mirror, or conduit or conveyor of God's truth to others.[7]

---

dedicated to "resurrecting," "reclaiming," and "reflecting" a theological vision for ministry. See, for example, Hiestand and Wilson, *The Pastor Theologian*; Strachan and Vanhoozer, *The Pastor as Public Theologian*; and Ferguson, *Some Pastors and Teachers*. For recent works akin to what this book is designed to be for pastors, see Wells, *God in the Wasteland*; *Losing Our Virtue*; *God in the Whirlwind*; *The Courage to be Protestant*; and Edwards, Ferguson, and Van Dixhoorn, *Theology for Ministry*.

6. Baxter, *The Reformed Pastor*, 41. Baxter's work was originally published in 1656, addressed to "my reverend and dearly-loved brethren, the faithful ministers of Christ, in Britain and Ireland."

7. Bridges, *The Christian Ministry*, 5–6. Bridges's work was originally published in 1830.

Introduction

Of course, this is not how the world views pastoral ministry. The world does not see pastors as a "conduit or conveyor of God's truth to others." At best, the non-believing world thinks pastors are doing a good work even if they're ultimately wasting their lives. At worst, pastors are propagators of hate-speech who are actually harming the culture. But Bridges knows better, and so do we.

Consider, for example, how the apostle Paul thinks about his life in his farewell address to the Ephesian pastors:

> You yourselves know how I lived among you the whole time from the first day that I set foot in Asia, serving the Lord with all humility and with tears and with trials that happened to me through the plots of the Jews; how I did not shrink from declaring to you anything that was profitable, and teaching you in public and from house to house, testifying both to Jews and to Greeks of repentance toward God and of faith in our Lord Jesus Christ. And now, behold, I am going to Jerusalem, constrained by the Spirit, not knowing what will happen to me there, except that the Holy Spirit testifies to me in every city that imprisonment and afflictions await me. But I do not account my life of any value nor as precious to myself, if only I may finish my course and the ministry that I received from the Lord Jesus, to testify to the gospel of the grace of God. (Acts 20:18–24)

The Apostle reminds his co-laborers how he lived among them the nearly three years he served the church in Ephesus. He recalls his humility and tears and the trials he suffered. Paul highlights the courage he exhibited by not failing to declare to them anything that was profitable in their walk with Christ. This rehearsal of his ministry was not intended to magnify the greatness of Paul, but to commend a particular vision for ministry to those who would remain in leadership at Ephesus. Paul always used biography to teach something about God and our life before him.

With this in mind, Paul tells the Ephesian elders what makes his life (and theirs) worth living. Paul could not separate his life from ministry. His life had value only insofar as he was faithful to the ministry given him—a ministry of testifying to the gospel of the grace of God. In other words, it did not matter to Paul what trials and sufferings awaited him in any city that God called him to because he considered his life "precious to himself" only in terms of faithfully finishing the ministry given him by God. Avoiding suffering would not be worth the cost of unfaithfulness in his calling.

Introduction

The way Paul *thought* about his life and ministry says something about the glory of the pastorate.

This is how a pastor must think. Our lives are a living testimony to the salvation of God. We consider our lives valuable or worthwhile or precious as we are faithful in this glorious work. A pastor hears Paul's conviction and finds it resonating in his heart. He says in one form or another, "Indeed, my life has value as it is a conduit of God's truth to people. Is there any greater vocation than to be a conveyor of the gospel to a lost world and in the care of a local church?"

There are many books on pastoral ministry available today. Even as many of these books are helpful in their unique contribution, pastors and the churches they serve need a vision for pastoral ministry that corresponds to the glory of the vocation. In the last century, the long-time pastor of Westminster Chapel in London, D. Martyn Lloyd-Jones, was invited to give a lectureship on preaching at Westminster Theological Seminary in Philadelphia. He opened by giving warrant for why he believed he was qualified to give a lecture series on preaching:

> But, ultimately, my reason for being very ready to give these lectures is that to me the work of preaching is the highest and greatest and the most glorious calling to which anyone can ever be called. If you want something in addition to that I would say without any hesitation that the most urgent need in the Christian Church today is true preaching; and as it is the greatest and most urgent need in the Church, it is obviously the greatest need of the world also.[8]

What qualified Lloyd-Jones to give lectures on preaching, in his mind, was how he *thought* about preaching. The exalted biblical-theological vision he had for preaching was the justification for his lectureship (of course, his faithful decades-long ministry of proclamation helped as well). I want to adapt the good doctor's words for the purposes of this book. Indeed, the exalted biblical-theological view of pastoral ministry I see in Scripture brings me to believe about the pastorate what Lloyd-Jones believed about preaching:

> But, ultimately, my reason for being very ready to write this book is that to me the work of *pastoring* is the highest and greatest and the most glorious calling to which anyone can ever be called. If you want something in addition to that I would say without any hesitation that the most urgent need in the Christian Church

---

8. Lloyd-Jones, *Preaching and Preachers*, 9.

Introduction

today is true *pastors*; and as it is the greatest and most urgent need in the Church, it is obviously the greatest need of the world also.

Resolutions are convictions of the mind that move the will. Of all men, pastors need to have resolve about the things most important to ministry. This book is built around twelve resolutions that together present a robust biblical-theological vision for ministry. And not only that—it's also personal. After nearly three decades in vocational ministry, I've come to see just how relevant and practical and needed these resolutions are to a pastor's faithfulness. My formal training as a church historian gives me an instinct to raise the dead and let them speak. In the pages of this book, you will hear many voices from church history that have shaped me and given me a particular vision for ministry. The church needs these voices. I offer them in the hope that, though dead, they will still speak in our time. I am convinced that how we *think* about pastoral ministry will largely determine how we *act* in ministry; and how we think about pastoral ministry must be informed by the truth of Scripture. It is my hope that God will use this book as one means of raising up a new generation of faithful pastors until that day when the chief Shepherd appears to bestow the unfading crown of glory on all under-shepherds worthy of the name (1 Pet 5:4).

1

God

> "The gospel . . . is not a doctrine of the tongue but of life. It is not grasped merely by the intellect and memory like other disciplines, but it is taken in only when it possesses the entire soul and when it finds a seat and place of refuge in the most intimate affection of the heart. . . . The gospel should penetrate into the most intimate affection of the heart, take hold of the soul, and have an effect on the whole human being."
>
> —John Calvin

> "For from him and through him and to him are all things. To him be glory forever. Amen."
>
> —Romans 11:36

Resolution 1: Resolved to pastor *coram Deo*—that is, before the face of God.

In his 1994 book *God in the Wasteland*, David Wells explains what is ailing the evangelical church:

Resolutions of a Pastor

> The fundamental problem in the evangelical world today is not inadequate technique, insufficient organization, or antiquated music, and those who want to squander the church's resources bandaging these scratches will do nothing to stanch the flow of blood that is spilling from its true wounds. The fundamental problem in the evangelical world today is that God rests too inconsequentially upon the church. His truth is too distant, his grace is too ordinary, his judgment is too benign, his gospel is too easy, and his Christ is too common.[1]

I believe Wells was right in 1994 and that his diagnosis is still relevant today. Who, after all, looks out upon evangelicalism as a whole and concludes that God is resting consequentially upon the church?

My argument is that the pastor plays a vital role in seeing that God rest consequentially upon the church; but before any program is suggested and implemented, the way to see this realized in the local church is to first ensure that God rests consequentially upon the pastor. To be sure, the pastor embracing a consequential God is easier said than done. Secularizing trends in Western civilization have only accelerated since the time of Wells's book, making the challenge for the pastor only harder.[2] There is a weightlessness to God that threatens to influence every aspect of pastoral ministry including preaching, teaching, discipleship, local evangelism, global missions, prayer, and counseling. The pastor is called to minister in a culture where Christianity has been marginalized to the degree that it no longer

---

1. Wells, *God in the Wasteland*, 30.

2. Mohler explains the essence of secularization: "Scholars debate the term aggressively, but it points to a process that has been taking hold in modern societies since the dawn of the modern age. It does not mean that all people in these societies become truly secular, or irreligious, but it does mean that Christianity, which forged the moral and spiritual worldview of civilization, is being displaced . . . . The key issue is that the society is distanced from Christian theism as the fundamental explanation of the world and as the moral structure of human society. Christian truth claims have lost all binding authority in the culture, and the loss of that binding authority is the most important fact." Mohler, introduction to *The Gathering Storm*, xiii. More recently, David Wells has helpfully explained how secularization is not so much a coherent philosophy, but a "diffuse, cultural environment." That is, secularization should be understood as a "cultural context" that "is not itself a religion, but because it has the power to shape how people construe the whole meaning of life, it functions like one." Wells, "Losing Our Religion," 803. Further, he asserts, "And in our time it is assumed that the whole meaning of life should be construed without reference to God. This is the 'normal' way of thinking. Our public square, as a result, becomes 'naked.' It has been stripped of any active divine presence or religious truth, as Richard John Neuhaus argued. This absence potentially exerts a powerful shaping force on the way that even Christian faith is articulated" (Wells, 808).

has any real influence. The God of the Bible rests inconsequentially upon the Western world—and this Godless culture has made its way into the church where the pastor serves.[3]

Secularization, of course, is not the pastor's only challenge. In addition to worldliness, the pastor must resist the continual onslaughts of the flesh and the devil. Indwelling sin is the great enemy within the pastor (Rom 7:15–25; see chapter 9), and the devil "prowls around like a roaring lion, seeking someone to devour" (1 Pet 5:8). The world, the flesh, and the devil conspire against the pastor in his efforts to reckon with God in utter seriousness.

A Tale of Taking God Lightly

The year was 1994. I had just graduated from the University of Washington with a degree in Political Science. When I chose that degree track, I assumed I would go on to law school and seek to change the world via Washington, DC. My political career, of course, would start local, but the goal was to go national, and sit in the seats of Congress, crafting and arguing for legislation that would change the world for the better. But during my senior year of college, my vocational goals began to radically change. As much as I loved my university courses (what wasn't to love in courses like The American City, Twentieth-Century American Foreign Policy, Political Philosophies of the Enlightenment, and Constitutional Law), my academic interests were migrating to the Bible, theology, and church history. Locke and Mill, you might say, were being overwhelmed by Luther and Calvin. I had a problem. My education and career "plan" were being interrupted by Providence. Indeed, the Lord had other plans for me.

My new direction was made clear, in part, by the wise counsel of a pastor in my life at the time. Jerry Theckston served as the senior pastor of Midway Evangelical Covenant Church in Seattle. I was introduced to Jerry by one of my roommates (I was living with four other guys in a house we rented close to campus) who had greatly benefited from Jerry's ministry during Young Life meetings in high school. Pastor Jerry apparently saw something in our ragtag group worth investing in, as he would come out to our house every other week for discipleship meetings that consisted of memorizing the book of James, reading various books he assigned, prayer,

---

3. For an analysis of how secularization has come to the church, see Mohler, *The Gathering Storm*, 19–38.

and eating something amazing that his wife Sue had baked. These meetings would also result in "assignments" beyond our reading and memorization. Pastor Jerry was determined not to let our Christianity become merely head knowledge that did not translate into practical love of our neighbors. This meant we needed to seek opportunities to serve in our local churches, as well as to witness on the streets of the university district. After all, as the book of James was teaching us, "faith apart from works is dead" (Jas 2:26). During that fateful last year of college, Pastor Jerry helped me see that God was not calling me to a career in law or politics, but to vocational ministry.

Not only was Pastor Jerry's investment greatly consequential in helping me discern my call to, and understanding of, ministry, but a parachurch ministry a group of us started that year proved to be radically formative as well. The Loft, as we called it, began as a partnership between my high school buddy Mark Driscoll and I as we set out to reach fellow "GenXers" with the gospel. In the 1990s, reaching particular demographic groups was all the rage in church planting circles, so without much thought we simply decided to launch a ministry that targeted our generation. Thankfully, Mark's father-in-law pastored a church in south Seattle (Trinity Church) and offered us the use of the building to hold our own weekly Sunday evening worship services. Mark and I would alternate Sundays so we could experience the responsibility for all aspects of the worship service, from preaching to music to testimonies or other elements of the liturgy that we wanted to try out. We were two guys with no formal training and a burden to preach and shepherd, but—not surprisingly—no church willing to give us a pulpit. So, we did what most evangelicals do when no one gives you an opportunity: we started our own thing.

I don't remember why we called it The Loft. It probably had something to do with the design of the Trinity Church sanctuary with its exposed beams along the ceiling of the A-frame church building. The name seemed warm and inviting and conducive to what we were trying to accomplish with the ministry, namely, fellowship around the Word among twenty-something urbanites. To at least my surprise, it started to work. People were coming in droves on Sunday nights to hear two young guys figure out how to preach, and to sing worship songs led by musician friends we recruited. And while Trinity Church wasn't a big building, it was greatly encouraging to see it at, or over, capacity each week. It was a blessing . . . and a curse.

A wise seminary professor once told me a helpful proverb about praise from people and the life of a preacher. He warned, "Flattery is like perfume.

It's intended to be sniffed not drank." My problem in the days of The Loft was that I was drinking in the praise—and it was making me spiritually sick. My "illness" came to a climax one Sunday night when I was preaching through 2 Timothy 1:6–7: "For this reason I remind you to fan into flame the gift of God, which is in you through the laying on of my hands, for God gave us a spirit not of fear but of power and love and self-control." The main thing I wanted to draw out of the text was the "spirit" that God had given us—a spirit not of fear but of power and love and self-control. The sad irony was that when it came to my vanity, I lacked self-control. I vividly remember the ordeal of trying to get through that sermon: losing my place in the outline, sweating, and feeling the penetrating eyes of people in the pews who I thought surely knew my corrupt craving for applause. When, after what felt like an eternity, my stumbling and stammering was done, I got out of the pulpit as quickly as I could, wanting nothing more in that moment but to be invisible.

Once I arrived home that night, God's merciful chastening continued. His hand was heavy upon me. I remember sitting late into the night in an old rocking chair we had in the living room. As I rocked back and forth, tears streaming down my face and at times finding it hard to breathe, I cried out to God, confessing my sin and pleading with him to forgive me. In those awful hours, I knew what the Lord wanted me to learn from this event: ministry would not be about me. I would not use the church for my own fame or platform or gain. If I was to be a pastor, it would be all about God's exaltation and the good of his people. I resolved in that moment to pastor for the glory of God. Through tears of joy and relief, God relented and set me on a course of living and pastoring *coram Deo*.

The Reformation for Today

What does the Latin phrase *coram Deo* mean? I was first introduced to it in a seminary class on Reformation theology. One of our textbooks was *Theology of the Reformers* by Timothy George. In it, George describes Martin Luther as an "existential" theologian. For Luther, "concern with God was a life-and-death matter, involving not merely one's intellect but one's whole existence."[4] George explains,

---

4. George, *Theology of the Reformers*, 58.

> Human existence is lived out *coram Deo*, "before God," or "in the presence of God." Calvin made a similar claim when he insisted that in every dimension of life human beings have "business with God" (*negotium cum Deo*). This has nothing to do with formal belief in God, hence Luther's rejection of the classical arguments for the existence of God. For Luther "God" can never be placed in quotation marks. The great sin of scholastic theology (and also, from Luther's perspective, of neo-Kantian philosophy) was precisely the attempt to make of God an ordering concept, the First Principle, or even Necessary Being. Such a procedure placed God at a distance, made God the object of natural inquiry, and thus exempted the human from deciding for or against God. But the God and Father of our Lord Jesus Christ is not a God we can discuss, or argue about, a God whose existence can be decided in the cool objectivity of a graduate seminar. The living God of the Bible is the God who meets us in judgment and mercy, the God who damns us and saves us. *Coram Deo* means that while we are always at God's disposal, God is never at ours. "To believe in such a God," Luther said, "is to go down on your knees."[5]

For Luther, because of who God is, life must be lived "on your knees." In other words, life is to be lived in a state of constant devotion to God, taking up every aspect of our lives into the exaltation of his name. It's the working out of 1 Corinthians 10:31 in all of life: "So, whether you eat or drink, or whatever you do, do all to the glory of God." For the Reformers, as for the Apostle, "whatever you do" is to be done to magnify the infinite worth of God.

The idea of living *coram Deo* is also embedded in Calvin's discussion of self-denial in his *Institutes of the Christian Religion*. Consider this section as Calvin draws out the implications of 1 Corinthians 6:19 ("You are not your own"):

> We are not our own: let not our reason nor our will, therefore, sway our plans and deeds. We are not our own: let us therefore not set it as our goal to seek what is expedient for us according to the flesh. We are not our own: in so far as we can, let us therefore forget ourselves and all that is ours.
>
> Conversely, we are God's: let us therefore live for him and die for him. We are God's: let his wisdom and will therefore rule all our actions. We are God's: let all the parts of our life accordingly strive toward him as our only lawful goal [Rom 14:8; cf. 1 Cor

---

5. George, *Theology of the Reformers*, 59.

6:19]. . . . Let this therefore be the first step, that a man depart from himself in order that he may apply the whole force of his ability in the service of the Lord.[6]

When Calvin writes that man ought to "apply the whole force of his ability in the service of the Lord" he is getting to the heart of living *coram Deo*.

Calvin's words remind me of a man named Ed Atsinger and his business, Salem Communications. Mr. Atsinger is one of the co-founders of the Salem Media Group, a major communications company headquartered in Camarillo, California.[7] After serving for three years as the executive producer of *The Albert Mohler Program*, a nationally syndicated radio show owned and operated by the Salem Radio Network, I was offered an editorial position at Salem's corporate headquarters. On one of my visits to Camarillo to discuss the role, I remember sitting across the desk from Mr. Atsinger, who at that time served as Salem's chief executive officer. It was rather intimidating, a fact I think he rather enjoyed. I don't remember everything we talked about at that meeting, but I'll never forget the warning he gave me. He said in a very matter-of-fact tone, "Should you decide to take this position, you need to know that I own all your vital energies." As you might imagine, I wasn't sure how to respond. I think I mumbled something like, "Of course." But even as it shocked me a bit, I understood the principle being established: as an employee of Salem Communications serving in their corporate offices, all my vital energies needed to go into advancing the mission of the company. Mr. Atsinger wanted me to understand the comprehensive nature of the position and the corporate culture I was entering.

The point of bringing up this story is to say something about living *coram Deo*. When we come to Christ in salvation, God "owns all our vital energies." All that we are is given in devotion to him. As children of God, "we make it our aim to please him" (2 Cor 5:9). We must see all of life in relation to God and his glory. God certainly doesn't expect less than Ed Atsinger. Indeed, God has his own "corporate culture" that he expects us to willingly embrace. This is the profound insight Joel Beeke offers as he considers the God-centered life:

---

6. Calvin, *Institutes* (McNeill), 1:690.

7. Even as my sense of call to pastoral ministry had not wavered, I sensed the Lord had further lessons for me to learn at Salem Communications as I continued to write my doctoral dissertation.

> In his relation to us, God has only rights and powers; He binds Himself to duties sovereignly and graciously only by way of covenant. In covenant, He assumes the duties and responsibilities of being a God unto us, but that does not detract from his being the first cause and the last end of all things. The universe is ruled not by chance or fate, but by the complete, sovereign rule of God. We exist for one purpose: to give Him glory. We have only duties to God, no rights. Any attempt to challenge this truth is doomed. Romans 9:20b asks, "Shall the thing formed say to him that formed it, Why hast thou made me thus?" God enacts laws for every part of our lives and demands unconditional obedience. We are called to serve Him with body and soul, in worship and daily work, every second of every day.[8]

The evangelical church today and her pastors need to reckon with God's demands of "unconditional obedience . . . every second of every day."

It is not surprising to find this theme of *coram Deo* thread throughout the great Reformation catechisms and confessions of faith. For example, this Reformation thinking is evident in the opening of the Heidelberg Catechism (1563):

> Q. What is your only comfort in life and death?
>
> A. That I with body and soul, both in life and death, am not my own, but belong to my faithful Savior Jesus Christ; who, with his precious blood, has fully satisfied for all my sins, and delivered me from all the power of the devil; and so preserves me that without the will of my heavenly Father, not a hair can fall from my head; indeed, that all things must be subservient to my salvation, and therefore, by his Holy Spirit, he also assures me of eternal life, and makes me sincerely willing and ready, henceforth, to live unto him.

Christians are people who derive all comfort in life and death from knowing that they are not their own, but belong wholly to Christ and, therefore, are "sincerely willing and ready . . . to live unto God." Similarly, the Westminster Catechism (1647) captures this idea with its memorable opening question: "What is the chief end of man?" Answer: "To glorify God and enjoy him forever." To glorify God and enjoy him forever is to live *coram Deo*.[9]

---

8. Beeke, *Living for God's Glory*, 41.

9. For a brief, helpful discussion of the primary confessions and catechisms from the Reformed tradition, and how they embody the idea of living a theocentric life, see Beeke, *Living for God's Glory*, 19–31.

The Puritan Quest for *Coram Deo*

The spiritual descendants of the Reformers, the Puritans, sought to live *coram Deo*. I recall in my young twenties being introduced to the Banner of Truth series "Puritan Paperbacks." I devoured them like a starving man devours food. Whether reading Thomas Watson's *The Godly Man's Picture*, or Richard Baxter's *The Reformed Pastor*, William Guthrie's *The Christian's Great Interest*, or Ralph Venning's *The Sinfulness of Sin*, William Gurnall's *The Christian in Complete Armour*, or Thomas Brooks's *Precious Remedies against Satan's Devices*, among others, I found in the Puritans a longing to live the God-centered life. J. I. Packer recognizes this in the Puritans when he outlines the first of several reasons why we need the Puritans in our own day:

> First, there are lessons for us in *the integration of their daily lives*. As their Christianity was all-embracing, so their living was all of a piece. Nowadays we would call their lifestyle holistic: all awareness, activity, and enjoyment all "use of the creatures" and development of personal powers and creativity, was integrated in the single purpose of honouring God by appreciating all his gifts and making everything "holiness to the Lord". There was for them no disjunction between sacred and secular; all creation, so far as they were concerned, was sacred, and all activities, of whatever kind, must be sanctified, that is, done to the glory of God.[10]

This Puritan effort to live the "integrated life"—to live *coram Deo*—is desperately needed in our day when the "disintegrated life" seems to prevail. It is all too common among professing Christians to divide their lives into the *sacred* and *secular*. This is a division not only foreign to the Puritans, but more importantly, to the Bible. The disintegrated life is at odds with the comprehensive call of God that sees all of life under the Lordship of Christ. The pastor, of all people, must understand this and incorporate a vision for the integrated life into his ministry.

The Augustinian Tradition

When it came to living *coram Deo*, the Reformers (and the Puritans after them) rightly saw themselves in the Augustinian tradition. Augustine (354–430), the church father and bishop of Hippo in modern-day Algeria,

---

10. Packer, *A Quest for Godliness*, 23–24.

illustrated living *coram Deo* in his spiritual autobiography *Confessions*. In this monumental work we see Augustine's understanding of a life absorbed in God, perhaps most vividly in this oft-quoted declaration:

> You are mighty, Master, and to be praised with a powerful voice: great is your goodness, and of your wisdom there can be no reckoning. Yet to praise you is the desire of a human being, who is some part of what you created; a human hauling his deathliness in a circle, hauling in a circle the evidence of his sin, and the evidence that you stand against the arrogant.
> But still a mortal, a given portion of your creation, longs to extol you. In yourself you rouse us, giving us delight in glorifying you, because you made us with yourself as our goal, and our heart is restless until it rests in you.[11]

True humanity can only be realized in the God-centered life. God, as Augustine knew, is the "goal" of our existence, the end for which we were created. Indeed, our hearts are consigned to never-ending restlessness unless we realize this goal of living for the glory of God. For Augustine, to live any other way than *coram Deo* was nonsensical. And worse, worthy of the curse of God. After heaping up words to try and describe the greatness of God, Augustine confesses that language betrays him from adequately extolling God: "And what have we said now, my God, my life, my holy sweetness, or what does anyone ever say in speaking of you? But woe to those who are silent about you; however garrulous they are in general, they are mute about what counts."[12] To live *coram Deo* is to never tire of finding words and cultivating a life that, however deficiently, exalts the glory of God.

The God Who Lives *Coram Deo*

The Bible is radically God-centered. In the Bible, we see that God lives *coram Deo*. This reality was impressed upon me while I was a seminary student at Trinity Evangelical Divinity School in the mid 1990s. I was taking a class titled Theology of Missions, and one of our required books was John Piper's *Let the Nations Be Glad: The Supremacy of God in Missions*. Unlike other people who learned of Piper's ministry through his seminal work *Desiring God: Meditations of a Christian Hedonist*—with its pithy motto, "God is most glorified in us when we are most satisfied in him"—*Let the Nations*

---

11. Augustine, *Confessions*, 3.
12. Augustine, *Confessions*, 3.

Be Glad was my introduction to Piper and his God-centered ministry. It was paradigm shifting for me.

I found Piper refreshingly out-of-step with contemporary evangelicalism. I sensed his "alien" status from the opening words of the first chapter: "Missions is not the ultimate goal of the church. Worship is. Worship is ultimate, not missions, because God is ultimate, not man. When this age is over, and the countless millions of the redeemed fall on their faces before the throne of God, mission will be no more. It is a temporary necessity. But worship abides forever."[13] In my copy of the book I have written in the margin, "Nice." I had found a kindred spirit—one who had not given over to the spirit of the evangelical age that in manifold ways peddled an anthropocentric understanding of the Bible. Before running to any particular program or strategy for missions, in this opening chapter Piper was determined to lay the essential biblical foundation of God's "God-centeredness." With relentless prose, Piper pressed the issue with paragraphs like this one:

> The ultimate foundation for our passion to see God glorified is his own passion to be glorified. God is central and supreme in his own affections. There are no rivals for the supremacy of God's glory in his own heart. God is not an idolater. He does not disobey the first and great commandment. With all his heart and soul and strength and mind he delights in the glory of his manifold perfections. The most passionate heart for God in all the universe is God's heart.[14]

If this was true, the implications for me were clear: because God lives *coram Deo*, then I must be radically God-centered in my life and ministry.

What I began to see still more clearly in those seminary days was how true it is to say, as Piper had, that "God is central and supreme in his own affections." The Bible makes this plain. For example, consider one of the key biblical texts for Piper's argument, Isaiah 48:9–11: "For my name's sake I defer my anger; for the sake of my praise I restrain it for you, that I may not cut you off. Behold, I have refined you, but not as silver; I have tried you in the furnace of affliction. For my own sake, for my own sake, I do it, for how should my name be profaned? My glory I will not give to another." In this text God says he defers his anger "for [his] name's sake," and restrains it "for the sake of [his] praise." Referring to his refining work and its purpose, God uses repetition to emphasize the point: "For my own sake, for my own sake, I do it." We see God act supremely *for God* when he asks rhetorically, "How

---

13. Piper, *Let the Nations Be Glad*, 35.
14. Piper, *Let the Nations Be Glad*, 39.

should my name be profaned?" And, finally, God leaves no doubt about the ultimate end of all that he does when he says emphatically, "My glory I will not give to another." To know what it means to live *coram Deo*, we look to the God-centeredness of God as seen in Isaiah 48:9–11, and other biblical passages that emphasis this truth.[15]

Another biblical text that makes this abundantly clear is Romans 11:33–36:

> Oh, the depth of the riches and wisdom and knowledge of God! How unsearchable are his judgments and how inscrutable his ways! "For who has known the mind of the Lord, or who has been his counselor?" "Or who has given a gift to him that he might be repaid?" For from him and through him and to him are all things. To him be glory forever. Amen.

The apostle Paul, in response to all the Lord has revealed to him up to this point in his letter to the Romans, bursts forth in praise to God. This doxology acknowledges God's infinite wisdom and knowledge, his perfect providence, his self-sufficiency, and sovereign majesty. We see Paul's utterly theocentric view of history. It is the essence of *coram Deo*. This text is the death knell to the self-centered life. Indeed, if Romans 11:36 is true, then the Godward life is the only rational way to live.

This is the point Paul makes as he opens the next section of the letter with an eye to what the gospel means for living the Christian life: "I appeal to you therefore, brothers, by the mercies of God, to present your bodies as a living sacrifice, holy and acceptable to God, which is your spiritual worship" (Rom 12:1). The main idea of this verse is seen in the exhortation to present our bodies to God. Paul is alluding to the old covenant sacrificial system, but with an all-important new covenant twist. In this arresting image of what it means to live the Christian life, Paul says that the sacrifice we daily offer to God is ourselves—all that we are. This, of course, is not an offering in the sense of making atonement for sin. Christ alone is the sufficient sacrifice for sin (Rom 8:1–4). Our "offering" of all that we are to God is in *response* to the salvation given to us. This is our reasonable service to God as a new creation in Christ (cf. 1 Cor 6:19–20; Gal 2:20). This is why we sing,

> Oh Father, use my ransomed life

---

15. For a list of many biblical passages that show God's zeal for his own glory arranged by subject, see Piper, *Let the Nations be Glad*, 41–46.

> In any way You choose;
> And let my song forever be
> My only boast is You.[16]

To live *coram Deo* is to say to God daily, *This ransomed life is yours, do with it whatever you please.* Another hymn that captures the essence of living the God-centered life is William Cowper's "God Moves in a Mysterious Way" (1774):

> God moves in a mysterious way
> His wonders to perform;
> He plants His footsteps in the sea
> And rides upon the storm.
>
> Deep in unfathomable mines
> Of never failing skill
> He treasures up His bright designs
> And works His sovereign will.
>
> Ye fearful saints, fresh courage take;
> The clouds ye so much dread
> Are big with mercy and shall break
> In blessings on your head.
>
> Judge not the Lord by feeble sense,
> But trust Him for His grace;
> Behind a frowning providence
> He hides a smiling face.
>
> His purposes will ripen fast,
> Unfolding every hour;
> The bud may have a bitter taste,
> But sweet will be the flower.
>
> Blind unbelief is sure to err
> And scan His work in vain;
> God is His own interpreter,
> And He will make it plain.

To live *coram Deo* is to see God riding upon the storms of life, working his sovereign will; it is to know that behind every heavy providence—the suffering we endure—stands the infinite wisdom of God. It is to believe that God's ways are higher than our ways and, therefore, to rest in this truth. Cowper's hymn powerfully echoes the radically God-centered biblical texts we've already considered (Isa 48:9–11; and Rom 11:33–36).

16. Kauflin, "All I Have Is Christ."

Marva Dawn makes what should be an obvious point, but often is not in evangelicalism, when she asserts, "The Bible is all about God."[17] The reason this is not so obvious to many readers of the Bible is due to the anthropocentric lens we bring to the text. Instead of asking what a particular biblical text reveals about God, many in the church today seem to default to questions like, *What does this text say about me?*, or *Where can I find myself in this text?* Bible studies and pulpit ministries are replete with application questions that ask things like, *How are you like David?*, or *How can you be more like Mary and less like Martha?*, or *How can we lead like Nehemiah?* The Scriptures become more of a self-help book rather than revelation of the triune God.

It wasn't long after my conversion that I was confronted with the radical God-centeredness of the Bible. This reality came crashing down on me when I first read Acts 17:24–25: "The God who made the world and everything in it, being Lord of heaven and earth, does not live in temples made by man, nor is he served by human hands, as though he needed anything, since he himself gives to all mankind life and breath and everything." The apostle Paul is animated by the idolatry permeating Athens. So steeped in idolatry are the Athenians that they even have an idol dedicated to "the unknown god" to help make sure they don't miss one (Acts 17:23). Paul pivots from the obvious idolatry to proclamation of the one true God when he says, "What therefore you worship as unknown, this I proclaim to you" (Acts 17:23). Paul proceeds to do just that: to proclaim the God who is and to declare the comprehensive demand the Creator makes on the world (Acts 17:24–31). This sermon excerpt may be titled, "The Call of God to All the Earth to Live *Coram Deo*." It is this God-centered view of life that is all too scarce in the church—the inevitable result, according to Wells, of a lost appetite for Scripture among evangelicals:

> Most profoundly, then, what has also been diminished through our lost appetite for the teaching of Scripture is a vision of God in his greatness, in his transcendence and holiness, as he stands over against the world in its sinfulness. This is always what is secured in the church's understanding when doctrine has its proper place in Christian understanding. The reason is that God's truth comes from God and when it is heard as he gave it, it takes us back to our center, to God as triune, to God in his greatness. To hear God's Word as the Word from *this* God is inevitably to become

---

17. Dawn, *In the Beginning, God*, 9.

God-centered. But it is this center that has become blurry, and this God-centeredness that is much scarcer.[18]

Pastoring *Coram Deo*

To understand what it means to pastor *coram Deo*, it is helpful to see clearly the opposite, or what it is *not* to pastor for the glory of God. The Bible does not leave us to wonder what this looks like. We see it in the faithless shepherds of Ezekiel 34:1–6:

> The word of the LORD came to me: "Son of man, prophesy against the shepherds of Israel; prophesy, and say to them, even to the shepherds, Thus says the Lord GOD: Ah, shepherds of Israel who have been feeding yourselves! Should not shepherds feed the sheep? You eat the fat, you clothe yourselves with the wool, you slaughter the fat ones, but you do not feed the sheep. The weak you have not strengthened, the sick you have not healed, the injured you have not bound up, the strayed you have not brought back, the lost you have not sought, and with force and harshness you have ruled them. So they were scattered, because there was no shepherd, and they became food for all the wild beasts. My sheep were scattered; they wandered over all the mountains and on every high hill. My sheep were scattered over all the face of the earth, with none to search or seek for them.

The metaphor of *shepherd* is being used to describe the leaders of Judah. Clearly, these shepherds are personally benefiting at great cost to the sheep. They are abusing their power by lording it over the people for their own selfish gain. Like contemporary prosperity pastors, these corrupt shepherds are using people to satisfy their own appetites for power and riches. The indictment is severe: "You eat the fat, you clothe yourselves with the wool, you slaughter the fat ones, but you do not feed the sheep" (v. 3). The consequences for the people are tragic. Those who remain under this tyranny are resigned to perish in gross neglect, while other sheep are scattered and lost, left to "become food for all the wild beasts" (v. 5).

Of course, God will not allow this to go on forever. After rehearsing his indictment on the faithless shepherds, God announces the judgement: "Thus says the Lord GOD, Behold, I am against the shepherds, and I will require my sheep at their hand and put a stop to their feeding the sheep.

---

18. Wells, *The Courage to Be Protestant*, 4.

No longer shall the shepherds feed themselves. I will rescue my sheep from their mouths, that they may not be food for them" (34:10). The Lord declares that he is "against the shepherds," a posture he undoubtably has toward many contemporary evangelical pastors who are in ministry not for God but for self.

In contrast to the faithless shepherds of Ezekiel 34, the apostle Peter demonstrates a better way—the way of the shepherd who labors *coram Deo*:

> So I exhort the elders among you, as a fellow elder and a witness of the sufferings of Christ, as well as a partaker in the glory that is going to be revealed: shepherd the flock of God that is among you, exercising oversight, not under compulsion, but willingly, as God would have you; not for shameful gain, but eagerly; not domineering over those in your charge, but being examples to the flock. And when the chief Shepherd appears, you will receive the unfading crown of glory. (1 Pet 5:1–4)

Peter gives the emphatic command to "shepherd the flock of God that is among you" with all the weight of apostolic authority. But notice that he doesn't merely give the command to shepherd, but governs the way in which this pastoral care is to proceed. It is the opposite way of the faithless shepherds seen in Ezekiel 34. The faithful shepherd works for the welfare of the flock that is among him, not some "virtual" flock on social media. The faithful shepherd serves willingly, not becoming embittered or resentful as if someone is forcing him to be a pastor. The faithful shepherd is not greedy for material gain, but is eager to pastor without an eye to worldly treasure. The faithful shepherd does not dominate anyone, but lays down his life for the flock as he emulates the Good Shepherd who laid down his life for his friends (John 15:13). And the faithful shepherd does all of this in anticipation of the ultimate reward that awaits: the unfading crown of glory.

Godward Is the Way

I remember well one of the final interviews I had during the hiring process to become the senior pastor of Immanuel Bible Church in Bellingham, Washington. The meeting was a Q&A on the final Sunday night of what had been a "candidating week" of events. One of the matriarchs of the church asked rather bluntly, "If we call you as our next senior pastor, in the first five years of your ministry where do you plan to take us?" I appreciated the question as it was intended to flesh out my philosophy of ministry and perhaps have me speak to particular programs I planned to implement. Without any hesitation, my response was, "Godward." I proceeded to give a brief sermon on Philippians 3:13–14 where the apostle Paul reminds the church in Philippi about his one passion in life: "Brothers, I do not consider that I have made it my own. But one thing I do: forgetting what lies behind and straining forward to what lies ahead, I press on toward the goal for the prize of the upward call of God in Christ Jesus." I wanted Immanuel Bible Church to join me in the glorious pursuit of Christ and conformity to him. In other words, I wanted a church to join me in living *coram Deo*.

To pastor before the face of God in all the wonderful and hard aspects of ministry is the subject of the chapters that follow. For now, let me say clearly what I hope is becoming self-evident for the reader. A pastor cannot lead people Godward if he himself is not going that direction. In other words, God must rest consequentially on the pastor if God would rest consequentially upon the church. And so, it starts with us. Fellow pastor, can you say with the psalmist, "My flesh and my heart may fail, but God is the strength of my heart and my portion forever?" (Ps 73:26) This is the heart-cry of a life lived *coram Deo*, and pastors of all people must strive for it. After all, if we are not living *coram Deo*, how can we expect our congregations to do so? In the nineteenth century, the Anglican bishop J. C. Ryle captured the essence of what it means to live and minister *coram Deo*:

> A zealous man in religion is pre-eminently a man of one thing. It is not enough to say that he is earnest, hearty, uncompromising, thorough-going, whole-hearted, fervent in spirit. He only sees one thing, he cares for one thing, he lives for one thing, he is swallowed up in one thing; and that one thing is to please God. Whether he lives, or whether he dies—whether he has health, or whether he has sickness—whether he is rich, or whether he is poor—whether he pleases man, or whether he gives offense—whether he is thought wise, or whether he is thought foolish—whether he gets blame, or whether he gets praise—whether he gets honor, or whether he gets shame—for all this the zealous man cares nothing at all. He burns for one thing, and that one thing is to please God and to advance God's glory. If he is consumed in the very burning, he cares not for it—he is content. He feels that, like a lamp, he is made to burn; and if consumed in burning, he has but done the work for which God appointed him.[19]

---

19. Ryle, *Practical Religion*, 174–75.

Brother pastor, may we burn for one thing: to please God and advance his glory. In other words, let us live and pastor *coram Deo*.

2

Scripture

"The whole Counsel of God concerning all things necessary for his own Glory, Man's Salvation, Faith and Life, is either expressly set down or necessarily contained in the Holy Scripture; unto which nothing at any time is to be added, whether by new Revelation of the Spirit, or traditions of men."
—London Baptist Confession (1689)

"Your word is a lamp to my feet and a light to my path."
—Psalm 119:105

Resolution 2: Resolved to pastor according to the sufficiency of Scripture.

A faithful pastor labors from a conviction that the Bible is sufficient for ministry. As the doctrine of inerrancy was embattled in a previous generation, today we are confronted with the question of the Bible's sufficiency. Is the Bible really all we need for faithful ministry? To ask this question is to put the focus on the *content* of ministry, and what the pastor thinks will produce gospel fruit. To understand and appreciate the sufficiency of Scripture for ministry, the pastor must see the connection between the sufficiency of Scripture and its *inspiration*. Therefore, this chapter rehearses the doctrine of Scripture with application made to corporate worship as well as other ministries of the church.

To survey the landscape of contemporary evangelicalism is to see pastors putting their faith in things other than the Bible for ministry effectiveness. Many pastors today seem to have bought into the lie that effective ministry is found in a building or a sound system or the clothes they wear or their charisma, props, websites, or apps—various means deemed necessary to supplement the Bible. All of these things are merely the *show* of ministry, not the *power* of ministry. Don't get me wrong: it's certainly good to have a building that's not falling apart, a sound system that doesn't glitch, websites that work, and preachers who don't come across disinterested in the pulpit. But when it comes to the question of what will give our ministries gospel success, we must look no further than the Word of God.

The Doctrine of Inspiration

We begin by recognizing what the Bible is, namely, the Word of God. The doctrine that explains this is *inspiration*, and is foundational for everything else we claim about the Bible. To say that the Scriptures are *inspired* is to say that they are "God-breathed"—that is, the product of God's Spirit. Explaining the meaning of the Greek word θεόπνευστος (*theopneustos*) in 2 Timothy 3:16, Paul Feinberg taught my Systematic Theology class at Trinity Evangelical Divinity School that the Bible is the "out-breathed breath of God." This, of course, is breathtaking. Before we consider the Bible's own testimony to its inspiration, a more exhaustive definition of inspiration is helpful.

What exactly are we affirming when we say the Scriptures are inspired? The nineteenth-century Princeton divine Charles Hodge explained inspiration as the "influence of the Holy Spirit on the minds of certain select men, which rendered them the organs of God for the infallible communication of his mind and will. They were in such a sense the organs of God, that what they said God said."[1] The influence of the Holy Spirit on "certain select

---

1. Hodge, *Theology*, 154. Hodge repeats the same idea a couple pages later when he asserts, "The sacred writers were the organs of God, so that what they taught, God taught" (156).

men" was so powerful and comprehensive that those men actually wrote the very words of God. Notice how Hodge explains this influence as "infallible." By infallible, he means that this "communication of [God's] mind and will" was incapable of erring given that it was the work of the "unable to err" Holy Spirit.

This, of course, does not necessitate a "dictation" view of inspiration, as if the human authors of Scripture were mere robots in the process of recording God's words. Again, Hodge is helpful: "As the believer seems to himself to act, and in fact does act out of his own nature; so the inspired penmen wrote out of the fullness of their own thoughts and feelings, and employed the language and modes of expression which to them were the most natural and appropriate. Nevertheless, and none the less, they spoke as they were moved by the Holy Ghost, and their words were his words."[2] The Holy Spirit worked through the natures of men—"their own thoughts and feelings"—even as he ensured that divine words were written. As Hodge explains, each of the human authors of Scripture "employed the language and modes of expression which to them were the most natural and appropriate." On this point, John Frame explains,

> Abraham Kuyper and Herman Bavinck called this process "organic" inspiration, to distinguish it from dictation or mechanical inspiration. Organic inspiration means that God used all the distinct personal qualities of each writer. God used the differences of heredity, environment, upbringing, education, gifts, talents, styles, interests, and idiosyncrasies to reveal his word. These differences were not a barrier that God had to overcome. Rather, they were God's chosen means of communicating with us. God's Word is complex and nuanced, multiperspectival. God used the organic complexity of human persons and the diversities among persons to communicate the complexity of his own personal word. He used human persons to communicate with us in a fully personal way.[3]

Understood this way, it is accurate to say that Scripture is both a divine *and* a human book. God, as the primary author of Scripture used unique human beings to reveal—infallibly—his words. Inspiration, therefore, is "a divine act that creates an identity between a divine word and a human word."[4] In the Bible, we have God's written revelation to the world.

2. Hodge, *Theology*, 157.
3. Frame, *Doctrine of the Word of God*, 142.
4. Frame, *Doctrine of the Word of God*, 140.

To further explain this truth, consider how the New Testament authors understood the Old Testament. Jesus affirmed the whole Old Testament as the Word of God (Matt 4:4-10; 5:19-20; 19:4-6; 26:31, 52-54; Luke 4:16-21; 16:17; 18:31-33; 22:37; 24:25-27, 44-47; John 10:34-35), even as he came to fulfill it (Matt 5:17-18; 26:24; John 5:46). And the apostle Paul, in 2 Timothy 3:16-17, affirms the whole Old Testament as the word of God (even as this passage is saying something true of *all* Scripture) when he states: "All Scripture is breathed out by God and profitable for teaching, for reproof, for correction, and for training in righteousness, that the man of God may be complete, equipped for every good work."

Not only did the New Testament authors understand the Old Testament as the inspired Word of God, but the apostles also understood that God had commissioned them to write God's Word alongside the Hebrew Scriptures. Paul, for example, affirms the divine origin of the words they taught when he writes to the Corinthians, "Now we have received not the spirit of the world, but the Spirit who is from God, that we might understand the things freely given us by God. And we impart this in words not taught by human wisdom but taught by the Spirit, interpreting spiritual truths to those who are spiritual (1 Cor 2:12-13). Rather than correcting the Thessalonians for the way they received the apostolic teaching, Paul commends them for their accurate understanding: "And we also thank God constantly for this, that when you received the word of God, which you heard from us, you accepted it not as the word of men but as what it really is, *the word of God*, which is at work in you believers" (1 Thess 2:13; emphasis added). Here we see the dual authorship of Scripture discussed above: what the Thessalonians heard from Paul they rightly accepted as the Word of God.

In terms of inspiration, it is important for the pastor to affirm two more aspects of this doctrine. The first has to do with the comprehensive nature of Scripture's inspiration, which can be explained using the term *plenary*. The word carries with it the idea of being *exhaustive*, *absolute*, or *total*. Think, for example, of a conference that includes "plenary sessions." By *plenary*, the conference organizers are describing sessions that are to include *all* conference attendees; this is in contrast to workshops or breakout sessions that include only subsets of the whole. "*Plenary* inspiration," Frame explains, "simply means that *everything* in Scripture is God's Word. To say this is merely to say that the entire canon is God's Word." He continues by drawing out the great implication of this for the Christian: "If the Bible is plenarily inspired, we may not pick and choose within the Scriptures, regarding one part as God's Word and another part as merely human."[5]

The second aspect of the doctrine of inspiration that is crucial to affirm is its *verbal* character. To say that the Bible is verbally inspired is to affirm that not only the *ideas* of the biblical authors are God-breathed, but the very *words* of Scripture are a product of God's Spirit. This means that Christianity is a *text-driven* religion. If we would know the mind of God then we must know the personal *words* God has given us in the Scriptures. As I demonstrate later in this chapter, the verbal inspiration of Scripture dictates what pastors do in light of being called "stewards of the mysteries of God" (1 Cor 4:1).

Sufficient Word, Sufficient God

Having established the inspiration of Scripture, we now come to the doctrine of the sufficiency of Scripture. One of the more helpful, clear, and succinct contemporary definitions of the sufficiency of Scripture comes from Wayne Grudem: "The sufficiency of Scripture means that Scripture contained all the words of God he intended his people to have at each stage of redemptive history, and that it now contains everything we need God to tell us for salvation, for trusting him perfectly, and for obeying him perfectly."[6] This definition is significant for several reasons, not least of which how it focuses our attention on the main thing: soteriology. John Feinberg states, "According to [Grudem's] definition, Scripture's sufficiency has to do with the most fundamental soteriological issues of all, namely, how to be saved and how to live out that salvation before God and mankind."[7] When I share Grudem's definition of sufficiency with my students I am quick to add that Grudem is not claiming that the doctrine of the sufficiency of Scripture claims and ensures that we always "trust [God] perfectly" and "obey [God] perfectly." But when we don't do so, the Scriptures are not at fault. Indeed, Scripture's sufficiency "is about the nature of Scripture's contents."[8] And the content of Scripture, as the product of God's Spirit, is sufficient for life

---

5. Frame, *Doctrine of the Word of God*, 143.

6. Grudem, *Systematic Theology*, 152. Feinberg invokes Grudem's definition in Feinberg, *Light in a Dark Place*, 684.

7. Feinberg, *Light in a Dark Place*, 684.

8. Feinberg, *Light in a Dark Place*, 684.

and godliness (2 Pet 1:3–4). One of the key biblical texts to establish this doctrine is found in 2 Timothy 3:14–17:

> But as for you, continue in what you have learned and have firmly believed, knowing from whom you learned it and how from childhood you have been acquainted with the sacred writings, which are able to make you wise for salvation through faith in Christ Jesus. All Scripture is breathed out by God and profitable for teaching, for reproof, for correction, and for training in righteousness, that the man of God may be complete, equipped for every good work.

Here the apostle Paul is reminding his young apprentice Timothy to remain devoted to the "sacred writings" which were not only sufficient to save him, but to build him up in the faith such that he would be "complete, equipped for every good work." Not just *some* good works but, given the sufficiency of Scripture, *every* good work. As Frame explains, "Scripture contains divine words sufficient for all of life. It has all the divine words that the plumber needs, and all the divine words the theologian needs . . . . And in that sense it is sufficient for science and ethics as well."[9] The very nature of Scripture as "breathed out by God" makes the Bible not only sufficient for *how* to be saved, but for *living out* this salvation in every sphere of life. That is, the Scriptures are "profitable for teaching, for reproof, for correction, and for training in righteousness" in a most comprehensive way—what Frame refers to as "the whole content of Scripture applied to the whole content of the Christian life."[10]

At this point, it is important to see the connection between the sufficiency of Scripture and the sufficiency of God. For when we claim the Scriptures are sufficient, we are really claiming that *God* is sufficient. This is a consequence of the doctrine of inspiration outlined earlier in this chapter. To make this still more clear, consider what R. Carlton Wynne claims about inspiration as "a verbal reflection of [God's] divine character"—character that is "personal, trustworthy, and true." He explains,

> In fact, the Bible so closely identifies God's Word with God himself that at one point the two appear as coordinate subjects in adjoining texts: "For the word of God is living and active, sharper than any two-edged sword, piercing to the division of soul and spirit, of joints and marrow, and discerning the thoughts and intentions

---

9. Frame, *Doctrine of the Word of God*, 221.
10. Frame, *Doctrine of the Word of God*, 221. Frame helpfully states, "Scripture contains all the divine words needed for any aspect of human life" (220).

of the heart. And no creature is hidden from his sight, but all are naked and exposed to the eyes of him to whom we must give account" (Heb. 4:12–13). As the written Word of God, the Bible lays bare the thoughts and attitudes of its hearers because God, its author, searches all heart and human plans (1 Chron. 28:9; Jer. 17:10).[11]

Given the doctrine of inspiration, therefore, when we say the Scriptures are sufficient, we are not merely trusting in some propositional truth statements or a dead letter. We are trusting in the living God to whom the word belongs. A wise pastor knows that the all-sufficient God comes to us by his Word and stands with us in life and ministry. It is the sufficiency of Scripture that allows us to say "Amen" to the promise of 2 Corinthians 9:8: "And God is able to make all grace abound to you, so that having all sufficiency in all things at all times, you may abound in every good work."

Historic Sufficiency

The sufficiency of Scripture as defined reflects what the church has historically believed, taught, and confessed. Consider, for example, Martin Luther's defense at the Diet of Worms (1521) when he was called upon to renounce his writings:

> Since then your serene majesty and your lordships seek a simple answer, I will give it in this manner, neither horned nor toothed: Unless I am convinced by the testimony of the Scriptures or by clear reason (for I do not trust either in the pope or in councils alone, since it is well known that they have often erred and contradicted themselves), I am bound by the Scriptures I have quoted and my conscience is captive to the Word of God. I cannot and will not retract anything, since it is neither safe nor right to go against conscience. I cannot do otherwise, here I stand, may God help me, Amen.[12]

Demonstrating his trust in the sufficiency of Scripture, Luther declared that he was "bound by the Scriptures" and "captive to the word of God." On the sufficient Scriptures he stood and would not recant unless the Word of God persuaded him that he was wrong in anything he wrote.

---

11. Wynne, "Scripture," 3.
12. Lindberg, *European Reformations Sourcebook*, 43.

Henry Bullinger, not before an imperial diet but before his congregation, proclaimed the sufficiency of Scripture in the second sermon of *The Decades* (1551):

> I will in few words declare unto you, dearly beloved, that in the word of God, delivered to us by the prophets and apostles, is abundantly contained the whole effect of godliness, and what things soever are available to the leading of our lives rightly, well, and holily. For, verily, it must needs be, that *that doctrine is full, and in all points perfect*, to which nothing ought either to be added, or else to be taken away.[13]

Clearly for Bullinger (and the other Reformers) this was not a doctrine left to the scholars of religion. The sufficiency of Scripture was a gracious doctrine for the church. Bullinger rightly pointed his congregation to the Scriptures for "the whole effect of godliness."

In the wake of the Reformation, Protestant churches developed a rich heritage of confessions that articulate clearly, among other essential doctrines, the sufficiency of Scripture. Take, for example, the Belgic Confession of Faith (1561). Article 7, "The Sufficiency of the Holy Scriptures to be the Only Rule of Faith," states,

> We believe that those Holy Scriptures fully contain the will of God, and that whatsoever man ought to believe, unto salvation, is sufficiently taught therein. For, since the whole manner of worship, which God requires of us, is written in them at large, it is unlawful for any one, though an apostle, to teach otherwise than we are now taught in the Holy Scriptures: nay, though it were an angel from heaven, as the apostle Paul saith. For, since it is forbidden, to add unto or take away anything from the word of God, it doth thereby evidently appear, that the doctrine thereof is most perfect and complete in all respects. Neither do we consider of equal value any writing of men, however holy these men may have been, with those divine Scriptures, nor ought we to consider custom, or the great multitude, or antiquity, or succession of times and persons, or councils, decrees or statutes, as of equal value with the truth of God, for the truth is above all; for all men are of themselves liars, and more vain than vanity itself. Therefore, we reject with all our hearts, whatsoever doth not agree with this infallible rule, which the apostles have taught us, saying, Try the spirits whether they are

---

13. Bullinger, *The Decades*, 61; emphasis added.

of God. Likewise, if there come any unto you, and bring not this doctrine, receive him not into your house.[14]

In the Belgic Confession, the Scriptures are said to "fully contain" and "sufficiently teach" all matters related to salvation. The Belgic Confession takes so seriously Scripture's sufficiency that it warns, "If there come any unto you, and bring not this doctrine, receive him not into your house."

Likewise, the Westminster Confession of Faith (1647) states, "The whole counsel of God concerning all things necessary for His own glory, man's salvation, faith and life, is either expressly set down in Scripture, or by good and necessary consequence may be deduced from Scripture: unto which nothing at any time is to be added, whether by new revelations of the Spirit, or traditions of men" (1.6).[15] The Church historic loves to confess the Scriptures as containing "all things necessary"—in other words, their sufficiency.

Shepherding in the Sufficient Word

The doctrine of the sufficiency of Scripture raises several implications for how pastors shepherd God's people. The first implication is summarized well by Feinberg: "Because of Scripture's sufficiency, we must make it the focus of both our preaching and teaching."[16] If we would shepherd God's people faithfully then we must make the Word of God central in all we do as pastors. This is the apostolic imperative when it comes to gospel ministry as seen in Paul's farewell address to the Ephesian elders: "Therefore I testify to you this day that I am innocent of the blood of all, for I did not shrink from declaring to you the whole counsel of God" (Acts 20:27). After all, pastors are "stewards of the mysteries of God" (1 Cor 4:1), and are charged with making "the word of God fully known" (Col 1:25). Furthermore, the apostle Peter reminds us that in the Scriptures "we have the prophetic word more fully confirmed, to which you will do well to pay attention as to a lamp shining in a dark place, until the day dawns and the morning star rises in your hearts" (2 Pet 1:19). The pastor takes heart that the sufficient Scriptures of both the Old and New Testaments are enough for both evangelism

---

14. Beeke and Ferguson, *Reformed Confessions*, 14–16.
15. Beeke and Ferguson, *Reformed Confessions*, 13; see also the 1689 Baptist Confession of Faith 1.6.
16. Feinberg, *Light in a Dark Place*, 704–5.

efforts (Rom 10:14) and discipleship goals (2 Tim 3:16–17). So, whether preaching and teaching for conversions or maturity in the faith, the Word of God must be central in all the pastor does, for it alone is sufficiently powerful to do the work of ministry. This means that all the "props" of ministry are not needed, or at least need to be seen for what they are: mere ornaments. Nothing but the sufficient Word of God has power for ministry fruit. This truth is liberating to the pastor who may have been deceived into thinking that unless he has the latest technology, for example, he cannot possibly expect ministry success. The Word of God does not need technology to make it *work*. And God's people do not need the Bible "dressed up" to make it powerful. It is sufficient in itself because of what it is: the Word of God. In 1886, Charles Spurgeon made this point in a sermon with a memorable illustration of a lion:

> Suppose a number of persons were to take it into their heads that they had to defend a lion, a full-grown king of beasts! There he is in the cage, and here come all the soldiers of the army to fight for him. Well, I should suggest to them, if they would not object, and feel that it was humbling to them, that they should kindly stand back, and open the door, and let the lion out! I believe that would be the best way of defending him, for he would take care of himself; and the best "apology" for the gospel is to let the gospel out.[17]

Given the sufficiency of God's Word, pastors simply need to "let it out."

Before Spurgeon, Luther spoke to the sufficiency of the Bible when he sought to explain the power of the Word:

> I will preach it, teach it, write it, but I will constrain no man by force, for faith must come freely without compulsion. Take myself as an example. I opposed indulgences and all the papists, but never with force. I simply taught, preached, and wrote God's Word; otherwise I did nothing. And while I slept [cf. Mark 4:26–29], or drank Wittenberg beer with my friends Philip and Amsdorf, the Word so greatly weakened the papacy that no prince or emperor ever inflicted such losses upon it. I did nothing; the Word did everything.[18]

A faithful pastor labors to sow the seed of God's Word, and then sleeps soundly each night knowing that God, in the power of the Holy Spirit, will give the increase according to his infinite wisdom and sovereign power.

17. Spurgeon, "Christ and His Co-Workers."
18. Luther, *Sermons I*, in *Luther's Works*, 51:77.

Scripture

As the apostle Paul explains to the Corinthian church, "I planted, Apollos watered, but God gave the growth" (1 Cor 3:6).

A second implication of this doctrine is the benefit to the pastor himself in terms of his own sanctification. This, of course, is desperately needed in contemporary evangelicalism given the tragic stories of yet another pastor succumbing to sin and being disqualified for ministry. The Word of God is not only sufficient for the sheep, but also for the shepherd who likewise is always a sheep in need of the Chief Shepherd. After discussing the ways in which God uses his Word to bless his people, Wynne turns his eye to pastors with the hope of their own growth in grace as they toil in the sufficient Scriptures on behalf of the church: "Even so, the pastor's Word-ministry to others will become a ministry of inner transformation to his own soul, ever conforming him to the image and glory of Christ (2 Cor. 3:18; 4:10)."[19] This is why the apostle pronounces this benediction over the Ephesian elders as he bids them farewell: "And now I commend you to God and to the word of his grace, which is able to build you up and to give you the inheritance among all those who are sanctified" (Acts 20:32). Paul knows that the pastors in Ephesus will be built up by the all-sufficient "word of [God's] grace." Indeed, it is God's sufficient Word that will grow us in holiness. As the psalmist states, "I have stored up your word in my heart, that I might not sin against you" (Ps 119:11). Our churches need pastors who are laboring in the Scriptures for their own sanctification as well as for the sake of those they shepherd.

A third implication of the sufficiency of Scripture for ministry has to do with wanting a Spirit-empowered ministry rather than one done in the flesh. I've never met a pastor who has told me he wants his church to lack spiritual power. As one would expect, it's always just the opposite. Pastors long for churches to experience the sovereign Spirit's power. The question is, how will that come about? Another way to ask it is, *How can I know if my ministries of preaching and teaching and counseling and evangelism and missions have Spiritual power?* The only way to ensure that our churches are Spirit-empowered churches is to make the Word of God the focus of all we do; for the Spirit works through the Word.

On this point the Reformer John Calvin is essential reading. In Calvin's theology there is a necessary connection between the work of the Spirit and the Word of God: "The Spirit wills to be conjoined with God's Word

---

19. Wynne, "Scripture," 8.

by an indissoluble bond, and Christ professes this concerning him when he promises the Spirit to his church."[20] Calvin further explains,

> And what wonder if Christ's bride and pupil be subject to her Spouse and Teacher, so that she pays constant and careful attention to his words! . . . In this way the church will distrust all the devisings of its own reason. But in those things where it rests upon God's Word the church will not waver with any distrust or doubting, but will repose in great assurance and firm constancy. So also trusting in the fullness of the promises it possesses, the church will have in them excellent means of sustaining its faith. Thus it will never doubt that the Holy Spirit is always with it, its best guide in the right path. But it will at the same time be mindful what use God would have us receive from his Spirit. "The Spirit," he says, "whom I shall send from the Father" [John 16:7] "will lead you into all truth" [John 16:13]. But how? Because, he says, "the Spirit will recall all that I have said to you" [John 14:26]. Therefore, he declares that we are to expect nothing more from his Spirit than that he will illumine our minds to perceive the truth of his teaching.[21]

The church, according to Calvin, will "never doubt that the Holy Spirit is always with it," so long as the church "rests upon God's Word." If we would have Spirit-empowered ministries then we must entrust ourselves to the sufficient Word of God—the very word the Spirit has constrained himself to. Indeed, the Spirit has bound himself to Scripture. Therefore, as the church does likewise, she can be assured of a Spirit-empowered ministry.

It is imperative for the pastor to never think he "graduates" from the Bible. This may be a particular temptation given all of the advice and helps that come to us year after year through our evangelical publishing houses and conferences. Some pastors may find themselves a few years into their first pastorates wondering when revival is going to break out, or wearied under the weight of various hardships that they have weathered. It is precisely at this moment that the pastor must remember the doctrine of Scripture and its sufficiency. This much-needed reminder may come in many ways, not least of which is through the songs of the church. It may be the simple verse of a children's song ("Jesus loves me this I know, for the Bible tells me so"); or, it may be one of the weightier hymns like "How Firm a

---

20. Calvin, *Institutes*, 4.8.13.
21. Calvin, *Institutes*, 4.8.13.

Foundation," where the opening stanza sings of the church's great foundation in the Word of God:

> How firm a foundation you saints of the Lord,
> is laid for your faith in his excellent Word!
> What more can he say than to you he has said,
> to you who for refuge to Jesus have fled?

When we consider what we've been given in the Scriptures—the very out-breathed breath of God—it seems more than appropriate to ask the rhetorical question of the hymn, "What more can he say than to you he has said?" The implied answer, of course, is *nothing*. In the Bible, God has given us *everything* we need for life and godliness. Therefore, we are resolved to pastor in the sufficiency of God's Word.

3

Gospel

> "The true church can be recognized if it has the following marks: the church engages in the pure preaching of the gospel; it makes use of the pure administration of the sacraments as Christ instituted them; it practices church discipline for the correcting of faults."
>
> —Belgic Confession (1561)

> "I am not ashamed of the gospel, for it is the power of God for salvation to everyone who believes."
>
> —Romans 1:16

Resolution 3: Resolved to be gospel-driven in ministry.

Surely Michael Horton is correct when he observes, "Distinguished from all religions, spiritualities, and philosophies of life, the Christian faith is, at its heart, a *gospel* (meaning 'Good News')."[1] The argument of this chapter is that the pastor's identity and priorities are established by the

---

1. Horton, *The Gospel-Driven Life*, 11.

gospel—the good news of Jesus Christ. The pastor above all is a "gospel minister." But before we consider how the gospel informs pastoral ministry, we have to be clear about what the Bible means when it speaks of the gospel. I begin my explanation of the gospel by first considering the state of contemporary evangelicalism with respect to the Good News.

Whatever Happened to the Gospel?

In his self-proclaimed "protest," *Christless Christianity: The Alternative Gospel of American Christianity*, Horton asks a very important question: "Judging by its commercial, political, and media success, the evangelical movement seems to be booming. But is it still *Christian*?"[2] Horton spends the remainder of his diatribe arguing that, in the main, evangelicalism is rapidly approaching a form of Christless Christianity. Horton explains,

> There need not be explicit abandonment of any key Christian teaching, just a series of subtle distortions and not-so-subtle distractions. Even good things can cause us to look away from Christ and to take the gospel for granted as something we needed for conversion but which now can be safely assumed and put in the background. Center stage, however, is someone or something else.[3]

It should come as no surprise to any thoughtful observer of the contemporary American church that at the center of the church's life is not Christ, but ourselves. We are reaping the rotten fruit of what Carl Trueman (and David Wells before him) explains as the "rise and triumph of the modern self."[4] The "triumph" has resulted in the displacement of God from the center of the church's life and replaced him with Self. In countless ways, contemporary evangelicalism is repeating the awful exchange that happened in the Garden of Eden millennia ago: we've rejected God as our rightful ruler and replaced him with ourselves.

Expelling the gospel from the center of the church, however, has not happened suddenly with loud bells and neon signs alerting us to this perilous path. In other words, what has gotten us here has been a series of incremental steps away from the gospel. "So much of what I am calling

---

2. Horton, *Christless Christianity*, 19. Horton refers to this work as a "protest" (20).

3. Horton, *Christless Christianity*, 20.

4. See Trueman, *Rise and Triumph of the Modern Self*; see also Wells, *God in the Wasteland*, 44–56.

'Christless Christianity,'" explains Horton, "is not profound enough to constitute heresy. Like the easy-listening Musak that play ubiquitously in the background in other shopping venues, the message of American Christianity has simply become trivial, sentimental, affirming, and irrelevant."[5] Where outright heresy would be relatively easy to detect, the loss of the gospel in the church has been happening over time rather "under the radar." One is reminded of the famous fable about a frog in a kettle of water being slowly boiled alive with the poor frog blissfully unaware.

Of course, what the world needs most is not us, but the gospel. This generation, like every generation, has need of a Savior. Therefore, pastors must be about the proclamation of the Savior *for* the world. This is the great news we herald and call people to believe: to bring glory to himself, God took on flesh and dwelt among sinful creatures to accomplish the salvation that only he could. By living a perfect life as the God-man in obedience to the law (active obedience) and dying an atoning death on the cross, and thereby satisfying God's just wrath for sin (passive obedience), Jesus Christ put away sin once for all of the elect. And to ensure that this salvation is accomplished, God conquered death by raising Jesus from the grave, opening the floodgates of eternal life to all those who would repent and believe this gospel before the Son of God returns to judge the living and the dead. Most surely, this is not a gospel of self, but the gospel of God—the only gospel that saves a world steeped in sin and darkness. The ultimate answer for the great problem of the human heart and its rebellion toward God is the gospel. Pastors, after all, are not ambassadors for self, but "ambassadors for Christ, God making his appeal through us.... For our sake he made him to be sin who knew no sin, so that in him we might become the righteousness of God" (2 Cor 5:20–21). That the gospel would be absent in the life of the church is no small irony given how the apostle Paul describes the gospel as a matter of "first importance": "For I delivered to you as of first importance what I also received: that Christ died for our sins in accordance with the Scriptures, that he was buried, that he was raised on the third day in accordance with the Scriptures" (1 Cor 15:3–4).

The Gospel for Christians?

Without trying to catalog all of the steps the American church has taken to marginalize the gospel, something Horton mentioned above gets to the

---

5. Horton, *Christless Christianity*, 21.

heart of the problem: "Even good things can cause us to look away from Christ and to take the gospel for granted *as something we needed for conversion but which now can be safely assumed* and put in the background." The gospel has been marginalized in large part because we have been taught to think the gospel is not for believers. The gospel, as Horton observes, was for conversion, but now we think we need to grow in faith—and surely this comes by another means than the gospel, right? Wrong. Pastors must reclaim the centrality of the gospel not only for our evangelistic efforts, but in discipleship as well. Indeed, the gospel is not only the means of conversion, but of growth in grace all the way to glory.

This all-important ministry principle came to me powerfully many years ago. My pastor at the time was taking several of us through the book of Romans. Our time in Romans 1:16–17 was incredibly instructive for me and left an indelible mark on my ministry. Here's the text: "For I am not ashamed of the gospel, for it is the power of God for salvation to everyone who believes, to the Jew first and also to the Greek. For in it the righteousness of God is revealed from faith for faith, as it is written, 'The righteous shall live by faith.'" Similar to how James says the tongue is a small member but makes great boasts (Jas 3:5), so it is with some words in Greek. Though small, γάρ (*gar*) is a really important Greek word. Indeed, this little conjunction—translated "for" in Romans 1:17—makes great boasts. It speaks to the "cause" or "reason" for why the gospel is the power of God for salvation (v. 16). The good news of Jesus Christ is the power of God for salvation because in the gospel a righteousness we so desperately need is revealed—not as a standard to meet, but as a gift to be received. This is the breakthrough understanding of this verse the great Reformer Martin Luther experienced causing him to refer to Romans 1:17 as "the very gate to Paradise."[6] The Heidelberg Catechism summarizes this teaching well:

> Question 60: How are you righteous before God?
>
> Answer: Only by true faith in Jesus Christ. Even though my conscience accuses me of having grievously sinned against all God's commandments, of never having kept any of them, and of still being inclined toward all evil, nevertheless, without any merit of my own, out of sheer grace, God grants and credits to me the perfect satisfaction, righteousness, and holiness of Christ, as if I had never sinned nor been a sinner, and as if I had been as perfectly obedient

---

6. Lindberg, *European Reformations Sourcebook*, 25.

as Christ was obedient for me. All I need to do is accept this gift with a believing heart.

In the gospel, "God grants and credits to me the perfect satisfaction, righteousness, and holiness of Christ." The result? Though utterly unworthy as a sinner, I am seen by God "as if I had never sinned nor been a sinner, and as if I had been as perfectly obedient as Christ was obedient for me." All I must do is "accept this gift with a believing heart."

So far, the gospel sounds like something we need for conversion, something that justifies us before a holy God. Indeed, it is. But not only this—though this reality is easily missed given our evangelical conditioning to think the gospel is only for conversion, that is, to save a person. Notice what Paul said to the Roman Christians in his extended greeting: "So I am eager to preach the gospel to you also who are in Rome" (1:15). When years ago, in my early twenties, my pastor showed me this, it was paradigm shifting for my understanding of ministry. I was at first befuddled to think Paul was eager to preach the gospel to believers, people *already* saved. After all, he had addressed the letter "to all those in Rome who are loved by God and called to be saints" (1:7)—a people with a faith in the Lord Jesus Christ so genuine and compelling that it was being "proclaimed in all the world" (1:8). Paul knew that the church in Rome, this local assembly of Christians, still needed the gospel. It would be to the church's peril to think they had graduated from the good news of Jesus Christ. Paul, for his part, was not going to let that happen, which is why he wrote eleven chapters explaining the gospel and another five applying it. To be sure, Paul has the gospel in mind when he explains his purpose in longing to come to Rome: "For I long to see you, that I may impart to you some spiritual gift to strengthen you—that is, that we may be mutually encouraged by each other's faith, both yours and mine" (1:11–12). The "spiritual gift" to strengthen them, and being "mutually encouraged by each other's faith," has at its heart the gospel of Jesus Christ. Strength and encouragement come by no other means.

So, whether for conversions or discipleship, pastors must keep the gospel central in their shepherding. Once the gospel is assumed or put in the background, churches are left without the very power of God "from faith for faith" (Rom 1:17). When this happens, churches are susceptible to pseudo-gospels. And Paul has strong language for these shams:

> I am astonished that you are so quickly deserting him who called you in the grace of Christ and are turning to a different gospel—not

that there is another one, but there are some who trouble you and want to distort the gospel of Christ. But even if we or an angel from heaven should preach to you a gospel contrary to the one we preached to you, let him be accursed. As we have said before, so now I say again: If anyone is preaching to you a gospel contrary to the one you received, let him be accursed. (Gal 1:6–9)

The Gospel for Pastors

Like churches as a whole, pastors are at risk of thinking they don't need the gospel. I know that sounds crazy to even suggest. After all, pastors are "gospel ministers." How could a pastor think he's graduated from the gospel?

I remember way back in 1995, when attending the Bethlehem Conference for Pastors, John Piper gave an address, "Charles Spurgeon: Preaching Through Adversity." Piper helpfully explained what can happen to a preacher when adversity is a constant companion:

> Preaching great and glorious truth in an atmosphere that is not great and glorious is an immense difficulty. To be reminded week in and week out that many people regard your preaching of the glory of the grace of God as hypocrisy pushes a preacher not just into the hills of introspection, but sometimes to the precipice of self-extinction.
>
> I don't mean suicide. I mean something more complex. I mean the deranging inability to know any longer who you are. What begins as a searching introspection for the sake of holiness, and humility gradually becomes, for various reasons, a carnival of mirrors in your soul: you look in one and you're short and fat; you look in another and you're tall and skinny; you look in another and you're upside down. And the horrible feeling begins to break over you that you don't know who you are any more. The center is not holding. And if the center doesn't hold—if there is no fixed and solid "I" able to relate to the fixed and solid "Thou," namely, God, then who will preach next Sunday?
>
> When the apostle Paul said in 1 Corinthians 15:10, "By the grace of God, *I am what I am*," he was saying something utterly essential for the survival of preachers in adversity. If, by grace, the identity of the "I"—the "I" created by Christ and united to Christ, but still a human "I"—if that center doesn't hold, there will be no

more authentic preaching, for there will be no more authentic preacher, but a collection of echoes.[7]

The word picture Piper uses of a carnival of mirrors vividly demonstrates what can happen to a preacher when he is bombarded with adversity over a sustained period: he forgets who he is.

In his address, Piper is asking how one preaches through adversity. My question is, how do we *pastor* through adversity? How do you stay in the ministry when the center is threatening to give way? I've pastored in a "carnival of mirrors," and it was no fun. In fact, it was one of the most difficult periods of time in my life. The adversity was so strong and the opposition so acute, there were mornings when I found myself pleading with God for the grace to continue. How did he answer my pleas? In part, by reminding me of who I am in Christ. In other words, I needed reminding that the gospel ultimately defines me, not my critics.

The Call Before the Call

In my pastoral ministry class at Southern Seminary, I have a lecture I love to give on a pastor's calling. Even as "calling" language is being questioned in our day,[8] I am still persuaded that it is a biblical idea and that it is imperative that a man be clear about his calling to pastoral ministry. Spurgeon knew this and warned of the "calamity" of a man entering ministry without being called:

> How may a young man know whether he is called or not? That is a weighty enquiry, and I desire to treat it most solemnly. O for divine guidance in so doing! That hundreds have missed their

---

7. Piper, "Charles Spurgeon."

8. Jamieson, *The Path to Being a Pastor*, 19–30. I find Jamieson's argument generally unhelpful for the primary reason that it puts the focus on the would-be pastor rather than God. Those who advocate for "calling" language are asking where this "aspiration" comes from. Knowing it is God who has granted the aspiration will be vital for the pastor when testing comes. Furthermore, calling language asks the same questions he seems to think are unique to those like him arguing for aspirational language. For example, if one says, "I'm called" he must test this call by considering the nonnegotiable qualifications that establish the calling in passages like 1 Timothy 3:1–7; Titus 1:5–9; and 1 Peter 5:1–4. And there should be corresponding affirmation by the church that the "internal" sense of call is legitimate, and not a mere subjective whim. Contrary to Jamieson, it still seems best to stay with the language of "internal" and "external" call with the corresponding safeguards to ensure, as much as possible, we haven't presumed on a pastorate.

> way, and stumbled against a pulpit is sorrowfully evident from the fruitless ministries and decaying churches which surround us. It is a fearful calamity to a man to miss his calling, and to the church upon whom he imposes himself, his mistake involves an affliction of the most grievous kind.[9]

Pity the church that has a pastor who "missed his calling" and should be doing any number of things other than pastoring.

As important as it is for a man be clear about his calling to pastoral ministry, it is not as important as remembering the call *before* the call. This is where gospel identity comes in and helps us avoid the carnival of mirrors that can be the undoing of a pastor. In this regard, I have found Dave Harvey and his book *Am I Called? The Summons to Pastoral Ministry* very helpful. He begins by establishing the centrality of God in the call to ministry and how God's initiative is paramount: "The call to ministry is about God's character and activity, about his mercy and love, and ultimately about his provision to those for whom he died. If the Caller's initiative is everything, then we must preoccupy ourselves with the ultimate Caller. It's that simple—and that profound."[10] This preoccupation with the ultimate Caller will lead us to consider what Harvey calls "the call before the call."

Before God calls us into ministry we must remember (and keep ever before us) the gospel truth that God first calls us to himself. Calling language is first and foremost about our calling to salvation. Consider, for example, Romans 8:30: "And those whom he predestined he also *called*, and those whom he *called* he also justified, and those whom he justified he also glorified." Predestined, called, justified, and glorified. The context of "called" in Romans 8:30 is salvation. Similarly, 1 Corinthians 1:9 teaches that we "were called into the fellowship of his Son, Jesus Christ our Lord," a reference clearly to salvation. Paul tells the Thessalonians of their common salvation when he says God "called you through our gospel, so that you may obtain the glory of our Lord Jesus Christ" (2 Thess 2:13–14).

The call before the call is what theologians designate God's *effectual call*. Wayne Grudem is helpful when he defines the effectual call as "an act of God the Father, speaking through the human proclamation of the gospel, in which he summons people to himself in such a way that they respond in saving faith."[11] The call to salvation precedes and grounds any secondary

---

9. Spurgeon, *Lectures to My Students*, 22.
10. Harvey, *Am I Called?*, 34.
11. Grudem, *Systematic Theology*, 843.

call to ministry. First and foremost, God calls us not to ministry but to fellowship with his Son in salvation. In other words, we are in Christ before we are ever in ministry. Knowing this is the only way to ensure that the center holds when affliction in ministry hits.

Why is it essential for a pastor to settle this primary call to Christ? Why is this vitally important? Harvey offers three reasons involving our identity, our adequacy, and our priorities. Let's consider each in turn. First, by settling the call before the call, we're reminded that God supplies our identity, not our ministry. In the gospel, we experience a true union with Christ through faith. This glorious truth reminds us that we are children of God before we're ever a pastor; and a child of God we always will be.

The importance of knowing this came home to me in a most profound way when I experienced the loss of my first wife to a five-year battle with cancer just after 7:00 p.m. on Sunday, February 2, 2014. Even as I slept very little that night, I remember waking up Monday morning having something like a crisis of identity. For the first time in sixteen years, I didn't wake up as Julia's husband. And if not Julia's husband, who was I? This question began a necessary process of reminding myself of my first calling as a follower of Jesus Christ, a redeemed sinner, a child of God. Grief and sorrow were conspiring to make me forget. I had to remind myself that my ultimate identity was not as Julia's husband. Marriage is by definition temporary or, as Piper has said, "momentary."[12] In contrast, my relationship with God in salvation is forever. The fight of faith in those critical days after Julia's homegoing centered on reminding myself that I am beloved of God and therefore can say with Paul in Romans 8:31–39,

> What then shall we say to these things? If God is for us, who can be against us? He who did not spare his own Son but gave him up for us all, how will he not also with him graciously give us all things? Who shall bring any charge against God's elect? It is God who justifies. Who is to condemn? Christ Jesus is the one who died—more than that, who was raised—who is at the right hand of God, who indeed is interceding for us. Who shall separate us from the love of Christ? Shall tribulation, or distress, or persecution, or famine, or nakedness, or danger, or sword? As it is written, "For your sake we are being killed all the day long; we are regarded as sheep to be slaughtered." No, in all these things we are more than conquerors through him who loved us. For I am sure that neither death nor life, nor angels nor rulers, nor things present nor things

---

12. Piper, *This Momentary Marriage*.

> to come, nor powers, nor height nor depth, nor anything else in all creation, will be able to separate us from the love of God in Christ Jesus our Lord.

Nothing "will be able to separate us from the love of God in Christ Jesus our Lord." My identity crisis was short-lived thanks to this glorious truth: that my identity in Christ is unchanging.[13]

Pastors must remember they are not their ministry. What do I mean by this? Take, for example, the pastor who defines himself by the applause or accolades of his church. When things are going well in the ministry, he feels great. He's living off the compliments, the encouragements, the respect that comes when people are happy with him. But what happens when a dark cloud of discontent on the part of the people moves over the church? What happens to that pastor when the encouragement turns to criticism? Who is he then? A crisis of identity can ensue unless the pastor remembers the call before the call.

Or consider how a pastor can be like a professional athlete. At some point, that athlete will have to hang up the cleats or shoes or gloves. Every athlete at some point "hits the cliff" and simply can't physically compete anymore.[14] When this happens, it is not uncommon for professional athletes to go through an identity crisis. Who are they, if not the one throwing touchdown passes, hitting homeruns, draining threes, or securing knockouts? When the uniform comes off, what is their identity?

Likewise, at some point a pastor will need to retire. Lord willing, our tenure as pastors is longer than a professional athlete's who, depending on the sport, may get to compete at the highest level into his or her late thirties. The point is, eventually we, too, will hit the cliff. Who will you be, pastor, when you no longer have an office at the church, sermons to prepare, and people asking for a meeting? Will you have an identity crisis that first morning you wake up without "Pastor" in front of your name? It is at this moment that you press into your unchanging identity that came with the call before the call: your identity in Christ. You never were your ministry. Since your conversion you have been a child of God. And a child of God you forever will be.

---

13. For an excellent book on the topic of identity in Christ, see Ferguson, *Children of the Living God*.

14. Even Tom Brady had to finally retire in 2023; and contrary to any signs suggesting otherwise, even LeBron James can't play forever.

Second, the call before the call reminds us where our adequacy for ministry comes from. Pity the pastor who thinks the weight of ministry is to be carried on his feeble and fallible shoulders. Consider these biblical texts that are intended to humble the proud and encourage the weak in ministry:

- "For while we were still weak, at the right time Christ died for the ungodly. For one will scarcely die for a righteous person—though perhaps for a good person one would dare even to die—but God shows his love for us in that while we were still sinners, Christ died for us" (Rom 5:6–8).

- "For consider your calling, brothers: not many of you were wise according to worldly standards, not many were powerful, not many were of noble birth. But God chose what is foolish in the world to shame the wise; God chose what is weak in the world to shame the strong; God chose what is low and despised in the world, even things that are not, to bring to nothing things that are, so that no human being might boast in the presence of God. And because of him you are in Christ Jesus, who became to us wisdom from God, righteousness and sanctification and redemption, so that, as it is written, 'Let the one who boasts, boast in the Lord'" (1 Cor 1:26–31).

- "Three times I pleaded with the Lord about this, that it should leave me. But he said to me, 'My grace is sufficient for you, for my power is made perfect in weakness.' Therefore I will boast all the more gladly of my weaknesses, so that the power of Christ may rest upon me. For the sake of Christ, then, I am content with weaknesses, insults, hardships, persecutions, and calamities. For when I am weak, then I am strong" (2 Cor 12:8–10).

According to these passages, God calls to himself people who are ungodly, weak, sinful, proud, unknown, and needy. He does this not only to humble us and magnify his greatness, but to encourage us in the truth that his grace is sufficient for us. His power is our sufficiency for ministry. The banner over our ministry efforts is the same as Paul's: "Such is the confidence that we have through Christ toward God. Not that we are sufficient in ourselves to claim anything as coming from us, but our sufficiency is from God, who has made us sufficient to be ministers of a new covenant" (2 Cor 3:4–6).

To hold to this conviction is typically far easier when starting a ministry than toward the end. Why? Because finishing seminary and entering the first pastorate can be overwhelming, and typically the pastor is still young enough to think he doesn't know everything. But as the years go by, if not careful, the pastor may think he knows it all, or at least has learned how to "succeed." He's become "good" at ministry. He can turn a phrase in the pulpit, say some things that sound wise in the counseling session, has become an expert in small talk, and can lead a good meeting. Subtly, he's started to trust in himself for his sufficiency. This ministry thing has gotten easy. But he should know better. The call before the call reminds him of the gospel. And so, he repents of his self-sufficiency and flees to the truth that apart from God, the pastor "can do nothing" (John 15:5). We must remember that a pastor is one "who serves by the strength that God supplies—in order that in everything God may be glorified through Jesus Christ" (1 Pet 4:11).

Third, the call before the call reminds the pastor that the gospel sets the priorities for ministry. After all, "mission creep" is a real thing, and if we're not careful we can find ourselves like Martha in Luke 10, very busy but not with the one thing needful. With the best of intentions, many pastors find themselves driven in ministry not by the gospel, but by the tyranny of the urgent—things that may not be bad in and of themselves, but not gospel priorities. William Edwards captures this concern well when he calls pastors to a theologically driven ministry:

> But the larger point is this: when a rich theological perspective is lost, so is the larger story for our ministry. Bereft of such a vision, we are left simply with the things immediately before us, our work defined primarily by our current activity rather than the age of consummation that has now come. Apart from this vibrant biblical vision, the pastor's attention will be limited to his own labors while missing the grand narrative that gives them true significance. When this occurs, the tasks of ministry become wearying in their repetition: sermons to prepare and worship to order with the approach of each Sunday; more counsel to offer, possibly with little hope of change if experience proves true; meetings with elders that focus primarily on pressing needs . . . . The immediate pressures and demands of pastoral ministry may cause us to lose sight of this final epoch of redemption in which we serve. And without this larger story, the burdens of ministry quickly become unbearable and the source of great discouragement. Ministry needs theology.[15]

In other words, the gospel must set the agenda for pastoral ministry.

15. Edwards, introduction to *Theology for Ministry*, xxiv–xxv.

Not only will the gospel guard the pastor against discouragement and the tyranny of pressing needs without a redemptive context, when the gospel sets our priorities, the glory of God becomes the end for all we do rather than our career. Far too many pastors today, it seems, are serving churches with one foot in and one foot out as their current ministry is simply a prelude to the next. When a pastor fixates on his career trajectory, it is a clear sign that the gospel is not driving his ministry. Ministry has become about the pastor's platform or influence, not the fame of Christ. Instead, pastors must think like John the Baptist when his disciples came to him seemingly frustrated with all the people going to Jesus to be baptized:

> Now a discussion arose between some of John's disciples and a Jew over purification. And they came to John and said to him, "Rabbi, he who was with you across the Jordan, to whom you bore witness—look, he is baptizing, and all are going to him." John answered, "A person cannot receive even one thing unless it is given him from heaven. You yourselves bear me witness, that I said, 'I am not the Christ, but I have been sent before him.' The one who has the bride is the bridegroom. The friend of the bridegroom, who stands and hears him, rejoices greatly at the bridegroom's voice. Therefore this joy of mine is now complete. He must increase, but I must decrease." (John 3:25–30)

John's response to these territorial disciples is a gospel-driven conviction: "He must increase, but I must decrease." Indeed, ministry is about the increase of Christ for the good of God's people. Our career path is not the reason for our ministries. Pastors exist to glorify God in the advance of the gospel.

This was certainly Paul's perspective as he gave his farewell address to the Ephesian elders after three years of serving together. After noting the imprisonments and afflictions that awaited him on his journey to Jerusalem, Paul reminded them of his purpose: "But I do not account my life of any value nor as precious to myself, if only I may finish my course and the ministry that I received from the Lord Jesus, to testify to the gospel of the grace of God" (Acts 20:24). Paul is telling the Ephesian pastors what makes his life valuable, what makes it precious to him: faithfulness in testifying to the gospel. That's it, but that's everything to Paul. A pastor should resonate deeply with Paul's metric for his life's value. A pastor is one who is called to ensure the gospel is preached, applied, and valued in the daily life of the church. After all, without the gospel, pastoral ministry is irrelevant.

Pastors must be resolved to be gospel-driven in ministry. The gospel is not only for unbelievers (to get them saved), believers (to build them up in discipleship), but for pastors laboring in the trenches of local church ministry. The gospel establishes the pastor's identity, reminds him of his sufficiency, and sets the agenda for all he does. Let us be *gospel* ministers from beginning to end.

4

Humanity

"It is difficult to exaggerate the importance of the doctrine of man."
—Anthony Hoekema

"[The tongue] is a restless evil, full of deadly poison. With it we bless our Lord and Father, and with it we curse people who are made in the likeness of God. From the same mouth come blessing and cursing. My brothers, these things ought not to be so."
—James 3:8–10

Resolution 4: Resolved to shepherd people according to a biblical anthropology.

In chapter 1, I introduced Pastor Jerry, and the "assignments" he gave me and my roommates during my senior year at the University of Washington. One of those assignments was to serve the homeless community in the University District of Seattle. There was no shortage of people in this category along University Avenue ('the Ave'), just a couple blocks from the main entrance to my alma mater. So, newly grounded in the bedrock truth of James 2:26 ("faith apart from works is dead"), I began praying and planning to put my faith to work in neighborly love among "the least of these" (Matt 25:40).

Before we went out, however, Pastor Jerry continued to establish theological foundations beneath us that would give motivation and persevering effort to our service. What, after all, is the great theological reason to love those the world would say are unlovable? In other words, what makes every human being infinitely valuable and, therefore, worth loving? Pastor Jerry took us again to the book of James, specifically James 3:5–12 with its warning about the "deadly poison" that is the tongue:

> So also the tongue is a small member, yet it boasts of great things. How great a forest is set ablaze by such a small fire! And the tongue is a fire, a world of unrighteousness. The tongue is set among our members, staining the whole body, setting on fire the entire course of life, and set on fire by hell. For every kind of beast and bird, of reptile and sea creature, can be tamed and has been tamed by mankind, but no human being can tame the tongue. It is a restless evil, full of deadly poison. With it we bless our Lord and Father, and with it we curse people who are made in the likeness of God. From the same mouth come blessing and cursing. My brothers, these things ought not to be so. Does a spring pour forth from the same opening both fresh and salt water? Can a fig tree, my brothers, bear olives, or a grapevine produce figs? Neither can a salt pond yield fresh water.

Verses 9–10 particularly gripped me, as they describe the incompatibility of blessing and cursing in the mouth of the follower of Christ. The great theological ground for not cursing any human being is clear: people are made in the likeness of God (v. 9). Image bearers require not only the absence of cursing from people, but the presence of blessing.

This realization at the age of twenty-two indelibly marked me with a vision of people akin to what Paul experienced when he had his eyes opened to the glory of Christ in the gospel. It's the vision of Christ and of people that results from amazing grace, making the blind see rightly. Here's how Paul describes it in 2 Corinthians 5:16–17: "From now on, therefore, we regard no one according to the flesh. Even though we once regarded Christ according to the flesh, we regard him thus no longer. Therefore, if anyone is in Christ, he is a new creation. The old has passed away; behold, the new has come." Indeed, new creations in Christ see the glory of God in the face of Christ and people *not according to the flesh*, but according to the image of God. Armed with new eyes, we embarked on our ministry of mercy to the image bearers of the University District.

The Image of God

It is one of the great mysteries and most profound truths in the Bible regarding humanity: we are created in the image and likeness of God. The significance of this biblical vision for humanity as it relates to pastoral ministry cannot be overstated. In this chapter, I set out the biblical teaching on the image of God and then explore the implications of it for pastors.

"Head and Crown of the Entire Creation"

Considering creation in general and humanity in particular, the Dutch theologian and churchman Herman Bavinck remarked, "The entire world is a revelation of God, a mirror of His virtues and perfections; every creature is in his own way and according to his own measure an embodiment of a divine thought. But among all the creatures only man is the image of God, the highest and richest revelation of God, and therefore head and crown of the entire creation."[1] What sets humanity apart from every other creature is the stunning truth that only humans have been stamped, as it were, with God's very image. Only humanity carries within it God's likeness. To begin to understand this, we must go back to the beginning where Moses gives us insight into the wonder of humanity's origin.

The key biblical passage is Genesis 1:26–31:

> Then God said, "Let us make man in our image, after our likeness. And let them have dominion over the fish of the sea and over the birds of the heavens and over the livestock and over all the earth and over every creeping thing that creeps on the earth." So God created man in his own image, in the image of God he created him; male and female he created them. And God blessed them. And God said to them, "Be fruitful and multiply and fill the earth and subdue it, and have dominion over the fish of the sea and over the birds of the heavens and over every living thing that moves on the earth." And God said, "Behold, I have given you every plant yielding seed that is on the face of all the earth, and every tree with

---

1. Quoted in Hoekema, *Created in God's Image*, 12.

seed in its fruit. You shall have them for food. And to every beast of the earth and to every bird of the heavens and to everything that creeps on the earth, everything that has the breath of life, I have given every green plant for food." And it was so. And God saw everything that he had made, and behold, it was very good. And there was evening and there was morning, the sixth day.

To this point in the narrative, we've seen God create each animal "according to its kind" (vv. 21, 24, 25). But now we see God creating man in his image and after his likeness (vv. 26–27). Furthermore, by creating humanity male and female we learn that God intends fellowship among his creatures as well as what will be described in more detail later in Genesis, namely, a marriage union designed to reflect the relationship between Christ and the church (Gen 2:24; Eph 5:32). And by granting dominion with the corresponding charge to "be fruitful and multiply," we understand that God ordained humanity to be his representatives on earth, working for a God-glorifying culture. In sum, to be in the image of God means that humanity is *like* God and *represents* God. As Grudem explains, "The Hebrew word for 'image' (*tselem*) and the Hebrew word for 'likeness' (*demût*) refer to something that is similar but not identical to the thing it represents or is an 'image' of. The word *image* can also be used of something that represents something else."[2]

It is also important to remember that the image of God, though corrupted by humanity's fall into sin, is still the indelible mark on all people since the creation of Adam and Eve, our first parents. We see this clearly in "the generations of Adam" as the image of God is passed down to his posterity: "This is the book of the generations of Adam. When God created man, he made him in the likeness of God. Male and female he created

---

2. Grudem, *Bible Doctrine*, 189. Or consider Calvin's argument: "There is no slight quarrel over 'image' and 'likeness' when interpreters seek a nonexistent difference between these two words, except that 'likeness' has been added by way of explanation. . . . The likeness of God extends to the whole excellence by which man's nature towers over all the kinds of living creatures. Accordingly, the integrity with which Adam was endowed is expressed by this word [image], when he had full possession of right understanding, when he had his affections kept within the bounds of reason, all his senses tempered in right order, and he truly referred his excellence to exceptional gifts bestowed upon him by his Maker." Calvin, quoted in Kerr, *Calvin's Institutes*, 45. And Charles Hodge contends, "All these distinctions, however, rest on a false interpretation of Gen. 1:26. The words [image] and [likeness] are simply explanatory one of the other. Image and likeness, means an image that is like. The simple declaration of the Scripture is that man at his creation was like God." Hodge, *Systematic Theology*, 2:96.

them, and he blessed them and named them Man when they were created. When Adam had lived 130 years, he fathered a son in his own likeness, after his image, and named him Seth" (Gen 5:1–3). To be in Adam's likeness, after his image, is to be in the image and likeness of God. Further evidence that the image of God is not lost in mankind after the fall is the basis for the judgment God inflicts on those who take the life of another: "And for your lifeblood I will require a reckoning: from every beast I will require it and from man. From his fellow man I will require a reckoning for the life of man. Whoever sheds the blood of man, by man shall his blood be shed, for God made man in his own image" (Gen 9:5–6). All of this brings David to echo Genesis 1:26–27 as he gives praise to God for the wonder of humanity:

> When I look at your heavens, the work of your fingers, the moon and the stars, which you have set in place, what is man that you are mindful of him, and the son of man that you care for him? Yet you have made him a little lower than the heavenly beings and crowned him with glory and honor. You have given him dominion over the works of your hands; you have put all things under his feet, all sheep and oxen, and also the beasts of the field, the birds of the heavens, and the fish of the sea, whatever passes along the paths of the seas. O LORD, our Lord, how majestic is your name in all the earth! (Ps 8:3–9)

God's majesty is seen in the "glory and honor" of his image as reflected in humanity.[3]

Sin has so marred the image of God that it is hard to see it, to behold the "glory and honor" of representing God in his likeness. Given this, how can we know what the image of God is? What does it look like? Is the image of God seen most clearly in our reasoning capabilities? Our moral sense? Our ability to make decisions? Of course, all these things are vital to our humanity and set us apart from the animals. But as Anthony Hoekema explains, that is to look inward at the self for the image of God rather than outward to Christ:

> Since Christ was totally without sin (Heb. 4:15), in Christ we see the image of God in its perfection. As a skillful teacher uses visual aids to help his or her pupils understand what is being taught, so God the Father has given us in Jesus Christ a visual example of what the image of God is. There is no better way of seeing the

---

3. To be sure, the author of Hebrews sees this passage ultimately fulfilled in Christ (see 2:5–8).

image of God than to look at Jesus Christ. What we see and hear in Christ is what God intended for man. If this is so, then the best way to learn what the image of God is not to contrast man with animals, as has often been done, and then to find the divine image to consist in those qualities, abilities, and gifts that man has in distinction from the animals. Rather, we must learn to know what the image of God is by looking at Jesus Christ. What must therefore be at the center of the image of God is not characteristics like the ability to reason or the ability to make decisions (as important as such abilities may be for the proper functioning of the image of God), but rather that which was central to the life of Christ: love for God and love for man. If it is true that Christ perfectly images God, then the heart of the image of God must be love. For no man ever loved as Christ loved.[4]

True humanity, humanity as it was intended by God at creation, is seen most clearly in the God-man Jesus Christ. That we learn what the image of God is by looking at Jesus Christ is at the heart of the gospel and what God is doing in saving us, namely, transforming us increasingly into the image of his Son.[5]

The Image of God and the Modern Self

One of the glories of God's creation of humanity is creation as male and female. As John Frame observes, "Genesis 1:27, which tells us that God created us in his image, also tells us that he made us male and female. Evidently sexual differentiation is something important, something vital to who we are."[6] Humanity as male and female is certainly "vital to who we are," as the Bible makes clear. This, of course, is a truth under constant assault in our day as the culture moves at breakneck speed into the normalizing of gender fluidity.

This effort to separate gender from sex is one of the themes of Carl Trueman's important book *The Rise and Triumph of the Modern Self*. His opening words help us see and feel something of the tectonic shift in thinking that marks our time:

---

4. Hoekema, *Created in God's Image*, 22.
5. This is the theme of chap. 9: holiness as *Christlikeness* through the renewing or restoring of the image of God in believers.
6. Frame, *Concise Systematic Theology*, 115.

Resolutions of a Pastor

> The origins of this book lie in my curiosity about how and why a particular statement has come to be regarded as coherent and meaningful: "I am a woman trapped in a man's body." My grandfather died in 1994, less than thirty years ago, and yet, had he ever heard that sentence uttered in his presence, I have little doubt that he would have burst out laughing and considered it a piece of incoherent gibberish. And yet today it is a sentence that many in our society regard as not only meaningful but so significant that to deny it or question it in some way is to reveal oneself as stupid, immoral, or subject to yet another irrational phobia. And those who think of it as meaningful are not restricted to the veterans of college seminars on queer theory or French poststructuralism. They are ordinary people with little or no direct knowledge of the critical postmodern philosophies whose advocates swagger along the corridors of our most hallowed centers of learning.[7]

Pastors today are ministering in a time of unprecedented gender confusion. The sexual revolution, what Trueman describes as "the radical and ongoing transformation of sexual attitudes and behaviors that has occurred in the West since the early 1960s," has a modern twist that presents a unique challenge to gospel ministers. The twist is the *normalization* of once deviant sexual behaviors. Trueman explains, "What marks the modern sexual revolution out as distinctive is the way it has normalized these and other sexual phenomena."[8] The primary way this normalization happens is by winning the war of words or language. According to Trueman, whoever controls the meaning of words, controls what is culturally normal while simultaneously marginalizing anyone with beliefs outside the new normal:

> The most obvious evidence of this change is the way language has been transformed to serve the purpose of rendering illegitimate any dissent from the current political consensus on sexuality. Criticism of homosexuality is now *homophobia*; that of transgenderism is *transphobia*. The use of the term *phobia* is deliberate and effectively places such criticism of the new sexual culture into the realm of the irrational and points toward an underlying bigotry on the part of those who hold such views.[9]

It *almost* feels like an unfair fight given all the weapons at the culture's disposal to infuse language with new meaning including but not limited to

---

7. Trueman, *Rise and Triumph of the Modern Self*, 19.
8. Trueman, *Rise and Triumph of the Modern Self*, 21.
9. Trueman, *Rise and Triumph of the Modern Self*, 21.

major media outlets, corporate America, pop culture, education systems, and professional sports. I say "almost" because what the pastor must remember is that we have words at our disposal that are altogether more powerful and effective than the words of the world; but we have to be willing to speak them.

The words I have in mind, of course, are the words of Scripture (recall chapter 2 on the doctrine of inspiration). My aim in this chapter is not to rehearse the doctrine of Scripture as much as to exhort pastors to apply it in our cultural moment. I often tell my students who are training for the pastorate to make it their aim to fill their churches with the vernacular of heaven—that is, be explicit in their use of biblical language to help people's minds be renewed according to Scripture (Rom 12:2). We have to win the language war at home, in the churches we serve. Otherwise, our church members will have minds shaped by the world and the central tenets of the new sexual revolution.

One vital area of doctrine that has seemingly lost the war of words in the culture as a whole and, it seems, in much of evangelicalism is the doctrine of sin. In postmodern thinking, sin, as David Wells observes, "is no longer defined in relation to God but, rather, it is thought of only in terms of the self." A person wouldn't be wrong to ask, "Whatever happened to sin?" Wells explains what has happened:

> In our Western secularized cultures, the understanding of sin has both contracted and lost its reference point. It has contracted in the sense that many of the failures and moral breaches previous generations recognized as sins are now seen as simply crimes. No one any longer calls them sins even though many are, in fact, violations of one or more of the Ten Commandments. And the same kind of process has happened at a psychological level. Many of the things that used to be sins are now only diseases. And sometimes these are not even clinically recognized diseases but simply maladies of the psyche. But all of this has happened because we are understanding all human behavior along a flat, horizontal level. We are not thinking of it vertically in relation to God. Sin, in consequence, "disappears."[10]

With secularization moving God to the "wasteland" (see chapter 1), it is no wonder sin has generally disappeared from the evangelical mind. But pastors cannot let this happen without engaging the war of words. That is,

---

10. Wells, "Losing Our Religion," 810.

the responsibility falls on us as pastors to reacquaint (or explain for the first time) the doctrine of sin vertically, with reference to God. For if we don't, the image of God will increasingly be defined in terms of self. Indeed, as authors like Trueman and Wells document, it already appears to be happening in much of evangelicalism: the image of God has become the image of Self.

The Bible, however, is relentless in defining sin vertically. Just a few examples will suffice. First, Genesis 3 and the narrative of the fall of mankind into sin demonstrates the vertical nature of sin. The whole point is that God's clear command was disobeyed, plunging the whole human race into ruin. We learn from the story of the fall that the essence of sin is rebellion against God. Second, we see Isaiah explain sin with an allusion to Genesis 3 when he declares, "All we like sheep have gone astray; we have turned—every one—to his own way" (Isa 53:6). Again, rebellion against God in an effort to be our own god. Third, Paul in the letter to the Romans, cannot fathom sin apart from reference to God. Consider Romans 1:24–25: "Therefore God gave them up in the lusts of their hearts to impurity, to the dishonoring of their bodies among themselves, because they exchanged the truth about God for a lie and worshiped and served the creature rather than the Creator, who is blessed forever! Amen." Paul would have us see all sins as a result of the awful exchange of God for idols. For Paul, after all, sin is not a falling short of the glory of self, but of God (Rom 3:23).

Humanity in the Age of AI

Not only are we living during a sexual revolution, but a technological revolution as well. Our digital age presents its own unique challenges for pastoral ministry and a biblical anthropology. What is happening to our understanding of humanity as we increasingly live our lives in virtual worlds and communicate with virtual assistants? What does a robust biblical anthropology have to say to artificial intelligence like ChatGPT or virtual reality platforms like Apple's Vision Pro? In what ways might our very humanity be at stake? And how can pastors help shepherd church members through these uncharted technological waters? While much more can and needs to be said about ministry in our digital age, one vital area of concern for pastors must be the relational aspect of our humanity that is threatened by today's technologies. Part of the essence of what it means to be human is the profound truth that we are made for relationship. Like God, who has always existed in the relationship of the Trinity, God's image bearers are made to be in relationship with him and each other. God is not an avatar, and neither are we. Relationship is an essential component of the image of God. Indeed, we are like him when we are in relationship.

To understand and appreciate the relational aspect of the image of God, we must begin with God's relationship with himself in the fellowship of the Trinity. We are given insight into the mystery of the Trinity in the creation narrative itself: "Then God said, 'Let us make man in our image, after our likeness'" (Gen 1:26). What is staggering about this verse and is perhaps missed in the wonder of being made in the image and likeness of God, is the use of the plural pronouns *us* and *our*. God is having an inter-Trinitarian conversation. God is deliberating among himself—the glorious Godhead of Father, Son, and Holy Spirit. Later in Genesis we see another use of the plural pronoun *us* as the Lord mercifully determines to frustrate the sinful plans of man in building "a city and a tower with its top in the heavens" to make a name for themselves: "Come, let *us* go down and there confuse their language, so that they may not understand one another's speech" (11:7; emphasis added). The mystery of the Trinity is revealed in a pronoun.

Turning to the New Testament, we see that Jesus (the Word) was with the Father from the beginning of creation: "In the beginning was the Word, and the Word was with God, and the Word was God. He was in the beginning with God" (John 1:1–2; cf. v. 14: "And the Word became flesh and dwelt among us, and we have seen his glory, glory as of the only Son from the Father, full of grace and truth"). At Jesus's baptism we see relationship in the love of the Father for the Son: "And when Jesus was baptized, immediately he went up from the water, and behold, the heavens were opened to him, and he saw the Spirit of God descending like a dove and coming to rest on him; and behold, a voice from heaven said, 'This is my beloved Son, with whom I am well pleased'" (Matt 3:16–17; cf. 17:5). During Jesus's high priestly prayer, we learn something of the relationship he had with the Father in eternity past: "And now, Father, glorify me in your own presence with the glory that I had with you before the world existed" (John 17:5).

Given the intimate relationship among the members of the Godhead, it follows that part of being made in the image and likeness of God is that we, too, are relational beings. First, we were made to have relationship with God. This is evident from the earliest pages of the Bible as God interacted with Adam and Eve in the garden. But it's seen most profoundly in the

Incarnation of the Lord Jesus Christ. Remaining what he was (God), he became what he was not (man) to accomplish salvation and thereby reconcile man to God. As the apostle Peter explains, "For Christ also suffered once for sins, the righteous for the unrighteous, that he might bring us to God" (1 Pet 3:18). When Peter says "bring us to God" he is speaking of the fulfillment of a covenant relationship between God and his redeemed people (cf. Jer 31:31–34). It's the breathtaking truth of what Jesus proclaims for his followers in John 10:14–15: "I am the good shepherd. I know my own and my own know me, just as the Father knows me and I know the Father; and I lay down my life for the sheep." How close is our relationship with Christ? How intimately will we know him? Jesus declares, "just as the Father knows me and I know the Father."

Even now, in the grace of the Lord's Supper, we experience our relationship with God in Christ. As Paul explains, "The cup of blessing that we bless, is it not a participation in the blood of Christ? The bread that we break, is it not a participation in the body of Christ?" (1 Cor 10:16) Through the ordinary means of bread and cup we experience our relationship with God, one expression of being "partakers of the divine nature" (2 Pet 1:4). These are the biblical realities that make sense of the Westminster Shorter Catechism's profoundly relational opening: "What is the chief end of man? Man's chief end is to glorify God, and to enjoy him forever."

Not only is the image of God the basis for our relationship with God, but it is also the foundation of our relationship with each other. Being created in the image and likeness of God is the ground for our relationships with fellow human beings. After all, the two greatest commandments according to Jesus are to love God *and* neighbor (Matt 22:37–40). Genuine neighbor love is not to be done in the Metaverse, but in the real world. It is no coincidence that as our lives move increasingly online our offline selves (our true selves) are lonelier and more isolated. In recent years, major studies have detailed the "epidemic of loneliness and isolation"[11] alongside books warning of the same.[12] As writer Meghan Houser observes, we've become a people "alone in the algorithm."[13] People were created by God to live in community, to flourish among each other—and this has everything to do with being created in the image and likeness of God.

---

11. See the 2023 report by U.S. Health and Human Services, "Our Epidemic of Loneliness and Isolation."

12. See, for example, Haidt, *The Anxious Generation*.

13. Houser, "AI Is a Hall of Mirrors," 73–77.

"Incarnational" Pastors

The image of God requires "incarnational" pastors. Pastors must resist the temptation to embrace technology at the expense of fostering real relationships. It shouldn't need to be said, but it does in our digital age: true discipleship is done in person. Pastors need to spend less time on social media interacting with *virtual* people and more time offline interacting with *real* people. I fear many pastors have believed the lie that a text message or email is sufficient for discipleship rather than seeing those media as simply a means to the end of shepherding God's people. After all, for a shepherd to truly care for the sheep, he must be physically present caring for them in concrete, practical ways. Incarnational pastors, for example, get out from behind the screen in preaching for the sake of communicating to those in attendance face to face, eye to eye. Preachers, after all, are called to be the very mouthpiece of God as we proclaim the very Word of God. In the classroom, incarnational pastors are "able to teach" (1 Tim 3:2), which means accurately explaining and applying the Scriptures, not merely hitting play on the DVD or streaming content. Incarnational pastors get out of the office, not relying on emails or texts as a "proxy pastor," but spending time "life on life" with God's people. When pastors are "incarnational"—physically among the people not mediated to them through technology—it will go far in helping church members know better the love of Christ in our impersonal, digital age. Consider the incredible opportunity we have for evangelism in our technological world: with unbelievers feeling increasingly isolated, the love of God will be felt when our churches move toward people in servant love. Incarnational pastors model this when they actually live and work among the broken people of the world—people pastors know are "harassed and helpless like sheep without a shepherd" (Matt 9:36). Whether in discipleship or evangelism, the image of God requires pastors to be "incarnational"—especially in our technological age.

Recapturing the Wonder

Christians of all people should be amazed by creation because we know it to be God's handiwork. This glorious truth marks the opening words of the Bible: "In the beginning, God created the heavens and the earth" (Gen 1:1; cf. John 1:1–3). As David surveyed creation he was moved to worship: "The heavens declare the glory of God, and the sky above proclaims his handiwork. Day to day pours out speech, and night to night reveals knowledge" (Ps 19:1–2). Thinking specifically of humanity David declared, "For you formed my inward parts; you knitted me together in my mother's womb. I praise you, for I am fearfully and wonderfully made" (Ps 139:13–14). After all, it was God himself who looked at all that he had made and pronounced it "very good" (Gen 1:31). Armed with the truth of Scripture, pastors proclaim to the world God's "very good" creation, including the glory and honor of humanity created in the image of God.

The sexual revolution is ugly. By this I mean that it is promoting a vision of life utterly at odds with God's beautiful design for humanity. In manifold ways, the vernacular of our day when it comes to sexuality is debased and corrupt. In contrast, pastors must engage Christians and non-Christians with the wonder of God's glorious design for humanity. The image of God is beautiful as we are in the likeness of the One who is altogether lovely, the God who "is light and in him is no darkness at all" (1 John 1:5). Even as sin has deeply marred the image of God in us, we know the heights from which we've fallen and the still greater heights that God in Christ is taking the redeemed. In this sense we must sound more like David when we speak of humanity as God's handiwork: "When I look at your heavens, the work of your fingers, the moon and the stars, which you have set in place, what is man that you are mindful of him, and the son of man that you care for him? Yet you have made him a little lower than the heavenly beings and crowned him with glory and honor" (Ps 8:3–5). It is this vision that pastors must embrace if we would win the war of language in our churches and commend again the beauty and wonder of God's design for humanity.

Shaping Toward Gratitude

How can pastors resist the distortions of the world and recapture the beauty and wonder of God's good design for humanity? Rather than be ashamed of a biblical anthropology, what motives might we have for gratitude? Petrus van Mastricht applies the doctrine of the image of God by suggesting that "a pious meditation on the divine image shapes us to gratitude toward our Creator, the one who so kindly conferred such excellent benefits."[14]

---

14. Mastricht, *Theoretical-Practical Theology*, 302.

Humanity

The first "motive" Mastricht gives to shape us to gratitude is to consider "the origin of the benefits, that is, the pure, unadulterated love of the Creator toward us."[15] Mastricht reasons,

> Is it not a token of singular goodwill to receive the image of a king or prince from his hand? Is it not likewise evidence of extraordinary divine affection, not only to create all things for the sake of man, but also to confer to man alone the likeness of his own wisdom, holiness, righteousness, dominion, and so forth, a likeness denied to all the other creatures?[16]

It is indeed "evidence of extraordinary divine affection" that God has made man in his image, a gift given no other creature. Due consideration of this fact should lead us to proclaim with the Psalmist, "Praise the LORD! Oh give thanks to the LORD, for he is good, for his steadfast love endures forever!" (Ps 106:1). A second motive for gratitude is what Mastricht calls "the end of the benefit." He asks, "To what great end did God bless man with his own image?" He answers as follows:

> Certainly not only for his own sake, but also for man's, namely, so that not only could man have a God similar to him, but also in turn, God could have man, that as his likeness he could love him, unite him to himself, receive him into eternal fellowship, and bestow upon him eternal blessedness and joy. For though conversation, and solid and constant friendship, are sometimes observed among those who are not equal, yet they are never observed among those that are entirely dissimilar, that is, in species and in morals. For there is no fellowship of men with beasts, and likewise no solid friendship of the pious with the impious (2 Cor. 6:15). Accordingly, neither does God admit anyone into the fellowship of eternal life and blessedness who is not to some extent similar to him.[17]

Our creation in the image of God is the foundation of our eternal blessedness and joy with God. Indeed, without it we would have no hope of fellowship with God. A third motive toward gratitude is how the image of God provides for "confidence and consolation in any adversities." Mastricht explains,

---

15. Mastricht, *Theoretical-Practical Theology*, 302.
16. Mastricht, *Theoretical-Practical Theology*, 302.
17. Mastricht, *Theoretical-Practical Theology*, 302.

> For if you are poor and needy, most destitute of the means of living, consider that nevertheless you are created in the image of God, and thus are much less to be deserted by God than the rest of the creatures who lack the image of God, those that are lifeless and irrational (Matt. 6:25–26); or if you are despised and rejected, consider that nevertheless you bear the image of God, the quintessence of the highest dignity; or if you are hated by the people, even pursued to death, consider that you were made in the image of God, and by it you are most safely protected, as by a divine fence (Gen. 9:6); and so forth.[18]

The "confidence and consolation" offered in a consideration of the image of God is deeply relevant in our age of loneliness and isolation. Furthermore, as the church enters into what Aaron Renn has helpfully described as the "negative world,"[19] the image of God will serve as a bulwark against the rising tide of opposition toward God's people. In considering each of these motives toward gratitude, pastors can see how "the uses of the divine image are various and eminent,"[20] and thus be better equipped to minister to their churches with a robust biblical anthropology.

Pastors must be resolved to minister according to a clear biblical anthropology in a world that sees with blurry eyes when it comes to the creation of man. Indeed, the image of God is lost in a sea of gender confusion and dehumanizing sexual ethics in what Trueman calls the "rise and triumph of the modern self." Add to this the unique challenges of our technological age, and the prospects for humanity seem bleak. Pastors, however, have an incredible opportunity to recast for modern ears the "glory and honor" of human beings in the image of God. What will be the result of this? Nothing less, and nothing greater, than churches growing in the two great commandments of love to God and neighbor. Why love to God? As Mastricht explains, "because he not only loved us, but he so loved us, that he conferred his own image upon us, and moreover, he rendered us similar to him, so that we could love him in return."[21] Why love to neighbor? Again, Mastricht is helpful when he considers how a biblical anthropology moves us toward neighbor:

---

18. Mastricht, *Theoretical-Practical Theology*, 303.
19. Renn, *Life in the Negative World*.
20. Mastricht, *Theoretical-Practical Theology*, 303.
21. Mastricht, *Theoretical-Practical Theology*, 303.

> When with love and reverence for the divine image which he bears together with us, we embrace him with the most intimate affection, and show this affection, on the one hand, by abstaining from all injury against his body and life (Gen 9:6), and against his honor and reputation (Jas 3:9), remembering that it is not swine, not donkeys or cats, with whom we deal, but those who bear the image of God; and on the other hand, by striving with all effort for their good, by duly looking out for both their nourishment and their clothing (Matt 25:35), that is, doing this as to the image of God.[22]

Indeed, it is not mere animals with whom we deal, but human beings indelibly marked with the image of God. These were the lessons Pastor Jerry embedded in me decades ago as he sent us out to the University district in Seattle. These are timeless truths of a biblical anthropology for pastors today.

---

22. Mastricht, *Theoretical-Practical Theology*, 303–4.

5

Church

"The Church is the mirror, that reflects the whole effulgence of the Divine character. It is the grand scene, in which the perfections of Jehovah are displayed to the universe."
—Charles Bridges

"I will build my church, and the gates of hell shall not prevail against it."
—Matthew 16:18

Resolution 5: Resolved to know and love the church.

MANY PASTORS TODAY ARE understandably concerned about a militant secularism threatening the church. The concerns involve the sexual ethics issues discussed in the previous chapter, protections for the unborn and elderly, ethnic strife, and persecution of Christians from an over-reaching state. These, among other issues, could tempt a pastor to think the way forward is apart from the church. This kind of thinking is a mistake, for the church is God's gift to the world for the very gospel hope it so desperately needs. On this point, Edmund Clowney is particularly insightful:

> The church, however, as the community of Christ's kingdom, can show the world an ethical integrity it must respect. When Peter describes the impact of Christian righteous deeds in a pagan world, he is thinking not of isolated saints, but of the *people* of God, called out of darkness into God's light. Christian witness that is limited to private religious experience cannot challenge secularism. Christians in community must again show the world, not merely family values, but the bond of the love of Christ. Increasingly the ordered fellowship of the church becomes the sign of grace for the warring factions of a disordered world. Only as the church binds together those whom selfishness and hate have cut apart will its message be heard and its ministry of hope to the friendless be received.[1]

In other words, what the world needs most is the church functioning as the people of God, a people "called . . . out of darkness into his marvelous light" (1 Pet 2:9).

One of the greatest temptations for a pastor is "mission creep." By this I mean the myriads of good and bad ideas that come to pastors on a yearly basis that threaten to derail a church from its central mission of gospel proclamation in all its forms. When this happens, not only are God's people led astray or left to wander aimlessly, but the world is given a distorted picture of the church. It's seen as something far less than what it is designed to be, resulting in a powerless witness to "another gospel," which is really no gospel at all. Therefore, this chapter is a call for pastors to know and love the church—to understand what a church is, and thereby care for it appropriately.

The Church and Her Mission

Charles Bridges (1794–1869), in his magisterial work *The Christian Ministry*, appropriately opens with a lofty definition of the church: "The Church is the mirror, that reflects the whole effulgence of the Divine character. It is the grand scene, in which the perfections of Jehovah are displayed to the universe."[2] For Bridges, a pastor cannot faithfully shepherd what he does not understand. This is why Bridges begins a book on pastoral ministry with a definition of the church. His definition is appropriately God-centered. The church is designed to reflect "the whole effulgence of the Divine

---

1. Clowney, *The Church*, 16.
2. Bridges, *The Christian Ministry*, 1.

character." That is, the radiance of God's character is to be reflected in the church. And notice the scope of this reflection of God's character according to Bridges: the universe. The church, in other words, is created by God to display the perfections of God *to the universe*—a "grand scene" indeed. This is the great mission of the church: to proclaim to the universe who God is.

How does this happen? How are the "perfections of Jehovah" reflected to the world through the church? To answer this question, we must define the church. What is its nature or essence? Can we get to the heart of it?

The People of God

In the New Testament, the Greek word for church is ἐκκλησία (*ekklēsia*) meaning "to call out." Put simply, the church is the "called-out ones" of God.[3] Though simply put, this is a most profound reality. The biblical witness of the church is to an assembly of people summoned by God out of the darkness of sin and death into worship of him, the one true God, in spirit and truth (1 Pet 2:9; John 4:23).

This idea of the church being the people of God is a favorite theme of the apostle Paul in his letters. For example, when Paul is giving his farewell address to the Ephesians elders, notice how he describes the church in Ephesus: "Pay careful attention to yourselves and to all the flock, in which the Holy Spirit has made you overseers, to care for the church of God, which he obtained with his own blood" (Acts 20:28). Paul sees the church as a "flock" of blood-bought people who are to be cared for by God-called overseers (cf. Eph 5:25). Likewise, in Colossians 1:13–14, Paul describes the church as a people brought out of the kingdom of this world and into the kingdom of Christ: "He has delivered us from the domain of darkness and transferred us to the kingdom of his beloved Son, in whom we have redemption, the forgiveness of sins." Indeed, in the gospel Paul sees the Lord creating a whole new community of people set apart for God:

> So then you are no longer strangers and aliens, but you are fellow citizens with the saints and members of the household of God, built on the foundation of the apostles and prophets, Christ Jesus himself being the cornerstone, in whom the whole structure, being joined together, grows into a holy temple in the Lord. In him you also are being built together into a dwelling place for God by the Spirit. (Eph 2:19–22)

3. Mounce, *Complete Expository Dictionary*, 110.

As this passage illustrates, the church is not a building or an idea or a metaphor. The church is a people who are "no longer strangers and aliens, but . . . fellow citizens with the saints and members of the household of God" (v. 19).

In understanding the church as the people of God, it is important to see the continuity the New Testament shares with the Old. After all, the New Testament pattern of God calling a people to himself in salvation (described in the book of Acts and explained in the epistles), is the continuation of a pattern first established in the Old Testament. For example, in Deuteronomy 4:10, God, speaking through Moses, commands, "Gather the people to me, that I may let them hear my words, so that they may learn to fear me all the days that they live on the earth, and that they may teach their children so." The author of Hebrews, after listing several Old Testament saints, explains, "And all these, though commended through their faith, did not receive what was promised, since God had provided something better for us, that apart from us they should not be made perfect" (Heb 11:39–40). This continuity between the Testaments with respect to the church is perhaps seen most clearly in 1 Peter 2:9 where the Apostle takes various Old Testament categories for God's people and applies them to the church: "But you are a chosen race, a royal priesthood, a holy nation, a people for his own possession, that you may proclaim the excellencies of him who called you out of darkness into his marvelous light." Whether considered as the Old Testament "congregation in the wilderness" (Acts 7:37–38) or the New Testament "household of God" (Eph 2:19), the church has always been, and will always be, an assembly of called-out ones for the glory and praise of God.[4] As Wilhelmus à Brakel observed, the church is "all the elect who

---

4. This definition is captured well by Grudem when he describes the church as "the community of all true believers for all time." Grudem, *Bible Doctrine*, 363. Likewise, R. C. Sproul states, "The Church refers to all the people who belong to the Lord, those who have been purchased by the blood of Christ." Sproul, *Essential Truths of the Christian Faith*, 217. J. I. Packer helpfully explains the church as the people of God *invisible* and *visible*; *triumphant* and *militant*; *universal* and *local*: "Essentially, the church is, was, and always will be a single worshiping community, permanently gathered in the true sanctuary which is the heavenly Jerusalem (Gal. 4:26; Heb. 12:22–24), the place of God's presence. Here all who are alive in Christ, the physically living with the physically dead (i.e., the church militant with the church triumphant) worship continually. In the world, however, this one church appears in the form of local congregations, each one called to fulfill the role of being a microcosm (a small-scale representative sample) of the church as a whole. This explains how it is that for Paul the one church universal is the body of Christ (1 Cor. 12:12–26; Eph. 1:22–23; 3:6; 4:4), and so is the local congregation (1 Cor. 12:27)." Packer, *Concise Theology*, 201.

have been called from the beginning of the world and are yet to be called until the end of the world. They are Christ's peculiar people (Titus 2:14)."[5]

Understanding the biblical teaching of the church as the people of God is particularly important for pastors to grasp in the age of "busy evangelicalism" when countless programs and ministries define our churches. If not careful, the church can begin to be seen as the management of programs rather than the shepherding of people. Knowing the church as the people of God will be a safeguard against this unbiblical thinking. After all, the "perfections of Jehovah are displayed to the universe" not through programs but people—a people locally assembled who are striving by the grace of God to be "imitators of God, as beloved children" (Eph 5:1). Furthermore, it is the people of God that ensure that the church is what Paul says it is, namely, "the pillar and ground of the truth" (1 Tim 3:15). When the church loses the truth as revealed in the Scriptures of the Old and New Testaments, there is no pillar and ground, but only the sinking sand of worldly wisdom. Church programs in themselves, no matter how well designed and intended, do nothing to establish the truth. God's people must do this.

Beloved of God

When my daughter was in high school, she made a beautiful collage around Romans 9:25 where God says something truly remarkable about the identity of those who are in Christ through faith: "As indeed he says in Hosea, Those who were not my people I will call 'my people,' and her who was not beloved I will call 'beloved.'" The church is God's "beloved" people. My teenage daughter thought this was worth framing and hanging on her wall (and still does).

This astonishing truth—that God calls us *beloved* in Christ—helps us understand why Jesus promises, "I will build my church, and the gates of hell shall not prevail against it" (Matt 16:18). All hell can break loose against the church, but Jesus will ensure that she stands. Why? Because as Paul explains, "Christ loved the church and gave himself up for her" (Eph 5:25). Jesus will "save to the uttermost" those for whom he died (Heb 7:25). Jesus did not die only to see the devil prevail against Christ's bride. The church triumphant sings with Paul, "No, in all these things we are more than conquerors through him who loved us. For I am sure that neither death nor life, nor angels nor rulers, nor things present nor things to come,

---

5. Brakel, *The Christian's Reasonable Service*, 5.

nor powers, nor height nor depth, nor anything else in all creation, will be able to separate us from the love of God in Christ Jesus our Lord" (Rom 8:37–39).

The Shepherd and the Sheep

Pastors must know and love the church as the people of God if they would remain faithful in ministry. By faithful, I mean caring for the people of God in a way that promotes their sanctification, their progress in practical holiness, on their way to heaven. Whether it's allowing for the "mission creep" mentioned earlier in this chapter or falling morally by failing to remember the immeasurable value of who they're called to shepherd, the pitfalls are many for the pastor who forgets the nature of the church as the people of God. To help us remember, contemporary evangelicalism needs the seventeenth-century Puritan pastor Richard Baxter. Here's a sample of Baxter exhorting pastors to remember the worth of Christ's church:

> It is the church of God that we must oversee and feed. It is that church that is sanctified by the Holy Spirit, is united to Christ, and is his mystical body. Oh, what a charge it is that we have undertaken! Shall we be unfaithful in such a charge? Have we been given the stewardship of God's own family, and shall we neglect it? God forbid! Christ walks among them. Remember his presence and keep all as clean as you can. The praises of the most high are in the midst of them. They are a sanctified, chosen people, a kingly priesthood, a holy nation, a choice generation, to show forth the praises of him who has called them (1 Pet. 2:9).
>
> Remember the price that was paid for the church that we oversee. As Paul says in this very text [Acts 20:28], God the Son purchased the church with his own blood. Oh, what an argument this is to enliven the negligent, and what an argument to condemn those who will not be awakened to their duty by it! Shall we despise the blood of Christ? Shall we think it was shed for those who are not worthy of our utmost care? Then let us hear those arguments of Christ whenever we feel ourselves grow dull and careless: "Did I die for them, and will you not look after them? They were worth my blood, and are they not worth your labor? Did I come down from heaven to earth, to seek and to save that which was lost (Luke 19:10), and will you not go to the next door or street or village and seek them? How small is your labor or humbling in comparison to mine! I debased myself to this, but it is your honor to be so

employed. I have done and suffered much for their salvation, and I have made you a coworker with me, and will you refuse the little that lies upon your hands?" Every time we look on our congregations, let us believingly remember that they are the purchase of Christ's blood and that we should regard them as such.[6]

It is for lack of this vision of the church that many pastors are found unfaithful in our day, and sheep walk around grossly malnourished. Pastors today must remember *who* they're shepherding. A biblical vision of the church as the people of God should chasten us and motivate us to be more careful in what and how we preach, teach, and care for the churches we serve.

In his helpful book on pastoral ministry, Timothy Witmer outlines four essential tasks of the faithful shepherd: knowing, feeding, leading, and protecting.[7] Each of these functions follows from a clear understanding of the church as the people of God. With the love of Christ, the pastor must *know* the people who make up his congregation both at the macro and micro levels. After all, how can a pastor care for people he doesn't know? In addition to knowing the sheep, faithful shepherds ensure that God's people are well nourished. This is accomplished as pastors faithfully *feed* the church a steady diet of the Word of God, the Scriptures of both the Old and New Testaments. Leadership in the church is servant-leadership, exhibited by pastors who *lead* sacrificially by laying down their lives for the sheep. Finally, faithful shepherds *protect* God's people from the "wolves" of heresy as well as various cultural "wolves," such as materialism, sensuality, pluralism, and relativism—worldly philosophies that threaten to shipwreck a person's faith. The ultimate protection pastors offer, of course, is the protection of the gospel—the good news of salvation from sin and death and the righteous wrath of God. Whether through public warnings from Scripture or private counsel in the Word of God, pastors labor to protect the church in the safe harbor of God's grace. In our cultural and ecclesiological moment, I want to emphasize the fourth function Witmer outlines, namely, protection.

---

6. Baxter, *The Reformed Pastor*, 93–94.
7. Witmer, *The Shepherd Leader*, 107–92.

Church

Holiness as Protection

According to the Council of Nicaea (AD 325) the church is "one, holy, catholic, and Apostolic."[8] Herman Bavinck makes use of this division as he describes the attributes of the church.[9] Regarding the holiness of the church, he states,

> The church is holy because it is a communion of saints. And believers are called saints, first of all, because they are objectively counted as saints in Christ by virtue of God's imputation to them of the righteousness of Christ. Second, believers are saints because, being born again of water and spirit in the inner self, they desire, with all seriousness of purpose, to live not only according to some but according to all the commandments of God (John 17:19; Eph. 5:25–27; 1 Thess. 4:3; Titus 2:14; Heb. 12:14; 1 Pet. 2:9). This attribute of the church, too, is spiritual, but not totally invisible. Although even the holiest have only a small beginning of this perfect obedience in this life, they nevertheless conduct themselves according to the Spirit and not according to the flesh.[10]

As Bavinck (and the Nicene Creed) recognizes, the church is both positionally and practically holy. As I argued earlier in this chapter, the church is the congregation of "called out ones," which means it is a "holy nation" (1 Pet 2:9); but as the redeemed of God, the church is to be holy in practice. Our spiritual holiness, as Bavinck explains, is "not totally invisible." The church is to display in practice what it is by position: holy unto the Lord. This is why church discipline, as a gift of God's grace to the church, is essential. Again, Bavinck is helpful as he makes the connection between the attribute of holiness and discipline:

> And discipline is a means given to the church by Christ so that the church may preserve its holy character. Such discipline must be exercised not merely in secret, say, by one brother over against another, but in the event of public sins it must be applied by the church to its members. How much of this holiness was still missing in the apostolic time the various epistles all report, and later ages frequently gave rise to a profound religious and moral decay. But after the lapse and decay the Spirit of Christ again and again

---

8. Van Dixhoorn, *Creeds, Confessions, and Catechisms*, 17–18.
9. Bavinck, *Reformed Dogmatics*, 4:320–25.
10. Bavinck, *Reformed Dogmatics*, 4:321–22; see also Bavinck, *Guidebook for Instruction in Christian Religion*, 165.

caused a revival and renewal to take place. This holiness of the church is also a characteristic which Christ earned for the church and which He works out, in and through the church.[11]

Church discipline, as an indispensable mark of the church, is one of the foremost ways Christ "works out, in and through the church" what he earned for her, namely, holiness.

From Bavinck to Bon Jovi

Just as rock band Bon Jovi in 1986 sang, "You give love a bad name," so the church in many ways has given discipline a bad name. Whether through poor teaching or practice (or both), church discipline is loathed in many quarters of evangelicalism such that one of God's great means of grace for his people is neglected. This reality should grieve a pastor's heart for he knows the neglect of church discipline leaves the church in a most vulnerable state.

Of course, church discipline has not always been out-of-favor in Protestant church history. Take, for example, the clear words of article 29 in the Belgic Confession of Faith (1561):

> The true church can be recognized if it has the following marks: The church engages in the pure preaching of the gospel; it makes use of the pure administration of the sacraments as Christ instituted them; it practices church discipline for correcting faults. In short, it governs itself according to the pure Word of God, rejecting all things contrary to it and holding Jesus Christ as the only Head.[12]

When I teach on this in my pastoral ministry class at Southern Seminary, it never fails to surprise at least some of my students to know that church discipline is part of our rich confessional history. Indeed, true churches are marked by the faithful practice of "church discipline for correcting faults." So, what went wrong?

There is no denying that poor leadership at the highest levels in some evangelical churches has caused a bad perception of church discipline. When leaders abuse their authority, betray the trust of church members, or fumble the administration of something as important as church discipline,

---

11. Bavinck, *The Wonderful Works of God*, 507.
12. Van Dixhoorn, *Creeds, Confessions, and Catechisms*, 102.

there is a justifiable negative reaction to it. I've heard credible stories among my students, for example, of churches moving far too quickly to the excommunication of church members; they lacked the necessary patient, loving pursuit of the person found in sin, in the hope of securing repentance. Rather, there was a rush to judgment and an all-too-eager desire to see the person removed from membership. The message communicated was not, "We love you in Christ and long for your freedom from this sin," but rather, "We are disgusted with your sin and ashamed of you, and don't want you a part of this fellowship any longer." When this happens, the damage to people and a right understanding of the gospel is incalculable.

Not only have unfaithful shepherds caused the neglect of church discipline, but our unique cultural moment has contributed as well. The church today is trying to grow up in a world that doesn't see "sins" that need to be corrected, but "emotions" that need therapy. In our day, there is a "mental health crisis" not a "sin crisis," and this worldly thinking has been infused into the church.

The warnings began in the mid 1990s with Cornelius Plantinga Jr.'s *Not the Way It's Supposed to Be: A Breviary of Sin* (1996), followed by David Wells's *Losing Our Virtue: Why the Church Must Recover Its Moral Vision* (1999). Then, in the early 2000s, sociologist Christian Smith began to document the shift among teenagers in *Soul Searching: The Religious and Spiritual Lives of American Teenagers* (2005), and he continued to document them as they became young adults in *Souls in Transition: The Religious and Spiritual Lives of Emerging Adults* (2009). The currents moving toward a therapeutic way of thinking with an emphasis on mental and emotional health have only gained momentum. Abigail Shrier's *Bad Therapy: Why the Kids Aren't Growing Up* (2024), and Jonathan Haidt's *The Anxious Generation: How the Great Rewiring of Childhood Is Causing an Epidemic of Mental Illness* (2024) are two important books that help us understand what's been happening to our nation's youth in recent decades, even if the solutions offered fall short of a much needed biblical-theological remedy.[13]

In more conservative evangelical churches, the worldly thinking of "health" and "well-being" isn't always obvious. It may be subtle and come in a way that at first blush seems biblical and, therefore, helpful. Take, for example, the popularity of 9Marks Ministries and its emphasis on "healthy" churches. The first edition of Mark Dever's *Nine Marks of a Healthy*

---

13. For a much needed contemporary biblical-theological diagnosis and remedy, see Gibson and Gibson, *Ruined Sinners to Reclaim* (2024).

Church was published in 2000, followed by a second edition (2004), third edition (2013); and the book is now in its fourth edition (2021). As a professor at the largest conservative Protestant seminary in the world, I can attest to the profound influence of 9Marks among my students in their way of thinking about the church: primarily in terms of health. But is this the most biblical way to think about the church as the people of God? Does the Bible emphasize *health* or *holiness*?

When health is emphasized over holiness, we should not be surprised if the faithful practice of church discipline is marginalized or altogether neglected. After all, church discipline is God's gift of grace to the church for her holiness. Consider why God disciplines his children in Hebrews 12:3–11:

> Consider him who endured from sinners such hostility against himself, so that you may not grow weary or fainthearted. In your struggle against sin you have not yet resisted to the point of shedding your blood. And have you forgotten the exhortation that addresses you as sons? "My son, do not regard lightly the discipline of the Lord, nor be weary when reproved by him. For the Lord disciplines the one he loves, and chastises every son whom he receives." It is for discipline that you have to endure. God is treating you as sons. For what son is there whom his father does not discipline? If you are left without discipline, in which all have participated, then you are illegitimate children and not sons. Besides this, we have had earthly fathers who disciplined us and we respected them. Shall we not much more be subject to the Father of spirits and live? For they disciplined us for a short time as it seemed best to them, but he disciplines us for our good, that we may share his holiness. For the moment all discipline seems painful rather than pleasant, but later it yields the peaceful fruit of righteousness to those who have been trained by it.

We are disciplined not that we may share in God's health, but "that we may share in his holiness" (v. 10). This is why the author of Hebrews adds this exhortation, "Strive for peace with everyone, and for the *holiness* without which no one will see the Lord" (12:14; emphasis added). Not the mere healthy but the holy "will see the Lord."

This, of course, is a very Pauline way of thinking about the church. Consider the way the Apostle understands marriage—specifically the way husbands are to love their wives—as a reflection of God's design for the church: "Husbands, love your wives, as Christ loved the church and gave himself up for her, that he might sanctify her, having cleansed her by the washing of water with the word, so that he might present the church to himself in splendor, without spot or wrinkle or any such thing, that she might be holy and without blemish" (Eph 5:25–27). Paul envisions a church presented to Christ not in great health, but in utter holiness. This makes complete sense as the church is the assembly of the redeemed, those who are chosen "in him before the foundation of the world, that we should be holy and blameless before him" (Eph 1:4). Chosen not for mere health, but for the beauty of holiness.

In this way, the apostolic witness is one. The apostle Peter reminds his readers that in Christ, they are part of God's holy congregation: "But you are a chosen race, a royal priesthood, a holy nation, a people for his own possession, that you may proclaim the excellencies of him who called you out of darkness into his marvelous light" (1 Pet 2:9). James commends true religion as being holy or "unstained from the world" (Jas 1:27). And John reminds believers that the pursuit of holiness is what children of God do: "Beloved, we are God's children now, and what we will be has not yet appeared; but we know that when he appears we shall be like him, because we shall see him as he is. And everyone who thus hopes in him purifies himself as he is pure" (1 John 3:2–3). Indeed, the majestic vision of John for eternity is one of God's people assembled in holiness, giving glory to God:

> Then came one of the seven angels who had the seven bowls full of the seven last plagues and spoke to me, saying, "Come, I will show you the Bride, the wife of the Lamb." And he carried me away in the Spirit to a great, high mountain, and showed me the holy city Jerusalem coming down out of heaven from God, having the glory of God, its radiance like a most rare jewel, like a jasper, clear as crystal. (Rev 21:9–11)

Health language doesn't come close to the transcendent picture John gives of the church. John doesn't envision a merely healthy Bride or healthy city coming down out of heaven. Like Paul in Ephesians 5, John sees the consummation of the church as "having the glory of God, its radiance like a most rare jewel, like a jasper, clear as crystal." This is breathtaking language as we behold the church presented in the splendor not of health, but of holiness. Language matters as it conveys meaning and, in this case, the meaning of church discipline is more accurately communicated with an emphasis on the biblical language of holiness—God's great design for his church.[14]

14. To be clear and charitable, *Nine Marks of a Healthy Church* includes church

This brief excursus on church discipline is not offered as a comprehensive explanation of what it is and how to most faithfully practice it in the local church.[15] The narrower goal has been to help shift the language around church discipline and why it is vital that pastors emphasize it in their biblical ecclesiology: church discipline is for the glory of God as displayed in his people increasingly walking in the freedom and beauty of holiness. With this ultimate end in view pastors can help bring the grace of church discipline from the margins of church life to its necessary center. This is not only a great protection to God's people but will help local churches better function as "the grand scene, in which the perfections of Jehovah are displayed to the universe."

The world is in desperate need of holy churches—churches that by the grace of God increasingly live as the people of God. A pastor knows and loves the church because he knows what the church is—namely, *people* Christ purchased with his own blood (Acts 20:28). Therefore, pastors will labor to see congregations live as "blameless and innocent, children of God without blemish in the midst of a crooked and twisted generation, among whom [they] shine as lights in the world" (Phil 2:15). A pastor's love for the church takes many forms, including the faithful practice of church discipline as seen in this chapter. We now turn to another indispensable way a pastor loves God's people: through the teaching of sound doctrine.

---

discipline as one of its marks. The point I'm making here is that *health* language isn't as biblical and, therefore, helpful as *holiness* language in accomplishing the very important goal 9Marks Ministries is aiming for, namely, the faithful practice of church discipline in local churches. Perhaps a fifth edition is needed: *Nine Marks of a* Holy *Church*.

15. For this I offer without any sense of irony, Leeman's helpful book *Church Discipline*.

6

Doctrine

"A culture for whom God is no longer present believes everything."
—David Wells

"But as for you, teach what accords with sound doctrine."
—Titus 2:1

Resolution 6: Resolved to teach sound doctrine.

A PASTOR MUST TEACH sound doctrine for the building up of the church in the faith. A pastor, of all people, knows that what we believe, teach, and confess makes all the difference in eternity for the people he is called to shepherd. This conviction animates his ministry in manifold ways, all of which involve the communication of sound doctrine. He sees himself as a pastor-theologian, teaching the great doctrines of the faith for the strengthening of the people he's called to serve.

Resolutions of a Pastor

The Disappearance of Theology

As a new believer, I could see it all around me: theology in the church didn't seem to matter much, if at all. I saw it in the Christian bookstores as I browsed the stacks. Row after row included various topical studies on Christian living or devotional books promising a closer walk with God or self-help gurus peddling their worldly ideas cloaked in various verses from the Bible. Strangely absent was robust theology. And it wasn't only in the brick-and-mortar Christian bookstores. Other than John MacArthur's "Grace to You," I couldn't find theology on the radio, either. Theology, I was told, doesn't *sell*. Theology is solely for academics or factious laypeople in the church who want to quarrel over the finer points of doctrine. Doctrine, after all, was not *practical*. Its only real utility was to divide people over teaching best left to the seminaries. Of course, what was being sold in the bookstores and broadcast on the radio reflected what existed in the typical evangelical church. With rare exceptions, this was the evangelical landscape of the 1990s.[1]

Something inside me knew this was not the landscape of the Bible. In those early years of my Christian faith, I was seeing in the Bible majestic mountains of theology, vast oceans of doctrine, and lush valleys of dogma. There was for me a great dissonance between the world of the Bible and that of contemporary evangelicalism. Like the child that looks around the playground and realizes he's different than most of his peers, I quickly came to see that my love for theology was not "normal." Indeed, I was rather odd in my love affair with doctrine. I remember, for example, how I would rise very early in the morning as a camp counselor at The Firs in Bellingham, Washington, so I could spend time with R. C. Sproul's *Chosen by God*, a wonderful introduction to the doctrine of election, before my cabin of kids would awake. I remember excitedly spending almost all my small stipend each month as a pastoral intern on books at Christian Book Distributors. I bought commentaries, works of systematic theology, history, and biblical theology because I couldn't make sense of my newfound faith otherwise. I loved those days of discovery—and still do. Even as my PhD is in history, I tell my students that my first love is theology. Evangelical indifference to theology in the 1990s did not make sense to me then, nor does it today.

---

1. The hollowing-out of theology in America is a story that began long before the 1990s. See, for example, my published dissertation *Broadcasting the Faith: Protestant Religious Radio and Theology in America, 1920–1950*.

Doctrine

One of the most astute observers of the evangelical landscape of the 1990s was David Wells, a theologian I introduced in chapter 1. In his seminal work *No Place for Truth*, I found a scholar who helped make sense of my intuition even as he likewise understood how hard it was to prove the thesis:

> The disappearance of theology from the life of the Church, and the orchestration of that disappearance by some of its leaders, is hard to miss today but, oddly enough, not easy to prove. It is hard to miss in the evangelical world—in the vacuous worship that is so prevalent, for example, in the shift from God to the self as the central focus of faith, in the psychologized preaching that follows this shift, in the erosion of tis conviction, in its strident pragmatism, in its inability to think incisively about the culture, in its reveling in the irrational. And it would have made few of these capitulations to modernity had not its capacity for truth diminished. It is not hard to see these things; avoiding them is what is difficult.[2]

The disappearance of theology, for Wells, is hard to prove among evangelicals because many of the traditional tenets of the faith are still professed. The problem is that mere profession is not enough to fundamentally shape a people. Even as orthodox theology is largely professed, it has been moved to the periphery of the Christian life. Theology is a distant voice being drowned out by the many different voices of modernity. Wells explains,

> It is not that the elements of the evangelical credo have vanished; they have not. The fact that they are professed, however, does not necessarily mean that the structure of the historic Protestant faith is still intact. The reason, quite simply, is that while these items of belief are professed, they are increasingly being removed from the center of evangelical life where they defined what life was, and they are now being relegated to the periphery where their power to define what evangelical life should be is lost . . . . At its center there is now a vacuum into which modernity is pouring, and the result is a faith that, unlike historic orthodoxy is no longer defining itself theologically.[3]

With theology marginalized to the periphery, the church in America has been left with a center that cannot hold.[4]

---

2. Wells, *No Place for Truth*, 95.
3. Wells, *No Place for Truth*, 108–9.
4. As Wells warns, "The stakes are high: the anti-theological mood that now grips the evangelical world is changing its internal configuration, its effectiveness, and its relation

The Apostolic Center

The apostles could not have imagined a faith without a theological center. We see this as early as the day of Pentecost as the Spirit is given, and Peter proclaims the gospel to people from all over the known world (Acts 2:14-41). In the course of the sermon, Peter explains weighty theological themes like the person and role of the Spirit (pneumatology), the person and work of Christ (Christology), and the role of the Father in overruling the sinful intentions of man (theology proper). In all of this, we see Peter proclaiming God as Trinity, an understanding of the Godhead that is richly theological. And we know that Peter's theological sermon was not an anomaly as the early church was established on more of the same: "And they devoted themselves to the apostles' teaching and the fellowship, to the breaking of bread and the prayers" (Acts 2:42). From the beginning of the church the apostles' teaching was at the center. According to Wells, this had everything to do with the apostles' understanding of the Scriptures:

> The apostles' understanding about the sole authority of Scripture, and hence its complete sufficiency, explains why Christianity took the form it did. From the very beginning it was doctrinally shaped. And this doctrine is important to the proper function of the Word of God in the life of the church. It is not as though the apostles had no other alternatives. There were many other options. But, under the inspiration of the Holy Spirit, they were led to cast Christian faith in a doctrinal way.[5]

Paul as Preeminent Pastor-Theologian

Given his significant role in the book of Acts and the epistles, the apostle Paul opens wide the window into the apostolic mandate for a theological faith. Shortly after his conversion, Paul "proclaimed Jesus in the synagogues, saying 'He is the Son of God'" (Acts 9:20). A look at Paul's whole body of work reveals that a Christ-centered, theologically-driven ministry

---

to the past. It is severing the link to historical, Protestant orthodoxy. It is emancipating contemporary evangelicals to form casual alliances at will with a multitude of substitutes for this orthodoxy. And the reason for this is that what that orthodoxy had and what contemporary evangelicalism so often lacks is a theology at its center that defines the faith and prescribes the sorts of intellectual and practical relations it should establish in the world." Wells, *No Place for Truth*, 96.

5. Wells, *The Courage to Be Protestant*, 195.

DOCTRINE

was not the naive zeal of a new convert, for the book of Acts ends with Luke explaining how Paul spent the "mature" years of his life: "He [Paul] lived there [Rome] two whole years at his own expense, and welcomed all who came to him, proclaiming the kingdom of God and teaching about the Lord Jesus Christ with all boldness and without hindrance" (Acts 28:30–31).

In addition to the "bookends" of Paul's ministry in Acts, we see his efforts to keep theology at the heart of pastoral ministry as he gives his farewell address to the Ephesian elders in Acts 20:18–32. In this charge to the pastors in Ephesus, Paul wants to cement in their minds what it means to shepherd the flock of God. At the center of his charge is the gospel; and this gospel carries with it great doctrines that need to be taught, which is why Paul reminds them that he "did not shrink from declaring to you anything that was profitable, and teaching you in public and from house to house, testifying both to Jews and to Greeks of repentance toward God and of faith in our Lord Jesus Christ" (vv. 20–21). He tells them that his life only has value insofar as he is faithful in testifying to "the gospel of the grace of God" (v. 24). Indeed, Paul could say that he was "innocent of the blood of all, for I did not shrink from declaring to you the whole counsel of God" (vv. 26–27). All of this required a theological understanding of the faith, something Paul was eager to keep at the center. In fact, Paul was so determined to protect the pure doctrine of the gospel that he didn't hesitate to vigorously warn the Ephesian pastors about false teachers: "I know that after my departure fierce wolves will come in among you, not sparing the flock; and from among your own selves will arise men speaking twisted things, to draw away the disciples after them. Therefore be alert, remembering that for three years I did not cease night or day to admonish every one with tears" (vv. 29–31). Paul describes unceasing, tearful effort in admonishing God's people to keep the faith even as unsound men were seeking to twist it. And, finally, Paul entrusts his co-elders to the one thing that will build up the church: sound doctrine. He says, "And now I commend you to God and to the word of his grace, which is able to build you up and to give you the inheritance among all those who are sanctified" (v. 32). He sounds like a faithful shepherd.

What we see in narrative form in the book of Acts, we see in Paul's epistles, specifically what are traditionally known as the "pastoral epistles" of 1 and 2 Timothy and Titus. Paul is very concerned that Timothy and Titus understand what an elder is to be and do. Both godly character and competency in teaching are nonnegotiable requirements for any man who would lead Christ's church. And the stakes could not be higher: "Keep a close watch on yourself and on the teaching. Persist in this, for by so doing you will save both yourself and your hearers" (1 Tim 4:16). Paul exhorts Timothy to guard his life and doctrine. Why? Because eternity is at stake for him and his hearers. For the purposes of this chapter, I want to focus on the "doctrine" side of Paul's concern for a pastor's life and teaching.

It is not uncommon for Christians today to talk about the character of their pastor (even if the virtues they are expecting are less than the holiness the Bible requires). Local churches in the main expect their pastor to be morally upright. What does not seem clear, however, is whether churches expect their pastor to teach sound doctrine. But to not have this clear expectation of their shepherd is to neglect holding their pastor to the apostolic imperative to "teach what accords with sound doctrine" (Titus 2:1). Paul is very concerned about *sound* or *healthy* doctrine. After all, a man is not qualified to be an elder if he is unable to teach faithfully the Scriptures. Consider, for example, how Paul opens his first letter to Timothy:

> As I urged you when I was going to Macedonia, remain at Ephesus so that you may charge certain persons not to teach any different doctrine, nor to devote themselves to myths and endless genealogies, which promote speculations rather than the stewardship from God that is by faith. The aim of our charge is love that issues from a pure heart and a good conscience and a sincere faith. Certain persons, by swerving from these, have wandered away into vain discussion, desiring to be teachers of the law, without understanding either what they are saying or the things about which they make confident assertions. (1 Tim 1:3–7)

A faithful pastor knows when someone is "swerving" from the truth. He can discern aberrant teaching and understand the difference between sound doctrine and "vain discussions." Finally, an elder cannot be swayed by error even when made with "confident assertions" because he is determined to establish the church on the truth of the gospel. Commenting on this passage, Carl Trueman notes,

> It is clear from this that Paul sees Timothy's task as an elder as involving the careful communication of the faith in a manner that focuses on the straightforward teaching of the gospel. The elder is to do this by avoiding the kind of, undoubtably fascinating but ultimately sterile, obsession with elaborate speculations that mark these problems at Ephesus. In other words, he is to have the maturity and discernment to know what exactly it is that he is to focus

on in terms of his teaching, and the knowledge to be able to do this effectively.[6]

Paul makes all of this still more clear when he outlines the qualifications for the office of elder. One of these necessary qualifications is "able to teach" (1 Tim 3:2). To this, Trueman observes, "It is important to stress that the ability to teach is nonnegotiable and clearly carries with it significant doctrinal freight. For Paul, one cannot be a teacher in the abstract: what one teaches, the content, is a vital part of the task; one can be a teacher only when one has sufficient mastery of this appropriate content to be able to teach it."[7] And this content, as we've seen, is "the whole counsel of God" (Acts 20:27). Paul elaborates on this essential qualification for an elder in Titus 1:9: "He must hold firm to the trustworthy word as taught, so that he may be able to give instruction in sound doctrine and also to rebuke those who contradict it." The ability to teach includes not only giving *positive* instruction in sound doctrine, but also knowing the content of the faith so well that the pastor knows when someone is contradicting it, and as a result, needing rebuke. The faithful teacher will not shrink back from issuing this rebuke because he knows the purity and unity of the church is at stake:

> Teach and urge these things. If anyone teaches a different doctrine and does not agree with the sound words of our Lord Jesus Christ and the teaching that accords with godliness, he is puffed up with conceit and understands nothing. He has an unhealthy craving for controversy and for quarrels about words, which produce envy, dissension, slander, evil suspicions, and constant friction among people who are depraved in mind and deprived of the truth, imagining that godliness is a means of gain. (1 Tim 6:2–5)

The great safeguard against the ungodliness Paul describes is pastors who lovingly and sincerely teach sound doctrine. This helps explain why Paul exhorts young Timothy to "follow the pattern of the sound words that you have heard from me, in the faith and love that are in Christ Jesus. By the Holy Spirit who dwells within us, guard the good deposit entrusted to you" (2 Tim 1:13–14). There is a "pattern of sound words" to be followed and a "good deposit" to be guarded. In other words, an apostolic center to the faith. The faithful pastor will ensure, through his teaching ministry, that

---

6. Trueman, *Crisis of Confidence*, 158.
7. Trueman, *Crisis of Confidence*, 159.

sound doctrine comes in from the margins and takes up its rightful place at the center of church life.

Delighting in Dogma

In the preface to the translated French edition of the *Institutes of the Christian Religion*, John Calvin offered the reader a brief word about the subject matter as incentive for reading it. Here's a portion of what he wrote:

> In order that my readers may better profit from this present work, I should like to indicate briefly the benefit they may derive from it. For, in doing this, I shall show them the purpose to which they ought to bend and direct their intention while reading it. Although Holy Scripture contains a perfect doctrine, to which one can add nothing, since in it our Lord has meant to display the infinite treasures of his wisdom, yet a person who has not much practice in it has good reason for some guidance and direction, to know what he ought to look for in it, in order not to wander hither and thither, but to hold to a sure path, that he may always be pressing toward the end to which the Holy Spirit calls him. Perhaps the duty of those who have received from God fuller light than others is to help simple folk at this point, and as it were to lend them a hand, in order to guide them and help them to find the sum of what God meant to teach us in his Word.... Thus, I exhort all those who have reverence for the Lord's Word, to read it, and to impress it diligently upon their memory, if they wish to have, first, a sum of Christian doctrine, and, secondly, a way to benefit greatly from reading the Old as well as the New Testament.[8]

Notice what Calvin says about his *Institutes*. First, it is not intended to be a substitute for Scripture, but a guide into the Scriptures. It is the Holy Scripture that alone "contains a perfect doctrine." Second, Calvin wrote his *Institutes* for those readers who "have not much practice in [the Bible]." In other words, it wasn't for the learned, but as a help to "simple folk"—the unlearned so that they could likewise benefit from "the infinite treasures of [God's] wisdom" embedded in the Scriptures. This leads to the third observation: how Calvin intended for the *Institutes* to serve the church as a "guide" or "help" so that God's people could faithfully find "the sum of what God meant to teach us in his Word."

---

8. Calvin, *Institutes* (McNeill), 1:6, 8.

The pastor as teacher of sound doctrine thinks likewise. A pastor sees his lifework as an effort to explain what Christianity is from the Scriptures of both the Old and New Testaments. Our dogma should be nothing more and nothing less than what the Bible teaches. It is the pastor's duty and delight to lead his congregation into the living waters of God's Word such that our churches say to God, "I will delight in your statutes; I will not forget your word" (Ps 119:16). A pastor understands that not all in the congregation have a seminary degree. The pews (or chairs) are, perhaps, full of the type of people Calvin pastored: "simple folk" who lack "practice" in the Scriptures. The faithful shepherd knows he's been given a great "stewardship from God . . . to make the word of God fully known" (Col 1:25). Therefore, a pastor sees his teaching as a "guide" or "help"—not to his popularity or fame—but to the church's greater understanding of the riches of God's Word.

A Confessing Theology

There was a time in church history when no one had to make a defense for doctrine's place at the center of the church's life. The question confronting the church for much of her existence was not *if* the church would seek to define itself theologically, but *what* theological commitments would define it. Not so in our time. Pastors today must make a defense for dogma. Its value cannot be assumed.

As a new believer no one had to tell me doctrine mattered. Immediately upon my conversion, I had an insatiable appetite for the Scriptures and wanted to know what they meant. I assumed the Bible must fit together as an organic whole because, after all, it was God's Word. And the "fitting together" resulted in dogma or the "pattern of sound words" Paul exhorted Timothy to teach (2 Tim 1:13). To my surprise (and dismay), the evangelical world I was reared in did not share my love affair with doctrine. More than "anti-theological" I found most people in the church "a-theological." Much like Ignorance in Bunyan's *Pilgrim's Progress*, these were people basically indifferent to theology, not seeing any real value in pursuing it. Three decades later not much has changed. And just as Ignorance became frustrated with Christian and Hopeful for their insistence that doctrine *does* matter, many in our churches today act likewise when we insist that what the church believes, teaches, and confesses matters for eternity, and that these truths should animate our lives before God. Confronted with an a-theological church, a pastor has a choice to make: will he become defensive and return frustration for frustration, or will he joyfully make the case for a confessional church?[9]

On the subject of a confessional church, I'm reminded of a helpful book published in 2000 when postmodernity was all the rage. Into this relativistic milieu came a work edited by Michael Horton that dared to suggest churches meet the challenges of postmodernity with *theology*. In *A Confessing Theology for Postmodern Times*, Horton and his team of writers set out to make what is old new again. In chapter 1, Charles Arand asks and answers the important question, "What is the value of church dogma?"[10] Pastors today would do well to consider Arand's fourfold explanation.

First, our Protestant confessional heritage provides "a framework and presuppositions for the reading of Scripture."[11] By this Arand means something similar to what Calvin meant in his preface to the *Institutes*: the church's dogma helps the reader of Scripture know what to look for by highlighting what is more or less important. "In a sense," Arand explains, "the church's dogma represents the 'accumulated insights' of those who have explored the Scriptures down through the centuries.... The church's confession and dogma provide an honest, 'up front' statement about its presuppositions: 'This is what we have discovered in Scripture and this is how we read the Scriptures.'"[12]

Second, our Protestant confessional heritage "provides a map for the reading of Scripture."[13] The church's dogma offers comprehensive summaries of what the church believes, teaches, and confesses. In this sense, creeds and confessions act as succinct "systematic theology" volumes or relatively brief expositions of the great doctrinal themes of the Bible. Arand explains,

> As documents that set forth the accumulated insights of the church over a period of centuries, the church's confessional and dogmatic writings might be likened to a collection of maps gathered into an atlas. Instead of mapping out geographical features, they map out the doctrinal terrain of the Scriptures.

---

9. By *confessional*, I have in mind not only the value of a church adopting a robust confession of faith as a teaching tool, but transparently positioning the church in the rich confessional heritage of Reformed Protestantism.

10. Arand, "Church's Dogma and Biblical Theology," 17–21.

11. Arand, "Church's Dogma and Biblical Theology," 18.

12. Arand, "Church's Dogma and Biblical Theology," 18–19.

13. Arand, "Church's Dogma and Biblical Theology," 19.

> This metaphor of a map or atlas is useful in understanding the reciprocal relation between the confessions and biblical writings. The confessions reproduce in miniature the doctrinal content of the Scriptures.[14]

What is important to see in Arand's understanding of the value of the church's dogma, is that, like Calvin, it is a guide into the Scriptures themselves. In this way, confessionalism is not seen as supplanting the Bible. Rather, the church's dogma is a faithful "map" of the Bible, alerting us to what must be seen and then faithfully guiding us as we go into the landscape of God's Word.

This leads to Arand's third point about the value of church dogma, namely, as hermeneutical guide. How we interpret the Bible is of utmost importance to the Christian life. After all, we must know accurately what God says in his Word, and hermeneutics is the practice of sound interpretive principles for doing so. A pastor should understand that the church's dogma is not a threat to Scripture, but Scripture's friend as our confessional heritage helps ensure we "present [ourselves] to God as one approved, a worker who has no need to be ashamed, rightly handling the word of truth" (2 Tim 2:15). Here's how Arand explains the church's dogma as hermeneutical guide:

> Maps are not intended to replace or avoid the trip through the country they survey. Indeed, there is no substitute for seeing the scenery of the countryside for yourself. Maps are merely a guide for actually taking the trip. Dogma is no substitute for reading and studying the Scriptures themselves. A traveler uses a map and embarks on a journey in order to arrive at a destination. The purpose of dogma is to "send us back into the Scriptures with more reader competence." It takes us to the center of the region. It points out highlights along the way: "Be sure to see this waterfall!" (e.g., don't miss the doctrine of the church). The purpose of dogma is to lead us unerringly to the gospel.[15]

---

14. Arand, "Church's Dogma and Biblical Theology," 19. Trueman, likewise, commends the church's dogma as helpful summaries of Christian truth: "They [creeds and confessions] offer more comprehensive and succinct summaries of Christian doctrine than anything else. Indeed, one might without hyperbole declare that, outside the Bible, the documents that contain more biblical truth per page than anything else are the great creeds and confessions of the church." Trueman, *Crisis of Confidence*, 151.

15. Arand, "Church's Dogma and Biblical Theology," 20.

Fourth, the church's dogma is a teaching tool that helps God's people learn the "pattern of sound words" (2 Tim 1:13) passed down through the centuries. The church, in other words, has a vernacular that each successive generation must learn. Our confessional heritage teaches us how to speak biblical truth while avoiding the doctrinal errors that have surfaced throughout church history. In this way, the church's dogma serves to renew our minds according to the Word of God, as Arand relates:

> Finally, dogma provides a pattern for thinking through and articulating the biblical message. This does not mean that one must simply quote Bible passages or must merely repeat the dogmatic sentences, but it does mean that one learns to think and speak in an orthodox way, in a way that conforms with the orthodox dogma . . . . Thus the early church's creedal and conciliar dogma functions like grammar or like the rules of chess. It does not dictate the specific sentences you will utter or the specific moves you will make, but it does determine the pattern for speaking or moving in an acceptable way.[16]

Reformation Faith for Today

The apostolic warning from James is almost enough to make a pastor resign or a seminary student drop out: "Not many of you should become teachers, my brothers, for you know that we who teach will be judged with greater strictness" (Jas 3:1). Not many, but some. And of the some who dare to teach the Word of God, a judgment of greater strictness. Why is this? Jesus said it plainly: "Everyone to whom much was given, of him much will be required, and from him to whom they entrusted much, they will demand the more" (Luke 12:48). Pastors, as we've seen, are entrusted with the daunting task of teaching the whole counsel of God (Acts 20:27). As "stewards of the mysteries of God" (1 Cor 4:1), pastors must ensure that they "make the word of God fully known" (Col 1:25), and "guard the good deposit" entrusted to them (2 Tim 1:14). Pastors, after all, are called to lead nothing less (and nothing greater) than "the church of the living God, a pillar and buttress of the truth" (1 Tim 3:15). Indeed, pastors have been given much and, therefore, much will be required. The nature of the trust gives warrant for the warning.

---

16. Arand, "Church's Dogma and Biblical Theology," 23.

Having echoed the apostolic warning, it now seems appropriate to ask, "What should be the content of the pastor's teaching ministry? What doctrines should he teach? What confessional heritage should be commended?

Reformed Theology

I am persuaded, first, from the Bible and, secondly, from the state of the world today, that pastors should happily and unapologetically teach from the Reformed tradition. Not only do I believe our Protestant confessional heritage is robustly *biblical*, I also believe it presents to the world a theology big enough for our time. With wars and rumors of wars in the news constantly as well as the moral confusion on everything from gender to marriage, to the protection of the unborn, Reformed theology presents a biblical framework; this theological foundation not only makes sense of the world as we see it, but also confronts the world with the truth of who God is, who we are, and what he has done to make what is wrong gloriously right. In addition to this, Reformed theology carries within it a God-centered impulse that is much-needed in our narcissistic culture. Evangelicalism for far too long has been awash in the cult of self. It is past time for pastors to reclaim and reintroduce the church to Reformation theology.

Jonathan Master outlines two convictions that gave rise to his book *Reformed Theology*. The first is that theological frameworks matter: "Knowing what we believe about God, humanity, worship, and salvation is important. More than important, it is vital. We need clear answers to the biggest questions in life and the most consequential matters of eternity. These answers must be true—everything depends on it."[17] Pastors, of all men, must believe truth matters for eternity. The stakes are that high.

But knowing what we believe matters not only for eternity, but for *today*. Again, Master is helpful: "Knowing these true answers and being able to articulate them is a powerful thing. . . . This kind of clarity and coherence brings stability to our lives, to our families, and to our witness to the world."[18] And theology matters, whether someone is a new believer or someone who is older in the faith: "If you are a new Christian, it is important for you to gain a foothold in the teaching of the whole Bible and to have ready answers for the biggest and most fundamental theological questions. If you have been a Christian for some time, you need to know

---

17. Master, *Reformed Theology*, 13.
18. Master, *Reformed Theology*, 13.

where you stand and to orient your worship, fellowship, and practice in a way that accords with your convictions. Having a basic theological framework is essential."[19] Like Calvin, pastor-theologians in our day must serve as "guides into the word of God," and Reformed theology helps gospel ministers do this most important "field guide" work.

The second conviction Master offers is that Reformed theology is a blessing. This claim may run counter to all you have heard about Reformed theology. After all, isn't this the theological "system" embraced only by ivory-tower theologians or angry social media "doctrinal police" who love controversy? Doesn't Reformed theology make people "robots" by denying "freewill," or teach a form of fatalism such that our choices don't matter? These are caricatures that need correction. Pastors believe Jesus when he says that he came to give life and give it abundantly (John 10:10). Sound, biblical doctrine is a blessing as it is truth *for* life. Master explains,

> Reformed theology, centered on Jesus Christ and rooted in the Scriptures, seeks to explain the whole Bible by showing God's work of salvation from beginning to end. It gives an honest assessment of humanity and good news about the nature of salvation. More than that, it shows how the Bible instructs us personally, teaching us how we should worship God and serve him in our everyday lives at home, at work, and in the church. Truth is always a blessing, but these truths give special life and clarity.[20]

What pastor wouldn't want this for his people?

On June 21, 2024, theologian Michael Horton remarked on X, "Many confessional churches seem content to live off the capital of the past. But it is not enough to invoke the slogans of the Reformation. We need to recover the fullness of biblical faith and practice in our own time and place." This, of course, is true. Churches shouldn't simply be content with empty slogans. True confessional churches don't just quote slogans, but sincerely believe them and strive to live accordingly. Pastors must lead in this effort toward a sincere faith.

The Reformation gave us many theologically rich slogans, in particular the five *solas*—a wonderful Latin word meaning *alone*. The following Latin phrases served to summarize the Reformers' theological convictions

---

19. Master, *Reformed Theology*, 13–14.
20. Master, *Reformed Theology*, 15.

Doctrine

about the essentials of Christianity. Together they help explain the heart of Reformed theology.[21]

- *Sola Scriptura* (Scripture Alone)

  This means that Scripture alone is the church's highest authority, and not man, tradition, government, or any other earthly authority. A faithful pastor delights in studying the Bible, God's inspired, inerrant, and sufficient Word, and longs for his congregation to delight in the Word of God as well. The Bible is the primary source for spiritual truth, the final authority on all matters of faith and life, and has the power to transform our lives (2 Tim 3:16–17; Heb 4:12).

- *Sola Gratia* (Grace Alone)

  This means that salvation is wholly owing to the grace or favor of God. His grace is not earned or merited or deserved in any way. It is God "who saved us and called us to a holy calling, not because of our works but because of his own purpose and grace, which he gave us in Christ Jesus before the ages began" (2 Tim 1:9). Pastors long to see the church increasingly stunned by the grace of God that saves (Rom 6:23; Eph 1:3–8).

- *Sola Fide* (Faith Alone)

  This means that faith is the instrument by which we lay hold of the promises of God in Christ. Salvation is not by faith in the merits of Christ *plus* works we might perform—whether church membership, baptism, aisle walking, or prayers prayed. Pastors rejoice to know "by grace you have been saved *through faith*. And this is not your own doing; it is the gift of God, not a result of works, so that no one may boast" (Eph 2:8–9; emphasis added).

- *Solus Christus* (Christ Alone)

  This means that our salvation is based solely on the finished work of Christ. Nothing needs to be added to the merits of Christ. Pastors love

---

21. For considering the five *solas* as a helpful starting point for understanding Reformed theology, see Master, *Reformed Theology*, 20–29. (This, of course, is not to deny the importance of the so-called "five points of Calvinism" or the emphasis that Reformed theology places on the covenants.)

to sing "in Christ alone our hope is found" as he is our all-sufficient Savior (1 Cor 1:30–31; Col 1:19–20; 2:13–15; Heb 10:8–14).

- *Soli Deo Gloria* (To the Glory of God Alone)

    This last of the five *solas* is the pinnacle of the others. It means that all of life is to be lived for the glory of God. God alone is to receive all glory, honor, and praise. It is a phrase that speaks to a radically God-centered life. Pastors love to proclaim the truth of Romans 11:36: "For from him and through him and to him are all things. To him be glory forever. Amen."

The Courage to Be Protestant

The church needs pastors who have the courage to be Protestant. By this I mean, pastor-theologians who see the biblical mandate to "teach what accords with sound doctrine" (Titus 2:1), and by God's grace, to set themselves to this glorious work. Our Protestant confessional heritage has not left us in the dark as to what we are to believe, teach, and confess. Of course, the world will shun our theology, and many in the church will reject it given its radically God-centered orientation. But by the Spirit's work through the Word, many will see and hear. Therefore, having the requisite skill in handling the Scriptures and the corresponding character required, pastors must resolve to offer to our churches and the world Reformation faith for today.

7

Prayer

> "A godly man cannot live without prayer."
> —Thomas Watson

> "Pray without ceasing."
> —1 Thessalonians 5:17

Resolution 7: Resolved to promote personal and corporate prayer.

In this chapter, I consider the necessity of prayer--what Calvin called the "chief exercise of faith, by which we daily receive God's benefits."[1] Spirit-empowered prayer is what fuels a pastor's ministry efforts as it daily reminds the shepherd of his utter dependency on God for any ministry fruit while also being the great means by which God pours out his grace. In other words, dependency and power are the reasons for personal and corporate prayer being at the heart of a faithful shepherd's work. And while

---

1. Calvin, *Institutes* (Lane and Osborne), 203.

a definition of prayer will be offered, one of the presuppositions behind this chapter is that more than a *theology* of prayer, what pastors need is the *will* to pray. Prayer is the natural heart cry of a child of God. After all, as Calvin observes, "faith unaccompanied by prayer cannot be genuine."[2] And, "The need for prayer, and its usefulness, cannot be emphasized too much."[3] Therefore, through biblical exegesis and examples from church history, this chapter primarily aims not to merely *define* prayer, but to stir in pastors a longing to *practice* it.

Augustine's God

In perhaps the greatest series of prayers ever recorded for posterity, Augustine of Hippo (354–430) opened his *Confessions* with this humble acknowledgment:

> You are mighty, Master, and to be praised with a powerful voice: great is your goodness, and of your wisdom there can be no reckoning. Yet to praise you is the desire of a human being, who is some part of what you created; a human hauling his deathliness in a circle, hauling in a circle the evidence of his sin, and the evidence that you stand against the arrogant. But still a mortal, a given portion of your creation, longs to extol you. In yourself you rouse us, giving us delight in glorifying you, because you made us with yourself as our goal, and our heart is restless until is rests in you.[4]

Over the next thirteen books, comprising nearly 500 pages, Augustine cries out to God in prayer, an extended version of what the apostle Paul describes in Romans 8:15: "For you did not receive the spirit of slavery to fall back into fear, but you have received the Spirit of adoption as sons, by whom we cry, 'Abba! Father!'"

My acquaintance with Augustine came thanks to a prompting by Martyn Lloyd-Jones. Let me explain. Back in the early 1990s, I was reading *Preaching and Preachers* and came across this paragraph:

> I have come to learn certain things about private prayer. You cannot pray to order. You can get on your knees to order; but how to pray? I have found nothing more important than to learn how to get oneself into that frame and condition in which one can pray.

---

2. Calvin, *Institutes* (Lane and Osborne), 203.
3. Calvin, *Institutes* (Lane and Osborne), 204.
4. Augustine, *Confessions*, 3.

> You have to learn how to start yourself off, and it is just here that this knowledge of yourself is so important. What I have generally found is that to read something which can be characterized in general as devotional is of great value. By devotional I do not mean something sentimental, I mean something with a true element of worship in it . . . . Start by reading something that will warm your spirit. Get rid of a coldness that may have developed in your spirit. You have to learn how to kindle a flame in your spirit, to warm yourself up, to give yourself a start . . . . When one finds oneself in this condition, and that it is difficult to pray, do not struggle in prayer for the time being, but read something that will warm and stimulate you, and you will find that it will put you into a condition in which you will be able to pray more freely.[5]

What Lloyd-Jones described was all-too-familiar to me. There were certainly times when I found it difficult to pray and needed something to warm my heart, to help put me in the right frame of mind to pray. I took Lloyd-Jones's advice and found something with "a true element of worship in it," Augustine's *Confessions*.

Outside the Bible, I've probably learned more about prayer from Augustine than anyone else. For example, the *Confessions* model deep reverence before God as Augustine never seems to forget *who* he is addressing: God Almighty, the sovereign King of the universe. We hear this in Augustine's humble refrain of "Master," "God," and "God the Master" before various sections of prayer. We see it in his constant acknowledgement of his sin and of God's transcendence. In addition to reverence, we also learn how convinced Augustine is that in Christ the child of God can "with confidence draw near to the throne of grace" (Heb 4:16). Both aspects of Augustine's prayers—deep reverence and confident approach—come through beautifully in the opening words of book 9:

> Master, I am your slave, I am your slave and the son of your female slave. But you have torn my chains apart; I will offer up a sacrifice, the praise of you. Let my heart and my tongue praise you, and let all my bones say, "Master, who is like you?" Let them say it, and you, answer me and says to my soul, "I am your rescue."
>
> But who am *I*, and what sort of person? What evil has been absent from the things I've done? And if not from the things I've done, then from the things I've said? And if not from the things I've said, then from my inclinations?

---

5. Lloyd-Jones, *Preaching and Preachers*, 181–82.

> Yet you, God, are good and compassionate. With your right hand, you explored the depths of my death, and from the floor of my heart you drained out the sea of rot. But the whole of what brough this about was that I stopped wanting what *I* had been wanting, and instead wanted what *you* wanted.
>
> But where was your right hand in that stretch of time so weighed down with its years? From what deep, what deepest, hidden place was my free choice in an instant called out—the choice to place my neck under your yoke, and my shoulders under your light load, the load that was yours, Jesus Christ, my helper, who bought me out of slavery?
>
> How delectably it happened, all of a sudden: all of those inane delectations weren't there any longer; I'd been terrified of losing them, but now I was delighted to turn them loose. You, my true, my highest sweetness, threw that nonsense out of me—threw it out and entered in its place; sweeter than any pleasure, though not felt in the body and the blood; brighter than any light, but more inward than any intimate retreat; loftier than any achievement that wins recognition—but those with a lofty self-regard can't know this.[6]

Augustine knew God liberated him from the bondage of sin and death making him a "slave" to God his "Master." There is no Master/servant confusion on Augustine's part. Yet he boldly approaches God through Christ, his great "helper" and the one who "bought [him] out of slavery." God in Christ had become Augustine's "highest sweetness."

In those early years of my Christian life, I found in Augustine a model for prayer worth emulating. The *Confessions* is probably what explains the way I generally begin my prayer time each morning, an opening salutation that reminds me of who I'm approaching as well as giving me confidence to come: "O God, my God, my Heavenly Father, I come before you in Jesus' holy and precious name. O God, please hear my prayer."

The Primacy of Prayer for Jesus

Early in Mark's gospel, we see the importance of prayer in the ministry of Jesus:

> And rising very early in the morning, while it was still dark, he departed and went out to a desolate place, and there he prayed. And

---

6. Augustine, *Confessions*, 238–39.

> Simon and those who were with him searched for him, and they found him and said to him, "Everyone is looking for you." And he said to them, "Let us go on to the next towns, that I may preach there also, for that is why I came out." And he went throughout all Galilee, preaching in their synagogues and casting out demons. (Mark 1:35–39)

Jesus had just spent the day prior teaching in the synagogue, healing Peter's mother-in-law, and healing the masses of people who came to him at sundown once the Sabbath had ended. Jesus, one might say, had experienced a crazy busy day of ministry; but this did not stop Jesus from "rising very early in the morning, while it was still dark," removing himself to a secluded place to pray (v. 35). For the Son of God, prayer was that important. The question is, why?

The first reason Jesus prayed has to do with the mystery of the incarnation. Not only was Jesus fully God, but also fully man. During the time of his humiliation, Jesus prayed to maintain communion with the Father. William Hendriksen is helpful when he observes that Jesus prayed "in order that the reservoirs of His body and soul might be replenished from His Father's inexhaustible resources."[7] Sinless though he was, as the God-man Jesus availed himself of prayer for the fulfillment of his earthly ministry. In passages like John 17, the high priestly prayer and in the Garden of Gethsemane, in the shadow of the cross, readers observe Jesus pouring out his heart to the Father for the accomplishment of redemption. As the author of Hebrews explains, "In the days of his flesh, Jesus offered up prayers and supplications, with loud cries and tears, to him who was able to save him from death, and he was heard because of his reverence" (5:7).

The second reason Jesus prayed was to leave us an example of dependence on God, a lesson pastors must ever learn. The reasoning goes something like this: if the One who was holy, blameless, pure, and set apart from sinners prayed earnestly to the Father, how much more should we? Prayer for the Christian is as essential as oxygen for breathing, water for hydration, and food for nutrition. It is spiritual sustenance for the soul. This is why we must heed the exhortation of Hebrews 4:16: "Let us then with confidence draw near to the throne of grace, that we may receive mercy and find grace to help in time of need."

Prayer, of course, is not always seen as essential. The essential nature of prayer was apparently lost on the disciples as we see in the text above,

---

7. Hendriksen, *Exposition of Luke*, 291.

specifically verses 36–37: "And Simon and those who were with him searched for him, and they found him and said to him, 'Everyone is looking for you.'" The word translated *searched* (κατεδίωξεν) is a vigorous term that could even mean "hunted." The idea behind the phrase "Everyone is looking for you" (πάντες ζητοῦσίν σε) is one of control, to make demands. The disciples evidently saw an opportunity for Jesus to leverage his newfound popularity, and removing himself from the scene for the sake of prayer seemed ridiculous. It wasn't expedient.

Before we are too hard on the disciples, isn't this often how we act in ministry? If we are not careful, prayer can be seen as an impediment to our work rather than the essential means of advancing the gospel. Paul, for example, wrote to the Colossians: "At the same time, pray also for us, that God may open to us a door for the word, to declare the mystery of Christ" (Col 4:3). The door for the Word will open, but not apart from prayer. The Apostle closed his second letter to the Thessalonians with a similar plea: "Finally, brothers, pray for us, that the word of the Lord may speed ahead and be honored, as happened among you" (3:1–2). The Word of the Lord will "speed ahead and be honored," but not apart from prayer.

An Ambitious Intern

I remember well my first pastoral internship when I was twenty-two years old. I shared an office with Dave Davies, the youth pastor of our church, who was in his late twenties and had a lot more ministry experience than me. I looked up to him in many ways even as we disagreed on several important doctrines related to the gospel. (I always enjoyed our spirited debates in that office as I was working out my theology and coming to my Reformed convictions.) Dave was patient with me as he recognized I was younger not only in age, but also in the faith. He would ask me questions to draw out of me what I believed, and would proceed to challenge me to know *why* I believed what I believed.

In addition to doctrine, Dave knew I needed to learn what a pastor *does* during the week. All my "jobs" in college were in banking, either in a local branch as a customer service representative or at a call center in a cubical on a headset. My experience in banking taught me to handle a lot of tasks, whether administrative or problem solving that needed immediate attention. At the call center, for example, there was a digital screen on the wall that showed all of the calls in queue—at any time there were

Prayer

dozens of people waiting to talk to a customer service representative like myself. No small anxiety overtook me as I looked up at the screen, watching the number of customers increase. I had learned that, generally speaking, people don't call the bank to tell them what a great job they're doing, and waiting for a long time to reach a real person was only exacerbating their frustration. So, I learned the art of quickly diffusing combustible situations with rapid-fire attention. It became a game to see how many calls I could successfully get through in an hour. In fact, my job depended on it.

No one had to train me to think like this. It came naturally. I arrived at the call center already wired this way, having been raised by a dad who was a "doer." My dad grew up in the small, midwestern town of Melvin, Iowa (population peaked at six hundred people, but just a fraction of that today). Upon graduation from high school, my dad left Melvin for the University of Iowa. After receiving his bachelor's and master's degrees, he left Iowa for upstate New York where he earned his PhD in economics at Cornell. After a brief teaching role at St. Lawrence University, my dad held various economic consulting positions with the government in Washington, DC, before leaving the public sector for a career in banking. I watched my dad climb the "corporate ladder," reaching the top rung as CEO of Pacific First Bank in Seattle, Washington. In my dad I saw the quintessential doer—he got things done. And I always wanted to be like him.

My propensity to be a "task master" and excelling at a high-volume, customer service center, however, was not the best training for ministry. I thought pastoring was all about being busy—busy with the *tasks* of ministry like planning events, recruiting volunteers, putting together worksheets, running copies, organizing games, buying food, setting up/taking down, etc. I approached ministry like a call center: get things done as quickly and efficiently as possible. And always have "measurables"—things you can check off at the end of the day as done. Sure, I was supposed to study the Bible, write lessons and sermons, meet with people, and pray. But those things were done not on "company time," but after hours. In those early months of my internship, I spent most of my time doing what Colin Marshall and Tony Payne have called "trellis work."[8]

Back to Dave. He saw in me this faulty approach to ministry. One day, in a gentle rebuke, he said to me, "Mike, you do know we pay you to study the Bible and pray." As you read this you may think this sounds crass. After all, putting "pay" and "Bible" and "pray" in the same sentence doesn't

---

8. Marshall and Payne, *The Trellis and the Vine*, 7–28.

sound very righteous. But Dave's point was profound. He was teaching me what should be at the heart of my ministry to the dear saints of our church: ministry of the Word and prayer. It was as if he had read Acts 6 and found it informative for contemporary ministry practice (which, of course, it is). It's the story of the apostles being tested in their leadership as a real problem is threatening the unity and harmony of the church. Indeed, ethnic conflict erupted over neglect of the widows in the church. Here's how Luke records it:

> Now in these days when the disciples were increasing in number, a complaint by the Hellenists arose against the Hebrews because their widows were being neglected in the daily distribution. And the twelve summoned the full number of the disciples and said, "It is not right that we should give up preaching the word of God to serve tables. Therefore, brothers, pick out from among you seven men of good repute, full of the Spirit and of wisdom, whom we will appoint to this duty. But we will devote ourselves to prayer and to the ministry of the word." (Acts 6:1–4)

The apostles recognize a real problem in the church. In other words, there is deficient care of God's people that needs to be remedied; and the temptation would be for the apostles to compromise their *primary* work for important but *secondary* work. Rather than compromise, the apostles address the problem in a way ("seven men of good repute, full of the Spirit and of wisdom") that does not draw them away from the primacy of prayer and the ministry of the Word.

Commenting on Acts 6 and the primary work of prayer and the ministry of the Word for pastors, Lloyd-Jones states, "Now there the priorities are laid down once and forever. This is the primary task of the Church, the primary task of the leaders of the Church, the people who are set in this position of authority; and we must not allow anything to deflect us from this, however good the cause, however great the need."[9] What Lloyd-Jones recognized is what the apostles learned from Jesus: prayer and the ministry of the Word is paramount.

Prayer Is Ministry

To demonstrate that prayer is one of the primary means God has ordained for his people to experience the blessings of salvation, I want to go to an

---

9. Lloyd-Jones, *Preaching and Preachers*, 30.

unlikely source, namely, Calvin. I say "unlikely" because one of many caricatures of Calvin is that he is the theologian that believes in God's sovereignty such that prayer is unnecessary. Contrary to this, Calvin writes,

> Prayer enables us to explore the riches which are treasured up for us with our heavenly Father. There is real contact between God and men when they enter the upper sanctuary, appear before him and claim his promises. We learn by experience that what we believed merely on the authority of his Word is true. There is nothing that we can expect from the Lord, for which we are not also told to pray. Prayer digs up the treasures which the Gospel reveals to the eye of faith. The need for prayer, and its usefulness, cannot be emphasized too much.[10]

Notice what profound claims Calvin makes. In prayer there is "real contact between God and men." Prayer is the means of true communion with God as we seek his heart for our lives. Prayer acts as a shovel that "digs up the treasures" of the gospel and applies them to our lives. "There is nothing," exhorts Calvin, "that we can expect from the Lord, for which we are not told to pray." This means that pastors must be men of prayer if we would see gospel fruit in our own lives and in the life of the churches we serve. Prayer is not something we do *before* or *after* ministry. Prayer *is* ministry. On this point, Calvin and Dave Davies agreed.

Toward a Definition of Prayer

To this point I've been assuming a definition of prayer while placing the emphasis on the action of prayer given its necessity. Now it is time to be clear about what prayer is with some motivations, particular to ministry, to practice it continually.

When most readers think of John Bunyan, the English Puritan, they likely think of *The Pilgrim's Progress*; but before I read *The Pilgrim's Progress*, I read Bunyan on prayer. I find his definition of prayer most helpful: "Prayer is a sincere, sensible, affectionate pouring out of the heart or soul to God, through Christ, in the strength and assistance of the Holy Spirit, for such things as God has promised, or according to his Word, for the good of the church, with submission in faith to the will of God."[11] According to Bunyan, prayer is first and foremost Trinitarian. Prayer is "to God, through

---

10. Calvin, *Institutes* (Lane and Osborne), 204.
11. Bunyan, *Prayer*, 13.

Christ, in the strength and assistance of the Holy Spirit." Prayer is an exercise in communion with the Godhead, each person having his specific role. This is important for the pastor to remember so that the majesty and mystery of the Godhead is ever before him. When we pray to the triune God, we are reminded of his transcendence and our finitude, his adequacy and our insufficiency. Trinitarian prayers are one of the best ways of remembering the Creator-creature distinction that is often lost in evangelicalism.

Bunyan proceeds to outline seven indispensable characteristics of genuine prayer. First, prayer must be "sincere." Without sincerity, Bunyan warns, none of our actions are regarded by God. He points to God's rejection of the insincere rebels of Hosea 7:13–14: "Woe to them, for they have strayed from me! Destruction to them, for they have rebelled against me! I would redeem them, but they speak lies against me. They do not cry to me from the heart, but they wail upon their beds." Bunyan observes, "It is rather for a pretense, for a show in hypocrisy, to be seen of men, and applauded for the same that they pray."[12] While Bunyan doesn't mention Jesus's hard words regarding the hypocrisy of the Pharisees, they are worth recalling: "And when you pray, you must not be like the hypocrites. For they love to stand and pray in the synagogues and at the street corners, that they may be seen by others. Truly, I say to you, they have received their reward" (Matt 6:5). In contrast to God's disdain for the hypocritical prayers of the ungodly, Bunyan notes the favor of God on the sincere prayers of the godly: "The prayer that has this [sincerity] in it as one of the principal ingredients is the prayer that God regards. Thus, 'The prayer of the upright is his delight' (Prov. 15:8)."[13]

Prayer, for Bunyan, must not only be sincere, but it must also be "sensible." By *sensible*, I take Bunyan to mean *biblical*. He explains, "It is not, as many take it to be, a few babbling prating, complimentary expressions, but a sensible feeling in the heart. Prayer has in it a sensibleness of diverse things; sometimes sense of sin, sometimes of mercy received, sometimes of the readiness of God to give mercy."[14] The "diverse things" prayer is sensible to are *gospel* things. Again, Jesus's instruction about prayer is relevant: "And when you pray, do not heap up empty phrases as the Gentiles do, for they think that they will be heard for their many words" (Matt. 6:7).

---

12. Bunyan, *Prayer*, 14.
13. Bunyan, *Prayer*, 14.
14. Bunyan, *Prayer*, 14.

Third, prayer is "an affectionate pouring out of the heart or soul to God through Christ." Bunyan explains with appropriate affection:

> O, what heat, strength, life, vigor, and *affection* there is in true prayer! 'As the heart panteth after the water-brooks, so panteth my soul after thee, O God' (Ps. 42:1). 'I have longed after thy precepts' (Ps. 119:40). 'I have longed for thy salvation' (Ps. 17:4). 'My soul longeth, yea, even fainteth, for the courts of the Lord; my heart and my flesh crieth out for the living God' (Ps. 84:2). 'My soul breaketh for the longing that it hath unto thy judgments at all times' (Ps. 119:20). O what affection is here discovered in prayer! You have the same in Daniel. 'O, Lord, hear; O Lord, forgive; O Lord, hearken and do; defer not, for thine own sake, O my God' (Dan. 9:19). Every syllable carries a mighty vehemency in it. This is called the fervent, or the working, prayer by James. And so again, 'And being in an agony, he prayed more earnestly' (Luke 22:44). He had his affections more and more drawn out after God for his helping hand. O how wide are the most of men with their prayers from this prayer! Alas! The greatest part of men make no conscience at all of the duty; and as for them that do, it is to be feared that many of them are very great strangers to a sincere, sensible, and affectionate pouring out of their hearts or souls to God. They content themselves with a little lip-labour and bodily exercise, mumbling over a few imaginary prayers. When the affections are indeed engaged in prayer, then the whole man is engaged, and that in such sort that the soul will spend itself, as it were, rather than go without that good desired, even communion and solace with Christ. And hence it is that the saints have spent their strength, and lost their lives, rather than go without the blessing (Ps. 69:3; 38:9, 10; Gen. 32:24, 26).[15]

All this affectionate pouring out of the heart to God is done only in and through Jesus Christ, his person and merits. We pray in his name, for he is our great High Priest who alone gives us access to God's throne of grace (Heb 4:14–16).

Fourth, true prayer must be done "by the strength or assistance of the Holy Spirit." Prayer, if genuine, must be Spirit-empowered. Bunyan warns of Spirit-less prayer: "If it be not in the strength and by the assistance of the Spirit, it is but like the sons of Aaron, offering strange fire (Lev. 10:1–2)."[16] That our prayers should be offered in the power of the Holy Spirit follows

---

15. Bunyan, *Prayer*, 16.
16. Bunyan, *Prayer*, 19.

given that the Christian life as a whole is to be lived in the Spirit (Gal 5:16–25).

A fifth characteristic of true prayer for Bunyan is prayer offered "for such things as God has promised." God's Word must be the content of all true prayer: "Prayer is only true when it is within the compass of God's Word; it is blasphemy, or at best babbling, when the petition is unrelated to the Book."[17] This means that a pastor must be a man of the Book. If our prayers would not diverge into mere worldliness—vain ramblings—then the Bible must shape our prayers. Pastors must be ever acquainted with the priorities of the apostles. What are the themes that animate their letters? How do they model for us the content of true prayer?

Sixth, true prayer is "for the good of the church." This is a profound insight by Bunyan, established on the mystery of the church's union with Christ. Bunyan explains,

> This clause covers whatsoever tends either to the honour of God, Christ's advancement, or his people's benefit. For God, and Christ, and his people are so linked together that if the good of the one be prayed for, the others must needs be included. As Christ is in the Father, so the saints are in Christ; and he that touches the saints, touches the apple of God's eye. Therefore pray for the peace of Jerusalem, and you pray for all that is required of you. For Jerusalem will never be in perfect peace until she be in heaven; and there is nothing that Christ more desires than to have her there. That also is the place that God through Christ has given her. He then that prays for the peace and good of Zion, or the church, asks that in prayer which Christ has purchased with his blood; and also that which the Father has given to him as the price thereof.[18]

The seventh and final aspect of true prayer for Bunyan is prayer that "submits to the will of God." This is the aspect of prayer that will nurture humility in us. We confidently approach the throne of grace through Christ in the power of the Holy Spirit, but as we boldly come, we humbly submit to God's will. Indeed, "the people of the Lord in all humility are to lay themselves and their prayers, and all that they have, at the foot of their God, to be disposed of by him as he in his heavenly wisdom sees best. Yet not doubting but God will answer the desire of his people that way that shall be most for

---

17. Bunyan, *Prayer*, 20.
18. Bunyan, *Prayer*, 21.

their advantage and his glory."[19] Jesus, of course, modeled this perfectly in the Garden of Gethsemane. In the shadow of the cross, Jesus endured one final temptation to abandon the mission of Calvary. His prayer ends with perfect submission: "Father, if you are willing, remove this cup from me. Nevertheless, not my will, but yours, be done" (Luke 22:42). With Bunyan's definition of true prayer before us, we close this chapter with the pastor's great motive for continual, earnest prayer: the gravity of gospel ministry.

"Help Us in This Awesome and Terrible Work"

I remember at first being stunned by Eric's prayer. Eric was one of our eleven elders at Immanuel Bible Church in Bellingham, Washington. I loved serving with those men because they understood something of the gravity of ministry. They were not playing religious games. As an example of this, Eric opened his prayer with these words: "Heavenly Father, please help us in this awesome and terrible work." I had never heard someone call pastoral ministry "terrible." But I knew what my co-laborer was thinking as he considered the gravity of shepherding God's people: "Who is sufficient for these things?" (2 Cor 2:16) Apart from the grace of God, no one. After all, what is a pastor but "the aroma of Christ to God among those who are being saved and among those who are perishing, to one a fragrance from death to death, to the other a fragrance from life to life" (2 Cor 2:15–16).

Eric's prayer reminded me of the wise words of Benjamin Warfield from a little booklet given me in seminary called *The Religious Life of Theological Students*: "I am sure that if you once get a true glimpse of what the ministry of the cross is, for which you are preparing, and of what you, as men preparing for the ministry, should be, you will pray, Lord, who is sufficient for these things, your heart will cry; and your whole soul will be wrung with the petition: Lord, make me sufficient for these things."[20] There it is; that is the key. When the pastor keeps before him the mission—what is at stake in the gospel—he will be moved into continual, earnest prayer. With the gravity of the ministry of the cross before us, how could we do otherwise?

---

19. Bunyan, *Prayer*, 22.
20. Warfield, *Religious Life of Theological Students*.

8

Preaching

> "I would say without any hesitation that the most urgent need in the Christian Church today is true preaching."
> —Martyn Lloyd-Jones

> "I charge you in the presence of God and of Christ Jesus, who is to judge the living and the dead, and by his appearing and his kingdom: preach the word."
> —2 Timothy 4:1–2

Resolution 8: Resolved to preach the Word.

PREACHING MUST BE CENTRAL in the work of the pastor and, therefore, in the life of the church. Preaching is not the only essential work of a faithful pastor. However, preaching, given what it *is* and what it *does*, must have a place of priority in the shepherd's labors.

Preaching

The Priority of Preaching

What does the world think about, if it thinks about them at all, when it thinks about preaching and preachers? Early in the semester, I often put this question to my preaching students. I introduce it something like this: "Imagine yourself on a plane, and as you often do when flying you begin having a conversation with the person sitting next to you. Inevitably, the question of what you do for a living comes up. Now, let's assume the person I'm talking to is not a Christian when he asks, 'So, what do you do for a living?' I answer honestly, 'I'm a Baptist preacher.' What is the gentleman sitting next to me thinking at that moment?"

My students have a variety of answers, none of them favorable. That unbeliever sitting next to me might think me a charlatan or mere "salesman for Christ." After all, the prosperity gospel is so ubiquitous in the culture that unbelievers may assume all preachers are really religious hypocrites, more interested in "fleecing" the sheep than actually caring for them. Another thought by the man sitting next to me may be of an angry "fire and brimstone" preacher who loves "condemning people to hell." A preacher, it may be thought, just loves to rail against sin, the secularization of the culture, and warn of hell and the judgment that is to come. Preaching is defined only by what it is *against*; or, perhaps the gentleman sitting next to me on that plane thinks a little more highly of preaching and preachers, and considers that I may be successful in helping people get along a little better in life each week with some pithy advice or Christianized "self-help." Preaching, in his mind, may offer marginal comfort in an otherwise difficult world as the preacher serves as a "life coach" or therapeutic counselor. There are other ideas I could list, but the common denominator of all the suggestions that my students offer is that all are woefully inadequate when it comes to a biblical understanding of preaching. The world just doesn't get it.

One pastor who understood the lofty place of preaching in the Bible was Martyn Lloyd-Jones, minister of Westminster Chapel in London during the mid-twentieth century. In 1969, Lloyd-Jones was giving a lectureship on preaching at Westminster Theological Seminary in Philadelphia. He opened by giving warrant for why he believed he was qualified to give a lectureship on preaching:

> But, ultimately, my reason for being very ready to give these lectures is that to me the work of preaching is the highest and greatest

and the most glorious calling to which anyone can ever be called. If you want something in addition to that I would say without any hesitation that the most urgent need in the Christian Church today is true preaching; and as it is the greatest and most urgent need in the Church, it is obviously the greatest need of the world also.[1]

For Lloyd-Jones, there is no higher calling than to preach the gospel of Jesus Christ. And while the church has many needs, there is no more urgent need than true, biblical preaching. Furthermore, at the risk of hyperbole, Lloyd-Jones claims that the "greatest need of the world" is preaching. It seems that for Lloyd-Jones these convictions are what ultimately qualifies any man to do a lectureship on preaching.

Where did Lloyd-Jones get this audacious idea for the primacy of preaching? Job security? After all, wouldn't we expect a preacher to say something like this to validate his life's work? Perhaps this was an instance of the "preacher" overwhelming the lecturer with a rhetorical flourish to elevate the topic in his listeners' imagination? A better explanation is that Lloyd-Jones was being *biblical* and *theological* in his evaluation of preaching's significance.

Jesus, the Apostle Paul, and Preaching

It is noteworthy that Mark in his Gospel opens with Jesus "proclaiming the gospel of God" (Mark 1:14). Mark is not concerned with birth narratives or establishing Jesus's Messianic lineage. Mark begins his narrative of the life and ministry of Jesus with him declaring, "The time is fulfilled, and the kingdom of God is at hand; repent and believe in the gospel" (Mark 1:15). Later in this opening chapter, Mark highlights the significance of Jesus's preaching ministry when he records his words to his disciples about why they must move on to the next town rather than stay in Capernaum: "And Simon and those who were with him searched for him, and they found him and said to him, 'Everyone is looking for you.' And he said to them, 'Let us go on to the next towns, that I may preach there also, for that is why I came out'" (Mark 1:36–38).[2] In this staggering statement Jesus makes it clear that his incarnation has everything to do with his preaching. The parallel passage in Luke's Gospel makes the point even more clearly: "And when it

---

1. Lloyd-Jones, *Preaching and Preachers*, 17. The reader will recall being introduced to this quotation in the introduction, with application made to pastoral ministry generally.

2. This passage was also considered in chap. 7 regarding prayer.

was day, he departed and went into a desolate place. And the people sought him and came to him, and would have kept him from leaving them, but he said to them, 'I must preach the good news of the kingdom of God to the other towns as well; for I was sent for this purpose'" (Luke 4:42–43). In other words, Jesus took on flesh and dwelt among sinful creatures to preach the good news.[3]

The importance of the preaching ministry of Jesus is further demonstrated when we see Jesus's ministry in the synagogue in Luke 4:16–21:

> And he came to Nazareth, where he had been brought up. And as was his custom, he went to the synagogue on the Sabbath day, and he stood up to read. And the scroll of the prophet Isaiah was given to him. He unrolled the scroll and found the place where it was written, "The Spirit of the Lord is upon me, because he has anointed me to proclaim good news to the poor. He has sent me to proclaim liberty to the captives and recovering of sight to the blind, to set at liberty those who are oppressed, to proclaim the year of the Lord's favor." And he rolled up the scroll and gave it back to the attendant and sat down. And the eyes of all in the synagogue were fixed on him. And he began to say to them, "Today this Scripture has been fulfilled in your hearing."

Jesus, preaching from Isaiah 61, makes it clear that he is the one Isaiah spoke of, the one who has come to "proclaim good news to the poor"; the one sent to "proclaim liberty to the captives and recovering of sight to the blind"; the one on mission to "proclaim the year of the Lord's favor." Jesus came to preach.

Did the apostle Paul learn anything from Jesus's example of preaching for the purpose of his ministry? Indeed. Here's a sample of biblical texts that demonstrate Paul's understanding of the priority of preaching [emphasis added]:

- "So I am eager to *preach* the gospel to you also who are in Rome" (Rom 1:15).
- "How then will they call on him in whom they have not believed? And how are they to believe in him of whom they have never heard? And how are they to hear without someone *preaching*? And how are they to

---

3. Of course, wonder upon wonder, Jesus would not only preach the good news, but through his life, death, and resurrection, he would actually *accomplish* the good news he proclaimed.

- preach unless they are sent? As it is written, 'How beautiful are the feet of those who *preach* the good news!'" (Rom 10:14–15)
- "Now to him who is able to strengthen you according to my gospel and the *preaching* of Jesus Christ. " (Rom 16:25).
- "For Christ did not send me to baptize but to *preach* the gospel, and not with words of eloquent wisdom, lest the cross of Christ be emptied of its power" (1 Cor 1:17).
- "For since, in the wisdom of God, the world did not know God through wisdom, it pleased God through the folly of what we *preach* to save those who believe. For Jews demand signs and Greeks seek wisdom, but we *preach* Christ crucified, a stumbling block to Jews and folly to Gentiles, but to those who are called, both Jews and Greeks, Christ the power of God and the wisdom of God" (1 Cor 1:21–24).
- "Woe to me if I do not *preach* the gospel!" (1 Cor 9:16)
- "Him we *proclaim*, warning everyone and teaching everyone with all wisdom, that we may present everyone mature in Christ" (Col 1:28).
- "I charge you in the presence of God and of Christ Jesus, who is to judge the living and the dead, and by his appearing and his kingdom: *preach the word*; be ready in season and out of season; reprove, rebuke, and exhort, with complete patience and teaching" (2 Tim 4:1–2).

All of these texts speak to the prominence of preaching in Paul's ministry—a pattern we see throughout the book of Acts by not only Paul, but Peter before him. Preaching the good news of Jesus Christ is an apostolic priority and, therefore, must be a priority for the pastor.

Demonstrating the priority of preaching in the ministry of Jesus and Paul is one thing, but asking and answering the question of "Why" is another. In other words, why is preaching so important? Why, along with prayer, should it be at the heart of a pastor's ministry? To answer this all-important question, I want to look at the glory of preaching in terms of what preaching *is* and what it *does*. Both what preaching is and what it does explains the priority of preaching.

Preaching

The Glory of What Preaching *Is*

Before I demonstrate what preaching is, it's important to consider what preaching is not. Preaching is not mere eloquence in speech, nor is preaching what Augustine called "eloquent nonsense":

> We must beware of the man who abounds in eloquent nonsense, and so much the more if the hearer is pleased with what is not worth listening to, and thinks that because the speaker is eloquent, what he says must be true.... A man speaks with more or less wisdom to the extent he has made more or less progress in the knowledge of the Scripture not just in knowing them but especially in understanding them correctly.... It is more important to speak wisely than eloquently.[4]

For Augustine, eloquent nonsense is attractive speech that is void of Scripture. It is worldly babble. What makes eloquent nonsense so dangerous is that hearers often confuse eloquence for truth. Augustine makes it clear that truth is found only in right knowledge and understanding of the words of Scripture. Therein lies true wisdom and speech worth hearing.

Charles Spurgeon, with characteristic vividness, exhorted preachers likewise as he described to his students what preaching is not:

> Sermons should have real teaching in them, and their doctrine should be solid, substantial, and abundant. We do not enter the pulpit to talk for talk's sake; we have instructions to convey important to the last degree, and we cannot afford to utter pretty nothings.... Alas! The indistinct utterances of many concerning the grandest of eternal realities, and the dimness of thought in others with regard to fundamental truths, have given too much occasion for the criticism! Brethren, if you are not theologians, you are in your pastorates just nothing at all. You may be fine rhetoricians and be rich in polished sentences; but without knowledge of the gospel, and aptness to teach it, you are but a sounding brass and a tinkling cymbal. Verbiage is too often the fig-leaf which does duty as a covering for theological ignorance. Sounding periods are offered instead of sound doctrine, and rhetorical flourishes in the place of robust thought. Such things ought not to be. The abounding of empty declamation, and the absence of food for the soul, will turn a pulpit into a box of bombast, and inspire contempt instead of reverence. Unless we are instructive preachers, and really feed the people, we may be great quoters of elegant poetry,

---

4. Augustine, *On Christian Doctrine*, 104–5.

and mighty retailers of second-hand windbags, but we shall be like Nero of old, fiddling while Rome was burning, and sending vessels to Alexandria to fetch sand for the arena while the populace starved for want of corn.[5]

So, if preaching is not "eloquent nonsense" and our pulpits simply a "box of bombast," what is preaching?

Preaching must be an exposition of Scripture. If our preaching is to be *Christian* preaching, our sermons must be an explanation and application of a passage (or passages) of Scripture. Indeed, the Christian preacher proclaims the Bible because he believes with the apostle Paul that "all Scripture is breathed out by God and profitable for teaching, for reproof, for correction, and for training in righteousness" (2 Tim 3:16). This conviction is summarized well by Haddon Robinson when he states, "Expository preaching at its core is more a philosophy than a method. Whether we can be called expositors starts with our purpose and with our honest answer to the question: 'Do you, as a preacher, endeavor to bend your thought to the Scriptures, or do you use the Scriptures to support your thought?'"[6] In addition to the doctrine of God, the most important doctrine to the preacher is that of Scripture (see chapter 2). True belief that the Bible is the Word of God will govern how preachers preach. In other words, the Christian preacher will make every effort, in the power of the Holy Spirit, to clearly explain and apply the Bible because of what he believes the Bible to be: the out-breathed breath of God (2 Tim 3:16). The nature of the Bible dictates the content of preaching. Christian proclamation, therefore, is formally bound to the Scriptures such that preaching must always be nothing other than the explanation and application of the Bible.[7] As J. I. Packer explains regarding a sermon,

---

5. Spurgeon, *Lectures to My Students*, 70, 72. Nearly a century later, James Stewart, in Spurgeon-like fashion, reasoned similarly when he cautioned preachers against making a sermon a "declamatory firework show": "Life and death issues are in your mouth when you preach the Gospel of Christ; and it is simply tragic trifling to make the sermon a declamatory firework show, or a garish display of the flower of rhetoric." Stewart, *Heralds of God*, 40.

6. Robinson, *Biblical Preaching*, 5.

7. Bryan Chapell makes this point when he explains, "Expository preaching attempts to present and apply the truths of a specific biblical passage." He continues, "An expository sermon may be defined as a message whose structure and thought are derived from a biblical text, that covers the scope of the text, and that explains the features and context of the text in order to disclose the enduring principles for faithful thinking, living, and worship intended by the Spirit, who inspired the text." Chapell, *Christ-centered*

Its *content* is God's message to man, presented as such. For the evangelical, this means that the source of what is said will be the Bible, and furthermore that a text will be taken (a verse, a part of a verse, or a group of verses), and the truth or truths presented will be, as the Westminster Directory for Public Worship put it, "contained in or grounded on that text, that the hearers may discern how God teacheth it from thence." The preacher will take care to make clear that what he offers is not his own ideas, but God's message from God's book, and will see it as his task not to talk for his text, but to let the text talk through him.[8]

Monologue from Heaven

We are now prepared to say exactly what preaching is: monologue from heaven. For when a preacher accurately proclaims the Word of God, we can confidently say that God is speaking through a human mouthpiece. Given this, there should be an identification of the sermon with the Word of God.[9] This claim is based on various biblical texts. For example, consider what Jesus tells the seventy disciples before he sends them out on their preaching mission: "The one who hears you hears me, and the one who rejects you rejects me, and the one who rejects me rejects him who sent me" (Luke 10:16; cf. John 13:20). If people hear (that is, receive) the words of the disciples, they are actually receiving God. If they reject the words of the disciples, they are actually rejecting God. Clearly, Jesus identified the words of his followers (the words taught them by Christ himself) with the Word of God.

This is the audacious claim of the apostle Paul in 2 Corinthians 5:20: "Therefore, we are ambassadors for Christ, God making his appeal through us." Indeed, God is appealing to the world through his Word; and this is what the expository preacher takes up every week. The Christian preacher,

---

Preaching, 30–31. Likewise, John Stott argues that exposition "refers to the content of the sermon (biblical truth) rather than its style (a running commentary). To expound Scripture is to bring out of the text what is there and expose it to view. The expositor pries open what appears to be closed, makes plain what is obscure, unravels what is knotted and unfolds what is tightly packed. The opposite of exposition is 'imposition,' which is to impose on the text what is not there." Stott, *Between Two Worlds*, 125–26.

8. Packer, "Why Preach?," 8.
9. See Adam, *Speaking God's Words*, 112–20.

as he faithfully proclaims the Word of God, is nothing less than "the messenger of the Lord of hosts" (Mal 2:7).

Our Protestant forefathers thought this way as well. Take, for example, Luther's understanding of what is happening in a sermon:

> John would say: Whoever would be in Christendom and be called a member or disciple of the Lord Christ must by all means hear God Himself. How, then, do I hear Him? A sectarian runs into a corner, closes his mouth, and need neither read nor hear; but he waits until our Lord God speaks with him, waits for the Spirit, and then says: Ah, this is what God teaches me! Nay, it's the devil on your head! To be taught by God Himself is to hear and learn the Lord Christ's Word from Him and to be sure that it is God's Word. This is hearing God Himself; and though an ass were to do the speaking, as in the case of Balaam (Num. 22:28), it would nonetheless be God's Word. Just so, you are hearing God the Father Himself when you hear a sermon from St. Paul or from me; and you do not become my pupil but the Father's pupil; for I am not speaking, but He is. Nor am I your master; but both of us have one Master and Teacher, the Father; and both of us are pupils too, except for the fact that the Father is speaking to you through me.[10]

Preaching for Luther is monologue from heaven.

Calvin, like Luther, taught that God, in the preaching event, is addressing his people through the mouth of a man. Take, for example, his comment on 1 Timothy 3:2, and how a pastor must be "able to teach":

> For St. Paul does not mean that one should just make a parade here or that a man should show off so that everyone applauds him and says, "Oh! Well spoken! Oh! What a breadth of learning! Oh! What a subtle mind!" All that is beside the point.... When a man has climbed up into the pulpit, is it so that he may be seen from afar, and that he may be pre-eminent? Not at all. It is that God may speak to us by the mouth of a man. And he does us that favor of presenting himself here and wishes a mortal man to be his messenger.[11]

For Calvin, preaching is evidence of God's kindness toward his church as he condescends to address his people "by the mouth of a man."[12] T. H. L.

---

10. Plass, *What Luther Says*, 1126.

11. Parker, *Calvin's Preaching*, 24–25.

12. Our Protestant confessional heritage teaches the identification of the sermon with the Word of God. For example, written by Heinrich Bullinger, the Second Helvetic

Parker, in his study of Calvin's preaching, explains how Calvin considered the preacher as "an envoy sent by God":

> He was careful to make the necessary distinction between the preacher and the Word of God. The preacher is not God, but an envoy sent by God. In himself he is nothing. All his authority and all the justification for his preaching lies in his ambassadorship, that is to say, in the two facts that God has called him to preach and that he preaches only what God in Holy Scripture commands him to preach. When, however, these two conditions are fulfilled, the preacher cannot retreat from the claim that the gospel which he preaches is the Word of God and as such demands the complete obedience of himself and his congregation.[13]

As God's envoy, the preacher's message, accurately derived from the Bible, is to be received not merely as a message from man, but as a word from God. In summary, preaching is glorious because of what it is: God speaking through the mouth of a man. In other words, it is monologue from heaven.

The Glory of What Preaching *Does*

The priority of preaching is seen not only in what it is, but also in what is *does*. Have you considered what actually happens when God is speaking through the mouth of a preacher? God is displaying his manifold glories, saving the lost, and sanctifying the saved. Let's consider each one of these activities of God in turn.

Displaying the Glories of God

The first thing preaching does is proclaim who God is. Lewis Allen explains, "Preachers have a single calling, to express who and what God is. This is our mandate, to declare what God has revealed about himself. What could be a greater task than being called to preach God?"[14] What a breathtaking

---

Confession (1566) makes the point thus: "Wherefore when this Word of God is now preached in the church by preachers lawfully called, we believe that the very Word of God is preached and received by the faithful" (1.4). In other words, the preaching of the Word of God *is* the Word of God in the sense that "sermons are the means by which the Word of God is applied to people." Adams, *Speaking God's Words*, 115.

13. Parker, *Calvin's Preaching*, 117.
14. Allen, *The Preacher's Catechism*, 35.

thought: a preacher is called to preach God; to hold him up to the church for all to see; to declare, "Behold your Maker." To display the glories of God to our churches means that we will preach as if God is real and his glory and honor the most important reality in the universe. Preachers believe this. Of course, on any given Sunday throughout evangelicalism, you would be forgiven for wondering if the one speaking actually believes that God is real and that he is the most important reality in the universe. Too often it seems as if the preacher believes he himself and his "audience" are the most important reality in the universe; and in terms of God being real, the levity and casualness of many preachers today is a tell that they don't actually believe that "it is appointed for man to die once, and after that comes judgment" (Heb 9:27). God-centered preaching—preaching that aims to display the glories of God—has been replaced by anthropocentric "messages" where man, not God, is sovereign.[15]

My deep appreciation for Post-It Notes began in seminary. I loved using yellow "stickies" to mark important pages in books and hold my place when I got to a good stopping point. I also began using Post-It Notes to write "notes to self." One such note I stuck on the bookshelf above my desk so it could stare at me every time I sat down to read or study my Bible. It read, "What does this text tell me about God?" This is the all-important question of any text of Scripture, and this is the necessary Godward step of any preacher as he begins his work of sermon preparation in any given passage of Scripture. The Post-It Note question is a safeguard or governor in the expositor's study to help ensure that he doesn't first go manward in the interpretation of a text. And this safeguard is needed given how hotwired we are to ask first, "What does this text say about me?" The expositor, however, has a precommitment in his sermon preparation: to discern what God's revelation (the Bible) says about God. The triune God is the "big idea" of the Bible, and he is who our churches need to behold, believe, and obey. A Post-It Note can help the preacher remember first things.

What does it sound like when a preacher is displaying the glories of God from the pulpit? What is he actually doing? He is beholding the attribute(s) of God from whatever text he's proclaiming, so that he can display this aspect of God to the church. For example, if I am taking up Genesis 1:3 ("And God said, 'Let there be light,' and there was light"), then I want to herald the creative *genius* and *power* of God to bring light out of darkness by his Word. I want to help the people of God gathered see a God

15. See Horton, *Christless Christianity*, 48–61.

who is so powerful and creative that he spoke light into existence. In his infinite *wisdom*, God determined that light was better than darkness for the world he created. Preachers help their congregations marvel at their Creator-God. Or consider taking up Isaiah 6 where we hear the song of the seraphim: "Holy, holy, holy is the LORD of hosts; the whole earth is full of his glory!" (v. 3) The glory of God's *holiness* is on display in the seraphim's refrain, and it's the preacher's job to help the church behold this stunning attribute of God against the backdrop of a fallen world where unholiness permeates everything. Perhaps the preacher is in Psalm 2, where in *sovereignty* God beholds the rebellion of the nations and "laughs." It continues, "The Lord holds them in derision" (v. 4). We could go on in considering the *faithfulness* of God from Jeremiah 31:31–34 as we behold the New Covenant promise, the love of God from John 3:16 in the giving of his Son, or the *justice* of God from Romans 2:6–11, where we learn that God will "render to each one according to his works." These are just some of the glories of God the preacher is determined to herald from the pulpit.

The rationale for proclaiming the glories of God from the pulpit was impressed upon me in seminary when I first read John Piper's *The Supremacy of God in Preaching*. This was an incredibly formative book for me as I was developing my own theology of preaching. By marshalling dozens of biblical texts and introducing me to the life and ministry of Jonathan Edwards, my preaching was put on a Godward trajectory that I've sought to maintain and grow in over nearly three decades. The following statements from the opening chapter entitled "The Goal of Preaching: The Glory of God" served as a breath of fresh air in the midst of the smog of man-centeredness permeating much of evangelicalism in the late 1990s:

- "God aims to exalt himself, not the preacher."
- "God the Father, God the Son, and God the Holy Spirit are the beginning, middle, and end in the ministry of preaching. Written over all ministerial labor, especially preaching, stand the words of the apostle: 'From him and through him and to him are all things. To him be glory forever (Rom. 11:36).'"
- "My burden is to plead for the supremacy of God in preaching—that the dominant note of preaching be the freedom of God's sovereign grace, the unifying theme be the zeal that God has for his own glory, the grand object of preaching be the infinite and inexhaustible being

of God, and the pervasive atmosphere of preaching be the holiness of God."

- "The keynote in the mouth of every prophet-preacher, whether in Isaiah's day or Jesus' day or our day, is 'Your God Reigns!' God is the King of the universe; he has absolute creator rights over this world and everyone in it. Rebellion and mutiny are on all sides, however, and his authority is scorned by millions. So the Lord sends preachers into the world to cry out that God reigns, that he will not suffer his glory to be scorned indefinitely, that he will vindicate his name in great and terrible wrath. But they are also sent to cry that for now a full and free amnesty is offered to all the rebel subjects who will turn from their rebellion, call on him for mercy, bow before his throne, and swear full allegiance and fealty to him forever. The amnesty is signed in the blood of his Son."

- "Behind and beneath the sovereign exercises of God's mercy as king is an unwavering passion for the honor of his name and the display of his glory."[16]

The God-centered vision of preaching outlined in those pages helped me see what must be at the heart of my preaching: God. It's no different today. The church continues to be in desperate need of preachers who are enthralled with the glories of God so that God, not man, is the great theme of our pulpits.

Preaching for Conversions

I love the Canons of Dort (1618–1619). Along with the Belgic Confession (1561) and the Heidelberg Catechism (1563), the Canons of Dort comprise the Three Forms of Unity, "the doctrinal standards of Dutch and German churches in the Reformed tradition."[17] Under the first (of five) main divisions of doctrine ("Divine Election and Reprobation"), article 3 reads,

> In order that people may be brought to faith, God mercifully sends proclaimers of this very joyful message to the people he wishes and at the time he wishes. By this ministry people are called to repentance and faith in Christ crucified. For "how shall they believe in him of whom they have not heard? And how shall they hear

16. Piper, *Supremacy of God in Preaching*, 19–24.
17. Van Dixhoorn, *Creeds, Confessions, and Catechisms*, 133.

without someone preaching? And how shall they preach unless they have been sent?" (Rom 10:14–15)[18]

Consistent with Romans 10:14–15, the Canons of Dort teach that God uses preaching to save the lost.

A pastor knows that people will end up in one of two places in eternity: heaven or hell. When a pastor steps into the pulpit, he's engaging in an intense warfare for the souls of his listeners. The preacher is battling against the world, the flesh, and the devil—given how powerfully each want to keep the congregation from beholding "the glory of God in the face of Jesus Christ" (2 Cor 4:6). Armed with the Word of God, the preacher labors in the Spirit of God for the conversion of sinners. Indeed, a pastor knows that the Word of God is the means God the Holy Spirit uses to save the lost. Consider Isaiah 55:10–11:

> For as the rain and the snow come down from heaven and do not return there but water the earth, making it bring forth and sprout, giving seed to the sower and bread to the eater, so shall my word be that goes out from my mouth; it shall not return to me empty, but it shall accomplish that which I purpose, and shall succeed in the thing for which I sent it.

Through the prophet Isaiah, God speaks of his word going forth from his mouth and doing what rain and snow do when it waters dry, barren land. And how does it go out from the mouth of the Lord? As we've seen in this chapter, it goes forth from the mouth of a man. The Word of God proclaimed through the preacher brings life where there was none. As the apostle Peter explains, a Christian is one who has been "born again, not of perishable seed but of imperishable, through the living and abiding word of God" (1 Pet 1:23). When the imperishable seed of the Word is proclaimed, God says "it shall not return to me empty, but it shall accomplish that which I purpose, and shall succeed in the thing for which I sent it." And according to the analogy used in Isaiah 55, one of the great things God sends his word forth to do is save the lost. And the preacher knows that "faith comes from hearing, and hearing through the word of Christ" (Rom 10:17).

This shouldn't surprise us. After all, there is an undeniable missionary heartbeat of God revealed in the Bible. Not only Isaiah 55, but earlier in the book we hear God pleading with the nations, "Turn to me and be saved, all the ends of the earth! For I am God, and there is no other" (Isa 45:22). This

---

18. Van Dixhoorn, *Creeds, Confessions, and Catechisms*, 135.

salvific appeal is consistent with the Abrahamic covenant of Genesis 12:3, where God promises Abram, "I will bless those who bless you, and him who dishonors you I will curse, and in you all the families of the earth shall be blessed." From Genesis we can go all the way to Revelation where we see this promise realized in the vision of John:

> And when he had taken the scroll, the four living creatures and the twenty-four elders fell down before the Lamb, each holding a harp, and golden bowls full of incense, which are the prayers of the saints. And they sang a new song, saying, "Worthy are you to take the scroll and to open its seals, for you were slain, and by your blood you ransomed people for God from every tribe and language and people and nation, and you have made them a kingdom and priests to our God, and they shall reign on the earth." (Rev 5:8–10)

This missionary zeal of God is seen beautifully in the earthly ministry of Jesus. He explains his dinner with Zacchaeus in terms of his mission to "seek and to save the lost" (Luke 19:10). He bid all who would hear: "Come to me, all who labor and are heavy laden, and I will give you rest. Take my yoke upon you, and learn from me, for I am gentle and lowly in heart, and you will find rest for your souls. For my yoke is easy, and my burden is light" (Matt 11:28–30). His heart for the lost is seen in his lament over Jerusalem: "O Jerusalem, Jerusalem, the city that kills the prophets and stones those who are sent to it! How often would I have gathered your children together as a hen gathers her brood under her wings, and you were not willing!" (Matt 23:37). And Jesus's resolve to gather all that Father has given him is seen in John 10:16: "And I have other sheep that are not of this fold. I must bring them also, and they will listen to my voice. So there will be one flock, one shepherd."

The preacher must take on this missionary heart of God in his preaching. The tone of our preaching must be a pleading for sinners to come to Jesus for the forgiveness of sins. The preacher knows eternity is at stake. Therefore, our preaching is never done with levity, but with the seriousness it demands. Sermons are an urgent appeal, as the apostle Paul demonstrates in his tone with the Corinthians: "Working together with him, then, we appeal to you not to receive the grace of God in vain. For he says, 'In a favorable time I listened to you, and in a day of salvation I have helped you.' Behold, now is the favorable time; behold, now is the day of salvation"

(2 Cor 6:1–2). It's texts like this, I imagine, that led Lloyd-Jones to urge seriousness in the pulpit:

> The preacher must be a serious man; he must never give the impression that preaching is something light or superficial or trivial . . . . What is happening is that he is speaking to them from God, he is speaking to them about God, he is speaking about their condition, the state of their souls. He is telling them that they are, by nature, under the wrath of God—"the children of wrath even as others"—that the character of the life they are living is offensive to God and under the judgment of God, and warning them of the dread eternal possibility that lies ahead of them. In any case, the preacher, of all men, should realize the fleeting nature of life in this world. The men of the world are so immersed in its business and affairs, its pleasures and all its vain show, that the one thing they never stop to consider is the fleeting character of life. All this means that the preacher should always create and convey the impression of the seriousness of what is happening the moment he even appears in the pulpit.[19]

With appropriate seriousness, a faithful preacher labors for conversions knowing that the Word of God is the means God the Holy Spirit uses to save the lost.

Preaching for Discipleship

Preaching is not only for displaying the glories of God and saving the lost, but also for sanctification. That is, preaching is one of the great means of discipleship at the pastor's disposal. Discipleship, after all, is about spiritual growth—or to put it more theologically, progressive sanctification. Our preaching aims to see Christians grow in Christlikeness.

When I lecture on this point to my preaching students at Southern Seminary and Boyce College, I usually open with this question: "What do you think most people in our churches think about when they think about discipleship?" The answers almost always have to do with one-on-one discipleship. The default thinking about discipleship in our churches seems to be either one person, or a small group of persons, *being discipled* by another person in the church. Interestingly, not once in nearly a decade of teaching

---

19. Lloyd-Jones, *Preaching and Preachers*, 85–86.

has the answer come back, "preaching." Whatever people think is happening in a sermon, discipleship doesn't seem to be it.

Preaching, however, is a God-ordained means of sanctification. Recall what I explained earlier about preaching as displaying the glories of God. With that in mind, consider 2 Corinthians 3:18, "And we all, with unveiled face, beholding the glory of the Lord, are being transformed into the same image from one degree of glory to another. For this comes from the Lord who is the Spirit." If we as preachers are doing our job, the congregation is "beholding the glory of the Lord" from a text of Scripture being expounded. And the apostle Paul says when this happens, we are "being transformed into the same image from one degree of glory to another." This work of the Spirit is what systematic theologians call *progressive sanctification*. In the words of the Westminster Shorter Catechism (Question 35):

> Q. What is sanctification?
>
> A. Sanctification is the work of God's free grace, whereby we are renewed in the whole man after the image of God, and are enabled more and more to die unto sin, and live unto righteousness.

Colossians 1:28-29 makes this same point: "Him we proclaim, warning everyone and teaching everyone with all wisdom, that we may present everyone mature in Christ. For this I toil, struggling with all his energy that he powerfully works within me." The preacher labors to proclaim Christ in the strength that God supplies so that people may be "mature in Christ." That is, sanctified. And surely Paul has people's growth in grace in mind as he exhorts Timothy to "preach the word; be ready in season and out of season; reprove, rebuke, and exhort, with complete patience and teaching" (2 Tim 4:2). If not for Christlikeness, why would Timothy preach the word defined as reproving, rebuking, and exhorting?

Training Churches in the Glory of Preaching

Pastors must teach their congregations about the glory of preaching, both what it *is* and what it *does*. Many faithful church members dutifully sit under hundreds of sermons over the years, and I wonder if they know why. The ways to train our churches in the glory of preaching are several. It can be done in membership classes, at congregational meetings, in Sunday school rooms, or at church conferences. While all of these ideas are good and needed, the best place to train a church in the glory of preaching is in the pulpit when a pastor is actually doing the work of exposition. More than teach it, we need to model it.

What would it mean for our churches if our members understood that during the preaching event God was actually addressing his people? What if our churches knew that when the Bible is proclaimed God is being displayed, people are being saved, and the saved are being sanctified? I think we would begin to see a great excitement and anticipation among our people for our Sunday gatherings. And as this happens and word gets out, an unbeliever may visit us for corporate worship and respond in faith: "falling on his face, he will worship God and declare that God is really among [us]" (1 Cor 14:25).

9

Godliness

> "It is a fearful thing to be an unsanctified professor, but much more to be an unsanctified preacher."
>
> —Richard Baxter

> "Keep a close watch on yourself and on the teaching. Persist in this, for by so doing you will save both yourself and your hearers."
>
> —1 Timothy 4:16

Resolution 9: Resolved to prioritize personal holiness.

A PASTOR MUST PRIORITIZE personal holiness in his own life even as he labors for holiness in the church. After all, the fundamental non-negotiable qualification for a pastor is to be "above reproach" (1 Tim 3:2; Titus 1:7).[1]

---

1. Albert Martin is helpful as he explains in part how the apostle Paul would have us understand the two "lists" of qualifications for an elder in 1 Timothy 3:1–7 and Titus 1:5–9 as a commentary on the main priority of being "blameless" or "above reproach": "Each list is only broadly suggestive of the fundamental requirement of being *blameless*, or *above reproach*. Two different Greek words, basically synonymous, meaning *blameless*,

Godliness

The path forward in holiness for the pastor is mortification. I can think of no better way to promote purity than by killing sin. The stakes couldn't be higher for the pastor's holiness. The English Puritan Richard Baxter warns pastors:

> Take heed unto yourselves lest your example contradict your doctrine and you lay stumbling blocks before the blind that may be the occasion of their ruin. Take heed unto yourselves lest you deny with your lives that which you say with your tongues and so be the greatest hinderers of the success of your own labors. This is the way to make men think that the word of God is merely an idle tale and to make preaching seem no better than prattling. He who means as he speaks will surely do as he speaks. One proud, surly, lordly word, one needless disagreement, one covetous action may cut the throat of many a sermon and destroy the fruit of all that you have been doing.[2]

In a later century but with the same concern, Scottish pastor Robert Murray M'Cheyne counseled a friend and fellow pastor likewise: "Remember you are God's sword—His instrument—I trust a chosen vessel unto Him to bear His name. In great measure, according to the purity and reflections of the instrument, will be the success. It is not great talents God blesses so much as great likeness to Jesus. A holy minister is an awful weapon in the hands of God."[3] In many ways today, talent is not lacking among leaders in the church. However, "great likeness to Jesus" seems to be at a premium.

My hope for the reader of this chapter is the same hope Thomas Watson had for the reader of his book *The Godly Man's Picture* in 1666:

> Christian Reader,
>
> The soul being so precious, and salvation so glorious, it is the highest point of prudence to make preparations for another world. It is beyond all dispute that there is an inheritance in light, and it is

---

are used in 1 Timothy 3:2 and Titus 1:7. In each case, what follows is, in a sense, a commentary with specific examples of what it means to be blameless . . . . Therefore, we should consider these two lists as specimens of some of the principal graces to be included in a description of blameless Christian character. By no means are either of these lists meant to be regarded as exhaustive. In comparing the two lists and trying to lay out in sequential form the specifics contained in them, I have sought to grasp the larger category, of which the specifics are illustrations or indications." Martin, *The Man of God*, 77–78.

2. Baxter, *The Reformed Pastor*, 33–34.
3. Bonar, *Memoir and Remains of M'Cheyne*, 282.

most strenuously asserted in Holy Scripture that there must be a fitness and suitability for it (Col. 1:12). If anyone asks, "Who shall ascend into the hill of the Lord?", the answer is, "He that hath clean hands and a pure heart" (Psa. 24:4). To describe such a person is the work of this ensuing treatise. Here you have the godly man's portrait and see him portrayed in his full lineaments. What a rare thing godliness is! It is not airy and puffed up, but solid, and such as will take up the heart and spirits. Godliness consists in an exact harmony between holy principles and practices. Oh, that all into whose hands this book shall providentially come, may be so enamoured with piety as to embrace it heartily.[4]

There is a temptation in ministry to think you've arrived. After all, gospel ministers are constantly exhorting people to holy living while trying to live a life worthy of emulation. People look to us for sound doctrine and a life consistent with this teaching; and if we're not careful, we might actually start to believe we have this whole sin thing under control. But that would be very dangerous thinking. Over every pastor's desk should be the apostolic warning from 1 Corinthians 10:12, "Therefore let anyone who thinks that he stands take heed lest he fall." The landscape of evangelicalism has become littered with fallen pastors—men who failed to "take heed."[5] The damage to Christ's church is incalculable. I offer this chapter as an exercise in taking heed so that pastors can make progress in holiness. As Charles Spurgeon warned, "For the herald of the gospel to be spiritually out of order in his own proper person is, both to himself and to his work, a most serious calamity; and yet, my brethren, how easily is such an evil produced, and with what watchfulness must it be guarded against!"[6]

To help us be still more watchful I will consider, first, the sanctification of the pastor; second, sanctification's great enemy; third, the mortification of the pastor with some practical helps to see this work accomplished in our lives.

---

4. Watson, *The Godly Man's Picture*, 7.

5. As I write this chapter, we are two weeks removed from the fall of yet another "famous" pastor due to an inappropriate relationship with a woman not his wife.

6. Spurgeon, *Lectures to My Students*, 8.

The Sanctification of the Pastor

Pastors, like all Christians, are being sanctified. This ongoing work can be understood more clearly against the backdrop of what Michael Horton and others have called "definitive sanctification." Horton writes, "Before we can speak of our being put to holy use and growing in grace . . . we must see that sanctification is first of all God's act of setting us apart from the world for himself."[7] This definitive work of setting apart can be seen in biblical texts like John 15:16, where Jesus says, "You did not choose me, but I chose you and appointed you that you should go and bear fruit and that your fruit should abide, so that whatever you ask the Father in my name, he may give it to you." The apostle Paul has definitive sanctification in mind when he declares, "And those whom he predestined he also called, and those whom he called he also justified, and those whom he justified he also glorified" (Rom 8:30). The predestination and calling of a person are a definitive *setting apart* for salvation—a glorious truth also seen in 1 Corinthians 1:9: "God is faithful, by whom you were called into the fellowship of his Son, Jesus Christ our Lord." The Christian is one who has been set apart for salvation in Christ.

But the Bible also speaks of sanctification in another way, a way that considers what is actually happening to a person who has been definitively set apart for God. Again, Horton is helpful when he writes about the inward transformation going on in the believer: "However, the New Testament . . . also speaks of this setting apart as an ongoing work within believers that renews them inwardly and conforms them gradually to the image of God in Christ. We are holy (definitive sanctification); therefore, we are to be holy (progressive sanctification)."[8] More help in our understanding comes from J. I. Packer. He explains progressive sanctification in relation to regeneration or the new birth:

> Regeneration is birth; sanctification is growth. In regeneration, God implants desires that were not there before: desire for God, for holiness, and for the hallowing and glorifying of God's name in this world; desire to pray, worship, love, serve, honor, and please God; desire to show love and bring benefit to others. In sanctification, the Holy Spirit "works in you to will and to act" according to God's purpose; what he does is prompt you to "work out your salvation" (i.e., express it in action) by fulfilling these new desires

7. Horton, *The Christian Faith*, 650.
8. Horton, *The Christian Faith*, 653.

(Phil. 2:12–13). Christians become increasingly Christlike as the moral profile of Jesus (the "fruit of the Spirit") is progressively formed in them (2 Cor. 3:18; Gal. 4:19; 5:22–25).[9]

More concisely, we have the Westminster Shorter Catechism (Q&A 35):

Q. What is sanctification?

A. Sanctification is the work of God's free grace, whereby we are renewed in the whole man after the image of God, and are enabled more and more to die unto sin, and live unto righteousness.

Every Christian pastor is being sanctified. By the Spirit of God, we are being enabled to "more and more" (progressively) die to sin and live a life worthy of the gospel. Now, wouldn't it be nice if this happened every day with no struggle, toil, or pain; no hiccups or setbacks? But surely the pastor, of all people, knows this is not the case. Our sanctification is not uninterrupted. Indeed, it has a great enemy that must be accounted for.

Sanctification's Great Enemy

The apostle Paul introduces us to sanctification's great enemy in Romans 7:21–25:

> So I find it to be a law that when I want to do right, evil lies close at hand. For I delight in the law of God, in my inner being, but I see in my members another law waging war against the law of my mind and making me captive to the law of sin that dwells in my members. Wretched man that I am! Who will deliver me from this body of death? Thanks be to God through Jesus Christ our Lord! So then, I myself serve the law of God with my mind, but with my flesh I serve the law of sin.

In verse 21, Paul says that he finds it "to be a *law* that when I want to do right, evil lies close at hand." He uses this law language again in verse 23 when he says, "I see in my members another *law* waging war against the law of my mind" [emphasis added]. By law, Paul means a *principle* or *operational principle*. Indwelling sin is a contrary law to the inclination to do good (an inclination Paul acknowledges that he has in vv. 21–22). And notice how this law or principle is always with us—it "dwells in my members," Paul says. In other words, everywhere we go this law is with us waging war

---

9. Packer, *Concise Theology*, 170.

against our God-given desire to walk in righteousness. Unlike a jacket, I can't leave this law at home or at the office. Where I go, it goes. I cannot get away from this enemy.

The Mortification of the Pastor

The pastor needs help against this great enemy. And great help comes from the seventeenth century in the teaching of John Owen. An English Puritan, Owen was a scholar, pastor, and preacher. Among the magisterial sixteen volumes that comprise his works are titles such as *The Glory of Christ* (vol. 1), *Communion with God* (vol. 2), *The Holy Spirit* (vol. 3 and, appropriately, where we find his essay, "Mortification of Sin"—27 pages of tough sledding, and in the context of 285 pages on the doctrine of sanctification); and *Temptation and Sin* (vol. 6 with its 648 pages dedicated to understanding the biblical teaching on temptation and sin). J. I. Packer, recognizing that Owen dealt with topics at a depth out-of-step with our relatively shallow evangelicalism, explains that Owen "wrote for readers who, once they take up a subject, cannot rest till they see to the bottom of it, and who find exhaustiveness not exhausting but refreshing."[10] Taking our cues from Owen, what is mortification? What does it mean to mortify sin?

To mortify means *to kill*. Owen calls mortification "the second part of sanctification."[11] If sanctification is *progressive holiness* in the life of the believer, mortification is the *progressive eradication* of sin in the believer. Owen explains, "Indwelling sin in the believer is the old man that must be killed, with all his faculties, properties, wisdom, craft, subtlety, and strength."[12] He continues, "[Mortification] is the weakening of sin's indwelling disposition . . . it is the alacrity, vigor, and cheerfulness of the Spirit or new man contending against lust."[13] To help us see that this "killing work" is ongoing, Owen reminds us that mortification "consists in a constant taking part with grace . . . against the principle, acts, and fruits of sin."[14] This is not a

---

10. Owen, *Sin and Temptation*, 18. In his introduction to Owens' work, Packer adds, "A Puritan model of godliness will most quickly expose the reason why our current spirituality is so shallow, namely the shallowness of our views of sin." Packer, introduction to *Sin and Temptation*, 24.
11. Owen, *The Holy Spirit*, 538.
12. Owen, *Sin and Temptation*, 154.
13. Owen, *Sin and Temptation*, 158.
14. Owen, *The Holy Spirit*, 543.

matter of on again/off again effort, but a *constant* cooperation with grace in seeking to destroy indwelling sin.

This is radical language—all this talk of mortifying, killing, and destroying sin. In our increasingly biblically illiterate churches, we may be tempted to think this is language exclusive to those "dour" Puritans, and not the language of the Bible. But the Bible talks this way; the Bible is ruthless in its discussion of sin. When it comes to sin, the Bible doesn't say to manage it, control it, befriend it, appease it, or merely avoid it. The Bible commands us to kill it. Consider Romans 8:12-13, which teaches, "So then, brothers, we are debtors, not to the flesh, to live according to the flesh. For if you live according to the flesh you will die, but if by the Spirit you put to death the deeds of the body, you will live." The Apostle says that the path of life is one where the deeds of the body are "put to death." Paul repeats this teaching in Colossians 3:5-6: "Put to death therefore what is earthly in you: sexual immorality, impurity, passion, evil desire, and covetousness, which is idolatry. On account of these the wrath of God is coming." Sin, the Apostle warns, is idolatry and brings wrath. Therefore, put it to death. And this isn't only the language of Paul, but of Jesus as well. In his earthly ministry, Jesus taught clearly on the reality of heaven and hell—eternal life and eternal death. The one who mortifies the flesh is the one who will inherit eternal life. The person who does not will be condemned in hell forever. This is the startling teaching of our Lord in Mark 9:42-48:

> Whoever causes one of these little ones who believe in me to sin, it would be better for him if a great millstone were hung around his neck and he were thrown into the sea. And if your hand causes you to sin, cut it off. It is better for you to enter life crippled than with two hands to go to hell, to the unquenchable fire. And if your foot causes you to sin, cut it off. It is better for you to enter life lame than with two feet to be thrown into hell. And if your eye causes you to sin, tear it out. It is better for you to enter the kingdom of God with one eye than with two eyes to be thrown into hell, "where their worm does not die and the fire is not quenched."

It's texts like these that led Owen to famously state, "Be killing sin or it will kill you."[15]

To more clearly understand what mortification is, it is helpful to understand what it is not. There are at least two misconceptions about mortification that need to be highlighted. First, mortification is not sinless

---

15. Owen, *Sin and Temptation*, 160.

perfection. In other words, it is not the final elimination of sin in this life. No one less than the apostle Paul himself, no stranger to the powerful sanctifying work of God in his life, acknowledged in Philippians 3:12–14, "Not that I have already obtained this or am already perfect, but I press on to make it my own, because Christ Jesus has made me his own. Brothers, I do not consider that I have made it my own. But one thing I do: forgetting what lies behind and straining forward to what lies ahead, I press on toward the goal for the prize of the upward call of God in Christ Jesus." And in 1 John 1:8 we read, "If we say we have no sin, we deceive ourselves, and the truth is not in us" (cf. Jas 3:2). The Bible nowhere holds out the hope of perfection in this life. Second, mortification is more than mere behavior modification. Mortification is not pretending sin is removed, or simply suppressing our sinful behavior through the "improvement of a quiet, controlled temperament."[16] Mortification is getting beyond the symptoms of sin (i.e., behavior) and taking aim at the root of sin—a root that lies in the heart. Believing as Jesus taught that "out of the overflow of the heart the mouth speaks" (Luke 6:45), the Christian prays like David in Psalm 139:23–24: "Search me, O God, and know my heart! Try me and know my thoughts! And see if there be any grievous way in me, and lead me in the way everlasting!"

Having defined mortification and clearing up two major misconceptions about what it is, I now want to ask, "How do we do it? How does a pastor (and any Christian for that matter) mortify the flesh?" Inspired by Owen, let me suggest fourteen ways the pastor can make progress in mortification.[17]

Strive for Universal Obedience

It is vital to start here given how easy it is to become fixated on one sin in our lives—as if it is the only one threatening us. Mortification needs to take account of the whole person. Owen explains that "without sincerity and diligence in a universality of obedience, there is no mortification of any one perplexing lust to be obtained."[18] That is, while you're fixated on any one lust, others may be your undoing. Owen warns,

16. Owen, *Sin and Temptation*, 155.
17. For help in thinking through some of these strategies, I am indebted to Hedges, *Christ Formed in You*, 135–46.
18. Owen, *Sin and Temptation*, 133.

> A man finds any lust to bring him into the condition formerly described; it is powerful, strong, tumultuating, leads captive, vexes, disquiets, takes away peace; he is not able to bear it; wherefore he sets himself against it, prays against it, groans under it, sighs to be delivered: but in the meantime, perhaps, in other duties—in constant communion with God—in reading, prayer, and meditation—in other ways that are not of the same kind with the lust wherewith he is troubled—he is loose and negligent. Let not that man think that ever he shall arrive to the mortification of the lust he is perplexed with. This is a condition that not seldom befalls men in their pilgrimage.[19]

Owen relates this approach to the man fixated on a particular illness with his body, giving all his attention to it, but neglecting his general health: "if he leave the general habit of his body under distempers, his labor and travail will be in vain."[20] Likewise in our battle with sin: "So will his attempts be that shall endeavor to stop a bloody issue of sin and filth in his soul, and is not equally careful of his universal spiritual temperature and condition."[21] It is this "universal obedience" the apostle Paul has in mind in 1 Corinthians 9:24–27:

> Do you not know that in a race all the runners run, but only one receives the prize? So run that you may obtain it. Every athlete exercises self-control in all things. They do it to receive a perishable wreath, but we an imperishable. So I do not run aimlessly; I do not box as one beating the air. But I discipline my body and keep it under control, lest after preaching to others I myself should be disqualified.

Beware Eternal Destruction

To promote the work of mortification, we must always keep the stakes before us. To be sure, Owen makes it clear that mortification should be pursued because of how sin causes a temporal loss of peace and strength.[22] But the even greater motivation for mortification is the eternal danger unchecked sin presents. As Owen warns, "God . . . will deliver none from destruction

---

19. Owen, *Sin and Temptation*, 133.
20. Owen, *Sin and Temptation*, 134.
21. Owen, *Sin and Temptation*, 134.
22. Owen, *Sin and Temptation*, 150–51.

that continue in sin; so that while anyone lies under an abiding power of sin, the threats of destruction and everlasting separation from God are to be held out to him (so Heb. 3:12; to which add Heb. 10:38)."[23] The threat of eternal ruin is a spur toward mortification.

Practice Self-Denial

The world says, "You just need a little *me* time." If someone said that to Owen, my guess is that he would have looked baffled and confused. He would have been perplexed because at the heart of the gospel is exactly the opposite message. Take, for example, Mark 8:34, where Jesus exhorts, "If anyone would come after me, let him deny himself and take up his cross and follow me." At the heart of discipleship is a denial of self. To not practice self-denial is, according to the apostle Paul, one of the marks of an enemy of God: "For many, of whom I have often told you and now tell you even with tears, walk as enemies of the cross of Christ. Their end is destruction, their god is their belly, and they glory in their shame, with minds set on earthly things" (Phil 3:18–19). When your god is your belly, you are living to satisfy your sinful passions and lusts, which is utterly contrary to the Christian life—and makes your heart a breeding ground for sin.

In Calvin's *Institutes of the Christian Religion*, the Reformer includes a chapter on the Christian life entitled "The Sum of the Christian Life, in Which We Discuss the Denial of Ourselves." This should be required reading for every pastor. After commending Romans 12:1–2 as God's gracious "method for organizing a person's life," Calvin concludes: "Now, this is a magnificent point: we are consecrated or dedicated to God so that, from now on, we may not think, speak, plan, or do anything except to his glory. After all, a sacred vessel may not be put to profane use without doing tremendous injury to God."[24] In other words, the Christian life is a complete reversal of a person's life apart from Christ. A Christian no longer lives for self, but for God and his glory. In prose characteristic of a sermon, Calvin further explains this point, part of which we saw in chapter 1:

> But if we are not our own but the Lord's, it is clear what error we should avoid and to what end we should direct all the activity of our lives. We are not our own; therefore, let neither our reason nor our will hold sovereignty over our plans and deeds. We are not our

---

23. Owen, *Sin and Temptation*, 151–52.
24. Calvin, *On the Christian Life*, 13.

own; therefore, let us not make this our goal, that we seek what is advantageous for us according to the flesh. We are not our own; therefore, as far as possible, let us forget ourselves and everything that is ours.

On the contrary, we are God's; therefore, let us live and die for him (Rom. 14:8). We are God's; therefore, let his wisdom and will govern all our actions. We are God's; thus, let every part of our life strive for him as our only authentic purpose. Oh, how greatly has that person profited who, when he has been taught that he is not his own, has taken away dominion and control from his own reason in order to grant it to God! You see, since the plague that is most effective in destroying human beings is when we submit to ourselves, so there is one safe haven of salvation: to neither know nor will anything on our own but simply to follow the Lord as he leads.[25]

The pastor, of all people, must settle this truth about the Christian life: we are not our own but belong to God. Freedom from sin and conformity to Christ begins with the practice of self-denial.

Battle Until Life Ends

There is no cease-fire in this war—mortification is a *habitual* weakening of sin through *constant* contention against it. Back to Romans 8:12–13, "So then, brothers, we are debtors, not to the flesh, to live according to the flesh. For if you live according to the flesh you will die, but if by the Spirit you put to death the deeds of the body, you will live." All the verbs in this passage emphasize an active, ongoing effort. Owen warns,

> Sin never wavers, yields, or gives up in spite of all the powerful opposition it encounters from the law of the gospel. If we only believed this, we would be less careless in carrying around that implacable enmity with us. It is well that those who are vigilant should weaken its force within them. But how sad is the deception of those who deceive themselves into thinking they have no sin (1 John 1:8).[26]

And because sin will always, to some degree, be active in us, Owen exhorts us to remain vigilant against sin: "Sin not only still abides in us, but is still

---

25. Calvin, *On the Christian Life*, 14.
26. Owen, *Sin and Temptation*, 19.

acting, still laboring to bring forth the deeds of the flesh. When sin lets us alone, we may let sin alone."[27]

Know There Can Be Great Victories

Given the power of the gospel, some sins in this life can be eradicated. This is great motivation to engage in warfare against indwelling sin. Owen writes, "Mortification succeeds in varying degrees and may completely triumph if the sin in question is not lodged too deeply within the natural temperament."[28] We believe this to be true because Christians are nothing less than a new creation in Christ: "From now on, therefore, we regard no one according to the flesh. Even though we once regarded Christ according to the flesh, we regard him thus no longer. Therefore, if anyone is in Christ, he is a new creation. The old has passed away; behold, the new has come" (2 Cor 5:16–17). As new creations in Christ we now, by the Spirit, "walk in newness of life" (Rom 6:4).

Beware Surprise Attacks

Sin loves to "come out of nowhere"—to spring up when we least expect it. This is what Owen called "involuntary surprisals." He warns, "Sin is never less quiet than when it seems to be most quiet, and its waters are for the most part deep, when they are still."[29] Sin is quiet like an enemy before an ambush. One of sin's strategies, according to Owen, is to induce a false sense of security as a prelude to a surprise attack. Therefore, the pastor must be vigilant and always at the ready to battle this merciless enemy. Recall how Jesus warned his sleepy disciples in the garden, "Watch and pray that you may not enter into temptation. The spirit indeed is willing, but the flesh is weak" (Matt 26:41).

Understand the Deceitfulness of Sin

First, Owen would have us understand how deceit *hides* the consequences or full truth of sin: "We also see the danger of sin's deception of the mind

---

27. Owen, *Temptation and Sin*, 11.
28. Owen, *Sin and Temptation*, 158.
29. Owen, *Temptation and Sin*, 11.

by examining the general nature of deceit. It consists in falsely presenting things to the mind in such a way that their true nature, causes, effects, or present conditions to the soul remain hidden. Thus, deceit conceals what should be exposed, whether it be circumstances or consequences."[30] Sin, in other words, presents only the desirable. Second, Owen would have us understand the *creeping* nature of deceit: "Deceit also operates slowly, little by little, so that its manipulation is not exposed all at once. In the story of the Fall, Satan acts in a sequence of steps. First, he removes the objection of death. Next, he offers them great knowledge. Then he suggests that they become gods. Each step hides aspects of reality and only presents half-truths."[31] Third, Owen would have us understand how deceit *twists* the truth. This is seen alarmingly in how sin deceives us into thinking grace is for licentiousness: "Here then is where the deceit of sin intervenes. It separates the doctrine of grace from its purpose."[32] The purpose of grace is holiness. But sin would have us believe it is for more sin. The apostle Paul addressed this heresy in Romans 6:1–2: "What shall we say then? Are we to continue in sin that grace may abound? By no means! How can we who died to sin still live in it?"

Make No Provision for the Flesh

Romans 13:14 states it plainly: "But put on the Lord Jesus Christ, and make no provision for the flesh, to gratify its desires." This is exactly what Jesus is teaching in Mark 9:43–48 where he calls for spiritual amputation when it comes to sin. The pastor must know himself and take pains not to put himself in a position of weakness. For the love of holiness, the pastor must ask himself questions like, "Should I watch that movie or show? Is this music good for my heart? Is social media edifying—is it promoting godliness in my life?" In every question of Christian liberty, what guides the pastor is a longing to see Philippians 4:8–9 realized in his life:

> Finally, brothers, whatever is true, whatever is honorable, whatever is just, whatever is pure, whatever is lovely, whatever is commendable, if there is any excellence, if there is anything worthy of praise, think about these things. What you have learned and

---

30. Owen, *Sin and Temptation*, 37.
31. Owen, *Sin and Temptation*, 37.
32. Owen, *Sin and Temptation*, 41.

received and heard and seen in me—practice these things, and the God of peace will be with you.

With too many stories in recent years of pastors falling due to unchecked sin in their lives, there is renewed discussion in evangelicalism of the value of the "Billy Graham Rule"—the code of conduct Graham and some of his associates adopted in an effort to avoid any circumstance that would put them in a potentially compromising moral situation or give the appearance thereof. (For example, being alone in a room with a woman not his wife was an application of the "code" for Graham.) While the debates continue over the merits of the Billy Graham Rule, it's good to recall that before Billy Graham there was the apostle Paul. When it comes to sin and temptation, Romans 13:14 remains undefeated. Pastors must strive to "put on the Lord Jesus Christ, and make no provision for the flesh, to gratify its desires."

Prayerfully Wield Your Spiritual Sword

Ephesians 6:17 teaches that part of God's armor for us in the battle against the world, the flesh, and the devil is "the sword of the Spirit, which is the word of God." This, of course, is how Jesus battled the temptations of the devil in the wilderness (Matt 4:1–11). If the Son of God used the Word of God to battle against temptation, how much more should we? The pastor says with the psalmist, "How can a young man keep his way pure? By guarding it according to your word. With my whole heart I seek you; let me not wander from your commandments! I have stored up your word in my heart, that I might not sin against you" (Ps 119:9–11). A practical way to battle sin with the Word of God is to pray the Scriptures. Scripture memory is essential, but it's only the first step. As we are memorizing the Word of God, we must pray those truths into our hearts. Prayer is how we "store up the word in our heart" and become fit for battle.

Replace Sin with Grace

By replacing sin with grace, we kill sin by nurturing the virtue that counters it. It's what we see the Apostle describing in Colossians 3:5–17, with his commands to "put to death" and "put on." The idea is to crowd out sin in our lives by filling our hearts with the graces that are sin's opposite.

For example, we kill lust by practicing purity; we wage war on pride by practicing humility; we counter greed with generosity and contentment; we crucify self-centeredness by serving others; we destroy anger by pursuing peace.

Stay in Community

Christians are saved to be in community—to be a vital member of Christ's church. The commands of Hebrews 3:12–13 and 10:24–25 are equally true for pastors. After all, would you rather go to war on your own or with an army at your side? In the battle against sin, there is strength in (godly) numbers. The church is God's gift to the pastor for his sanctification (see chapter 5). A pastor first and foremost strives to be a faithful church member and as he does, he experiences the love and care of God's people for his holiness. The local church is not only something a pastor oversees; he is also a covenant member. The community of God's people is designed to be a community of grace whereby "we all, with unveiled face, beholding the glory of the Lord, are being transformed into the same image from one degree of glory to another. For this comes from the Lord who is the Spirit" (2 Cor 3:18). Knowing this, a pastor must stay embedded in the very community he is called to serve.

Look to the Cross

We put sin to death only in the context of Christ's ultimate victory over sin at the cross. Provision for our victory has been made in his victory. The banner over our war against indwelling sin is Galatians 6:14: "But far be it from me to boast except in the cross of our Lord Jesus Christ, by which the world has been crucified to me, and I to the world." Indeed, we fight in the triumph of Christ (2 Cor 2:14; Col 2:13–15). Therefore, we battle with the confidence that when we fail, we are not abandoned by our God. This is motivation to get up and get back to the frontlines, knowing that the ultimate victory is assured.

Depend on the Holy Spirit

This war is not fought in the flesh. Our only hope in mortification is to battle in the strength that God supplies. And that strength is himself. As we've seen, it is "by the Spirit" that we put to death the deeds of the body (Rom 8:13). Only as we "walk by the Spirit" will we "not gratify the desires of the flesh" (Gal 5:16). Owen cautions, "All other ways of discipline are in vain. All other helps leave us helpless. Mortification is only accomplished 'through the Spirit.'"[33]

Think Much of the Excellency of God

This is the pinnacle of all our labors to kill sin. When we think much of the excellency of God, we will have a right view of self. Both a high view of God and clear view of ourselves in relation to God will "strike deep at the root of any indwelling sin," as Owen explains:

> Be much in thoughtfulness of the excellency of the majesty of God and your infinite, inconceivable distance from him. Many thoughts of it cannot but fill you with a sense of your own vileness, which strikes deep at the root of any indwelling sin. When Job comes to a clear discovery of the greatness and excellency of God, he is filled with self-abhorrence and is pressed to humiliation (Job 42:5–6). And in what state does the prophet Habakkuk affirm himself to be cast upon the apprehension of the majesty of God? "With God," says Job, "is terrible majesty." Hence were the thoughts of them of old, that when they had seen God they should die. The Scripture abounds in this self-abasing consideration, comparing the men of the earth to "grasshoppers," to "vanity," the "dust of the balance," in respect of God. Be much in thoughts of this nature, to abase the pride of your heart, and to keep your soul humble within you. There is nothing [that] will render you a greater indisposition to be imposed on by the deceits of sin than such a frame of heart. Think greatly of the greatness of God.[34]

---

33. Owen, *Sin and Temptation*, 153.
34. Owen, *Sin and Temptation*, 1165–66.

The Call to Take Heed

In one sense, the reasons for a pastor falling are many. But in another sense, the reason is single: a pastor falls when he fails to take heed. Richard Baxter knew this, and therefore warned pastors in his day to take heed to themselves. What was needed in seventeenth-century England is utterly relevant for our day:

> Take heed to yourselves, for you have a depraved nature, and sinful inclinations, as well as others. If innocent Adam had need of heed, and lost himself and us for want of it, how much more need have we! Sin dwells in us, when we have preached ever so much against it; and one degree prepares the heart for another, and one sin inclines the mind to more. If one thief be in the house, he will let in the rest; because they have the same disposition and design. A spark is the beginning of a flame; and a small disease may cause a greater.... In us there are, at the best, the remnants of pride, unbelief, self-seeking, hypocrisy, and all the most hateful, deadly sins. And does it not then concern us to take heed to ourselves?[35]

Taking heed to ourselves—resolving to live in radical holiness—will not always be met with evangelical support. Due to a functional antinomianism that seems to permeate the American church, when a pastor emphasizes personal holiness in his own life and in the life of the church, the pushback is real. The pastor may hear in one form or another a collective "Relax" from his congregation (including, perhaps, his fellow pastors), the implication being that all this talk and effort toward holiness, if left unchecked, will lead them to be "legalists" or "fundamentalists" at worst, "killjoys" at best.

Of course, this reaction against the pursuit of holiness is not unlike what the Puritans experienced as they were scornfully labeled "precisionists" and "puritans" (the term was originally used as a pejorative) given their perceived "extreme" views on personal holiness. It is akin to the reaction to Philip Spener, the German Pietist, as he introduced twice weekly "small group" meetings in his home for "religious conversations," prayer, and Bible study for the purpose of cultivating personal holiness. People derisively referred to these groups as "gatherings of the pious." Hence, *Pietism* was born. The reactions today can be similar to what the Wesleys (brothers Charles and John) and George Whitefield experienced at Oxford

---

35. Baxter, *The Reformed Pastor*, 73.

University in the late 1720s and early 1730s with the advent of their "Holy Club"—a small group of students determined to help one another live a disciplined and "methodical" life (from which the pejorative "Methodist" originated) for the sake of promoting personal holiness. These historical examples are encouraging reminders that efforts toward holiness have always been resisted in the church and will continue to be in our day. When the resistance comes, we must be resolved to hear the apostolic encouragement: "As obedient children, do not be conformed to the passions of your former ignorance, but as he who called you is holy, you also be holy in all your conduct, since it is written, 'You shall be holy, for I am holy'" (1 Pet 1:14–16).

The discipline of mortification is one way a pastor takes heed to himself. Again, Baxter is helpful in sounding the alarm and warning of the ultimate peril of not taking heed:

> You yourselves have a heaven to win or lose. You have souls that must be happy or miserable forever. Therefore, it concerns you to begin at home and to take heed unto yourselves as well as unto others. Preaching well may succeed to the salvation of others without the holiness of your own hearts or lives. It is possible at least, though less likely. But it is impossible that preaching well should serve to save yourselves. "Many will say to me in that day, 'Lord, Lord, have we not prophesied in your name?'" They will be answered with "I never knew you, depart from me, you who work iniquity" (Matt 7:22–23) . . . . Believe it, brethren, God is no respecter of persons. He does not save men for their clerical clothes or callings. A holy calling will not save an unholy man.[36]

In speaking this way Baxter is simply echoing the apostle Paul in his exhortation to Timothy: "Keep a close watch on yourself and on the teaching. Persist in this, for by so doing you will save both yourself and your hearers" (1 Tim 4:16). Churches need holy ministers. May our pursuit of holiness in the power of the Holy Spirit bear much fruit in our day for the glory of God and the good of the churches we serve.

---

36. Baxter, *The Reformed Pastor*, 35–36.

10

Suffering

"Pastors and their people must suffer."
—John Piper

"Share in suffering as a good soldier of Christ Jesus."
—2 Timothy 2:3

Resolution 10: Resolved to suffer for the sake of Christ.

On July 18, 2021, prosperity preacher Casey Treat delivered a sermon to his Seattle megachurch (founded 1980) titled "Force of Faith."[1] He began by informing his audience of "two things that changed everything" in his life, at the age of nineteen, when he experienced a conversion to Christianity in a drug rehabilitation center. The two things were the need to renew his mind according to Scripture and to use his faith so that he would "not be limited by this world." Treat explained, "That's how Wendy [wife] and I are celebrating our forty years of marriage, healthy and strong and whole.

---

1. Treat, "Force of Faith."

Yesterday we were out on our bicycles, rode for twenty-five miles and we said, 'It's still working! It's still working!'" Treat went on to credit prosperity pastors Julius Young and Frederick Price, his two "spiritual fathers in the faith," with teaching him these spiritual techniques to "leave [his] depressions, fears, anxieties, addictions, poverty—all of that, behind."[2]

The Prosperity Gospel

Not only is the prosperity gospel "still working" for Casey and Wendy Treat, but based on its proliferation, not only in America but around the world, it's apparently still working for millions of other people as well. Consider the American context alone. According to Kate Bowler in *Blessed: A History of the American Prosperity Gospel*, in 2011, one million people were attending American prosperity megachurches with the largest of these churches, Joel Osteen's Lakewood Church in Houston, boasting 38,000 members.[3] Some of the most recognized names in American Christianity over the last one hundred years are associated in one form or another with the prosperity gospel—names like Oral Roberts, Kenneth Hagen, Kenneth Copeland, Frederick Price, John Hagee, Joyce Meyer, T. D. Jakes, Joel Osteen, and Creflo Dollar, to name some. Institutions such as Oral Roberts University and Rhema Bible Training Center (part of Hagen's ministry empire) have given the movement national recognition, and served as somewhat of a unifying force among the many disparate prosperity gospel churches spread throughout America in urban, suburban, and rural locations. Not only are prosperity churches and ministries not geographically limited, prosperity preaching also translates well into all the major media, whether print, radio, television, or internet. Indeed, as Casey Treat declared, the prosperity gospel is "still working."

It's one thing to describe the ubiquity of the prosperity gospel, but quite another to explain it. What exactly is the prosperity gospel? "Though it is hard to describe," observes Bowler, "it is easy to find. The prosperity gospel is a wildly popular Christian message of spiritual, physical, and financial mastery that dominates not only much of the American religious scene but some of the largest churches around the globe."[4] While the prosperity gospel has spread throughout the world, it has its roots in American

2. Treat, "Force of Faith."
3. Bowler, *Blessed*, 181.
4. Bowler, *Blessed*, 3.

soil. Indeed, it is in many ways the Americanization of Christianity. Bowler explains how the prosperity gospel is a particular "American blessing": "But rather than sacralizing the founding of the United States or visions of manifest destiny, the prosperity gospel was constituted by the deification and ritualization of the American Dream: upward mobility, accumulation, hard work, and moral fiber."[5] Its global persistence, however, is due to more than the appeal of the American Dream. After all, the American Dream doesn't explain the prosperity gospel's proliferation in a place like Ethiopia where its popularity is on par with America. It has to do with its "comprehensive approach to the human condition":

> Why has it become so successful in so many places? We must not think that it is simply the lure of financial success. The prosperity movement offers a comprehensive approach to the human condition. It sees men and women as creatures fallen, but not broken, and it shares with them a "gospel," good news that will set them free from a multitude of oppressions. . . . The prosperity gospel's chief allure is simply optimism.[6]

What began as a baptized American Dream became the comprehensive answer to the human condition since the fall. A movement hatched inside Pentecostalism in the early twentieth-century "soon found that its universal reassurances could carry it far beyond any denominational or sectarian home."[7] A global movement was born.

Surprisingly, given its dominance within American religion and global Christianity, the prosperity gospel has received scant scholarly attention.[8] It has become clear that the prosperity gospel is here to stay, and is only growing in influence. Therefore, further study of the prosperity gospel is needed and scrutiny given in the light of Scripture. In this chapter, I argue that the prosperity gospel is inconsistent with a Pauline theology

---

5. Bowler, *Blessed*, 226.

6. Bowler, *Blessed*, 232.

7. Bowler, *Blessed*, 42.

8. While much scholarly attention in the twenty-first century has been given to relatively small religious movements in America, like Christian Nationalism, Kate Bowler seems to be alone in her scholarly work on the prosperity gospel (see Bowler, *Blessed*). The reasons for this may have to do with the lack of transparency the various prosperity ministries practice, making it difficult for outsiders to research particular churches or ministers. Or, perhaps, prosperity gospel preachers are not deemed serious objects of study given their charlatan persona and thereby underestimating their influence.

of suffering. More specifically, when a Pauline theology of suffering is seen in its connection to glory, the prosperity gospel is seen for what it truly is: namely, a different gospel, which is really no gospel at all. Pastors, therefore, must reject the prosperity gospel in all its forms, and be willing to suffer for the sake of Christ and his church.

A Pauline Theology of Suffering

In Bunyan's classic allegory of the Christian life, *The Pilgrim's Progress*, the main character, Christian, soon after coming to the cross and having his burden removed, finds himself at the foot of Difficulty Hill. Joining him are two fellow-travelers, Formalist and Hypocrisy. As the three gaze upon the Hill with its steep, treacherous terrain, both Formalist and Hypocrisy think better of going straight up its face, opting to take two easier paths around the base of the Hill. Formalist chooses the path to the left called Danger while Hypocrisy chooses the path to the right called Destruction. Both paths live up to their name as Formalist perishes in a dark wood, and Hypocrisy falls to his death over a steep cliff. Christian, meanwhile, proceeds up the face of Difficulty Hill at first running along rather effortlessly. But this soon changes as Christian's running slows to a crawl on his hands and knees as he, with great difficulty, finally makes it to a pleasant arbor, a place of refreshment provided by the King for weary travelers.

It is significant that Bunyan introduces Christian to the Hill of Difficulty shortly after having his burden removed at the cross. For Bunyan knows that this is the way to the Celestial City, and Christian would need to learn this sooner rather than later. Indeed, not only did his journey not become *easier* after having his burden removed, it actually become *harder*. And this is where the prosperity gospel goes so tragically amiss by depicting Christianity as a faith without Difficulty Hill.[9]

9. Before Bunyan, Calvin saw with rare insight God's good design in weaning us away from this world—in order to set our minds on things above—by ensuring that life this side of heaven is "miserable in countless ways." He explains, "We make progress through the discipline of the cross, therefore, only when we learn that this life, considered in itself, is troubled, tumultuous, and miserable in countless ways, and in no respect is it completely happy; that all the things considered to be its benefits are unreliable, inconsistent, empty, and ruined by their accompanying evils. And at the same time, we determine from this that we are to seek and hope for nothing in this life except struggle. When we consider our crown, we must lift our eyes to heaven. We must hold this to be true, that the mind is never earnestly motivated to desire and mediate on the future life unless it is first infused with a contempt for the present life." Calvin, *On the Christian*

Resolutions of a Pastor

One of the clearest biblical texts that undermines the prosperity gospel is Romans 8:12–17. For in this passage, we see the apostle Paul's teaching about the necessity of suffering in the Christian life:

> So then, brothers, we are debtors, not to the flesh, to live according to the flesh. For if you live according to the flesh you will die, but if by the Spirit you put to death the deeds of the body, you will live. For all who are led by the Spirit of God are sons of God. For you did not receive the spirit of slavery to fall back into fear, but you have received the Spirit of adoption as sons, by whom we cry, "Abba! Father!" The Spirit himself bears witness with our spirit that we are children of God, and if children, then heirs—heirs of God and fellow heirs with Christ, provided we suffer with him in order that we may also be glorified with him.

Paul begins this pericope by demonstrating that a Christian does not live "according to the flesh" (v. 12). That is, Christians do not live under the tyranny or mastery or dominion of sin. As he explained earlier in chapter 8, "There is therefore now no condemnation for those who are in Christ Jesus. For the law of the Spirit of life has set you free in Christ Jesus from the law of sin and death" (8:1–2). The Christian's freedom in Christ makes living according to the flesh impossible. This is a theme the Apostle took up in chapter 6 when he asked, "What shall we say then? Are we to continue in sin that grace may abound? By no means! How can we who died to sin still live in it? . . . We know that our old self was crucified with him in order that the body of sin might be brought to nothing, so that we would no longer be enslaved to sin. For one who has died to sin has been set free from sin" (6:1–2, 6–7). The Christian is a debtor not to the flesh, but to the Spirit. Knowing this is of utmost importance, given that eternity is at stake: "For if you live according to the flesh you will die but if by the Spirit you put to death the deeds of the body, you will live" (v. 13).

Children of God

Having established that Christians are Spirit-led people, the Apostle proceeds to outline what is the true identity of a Christian, namely, a child of God: "For all who are led by the Spirit of God are sons of God. For you did not receive the spirit of slavery to fall back into fear, but you have received the Spirit of adoption as sons, by whom we cry, 'Abba! Father!'" (vv. 14–15).

Life, 48–49.

If you are led by the Spirit of God—that is, if you're a Christian—then you are a child of God. No slavery to sin with its corresponding fear of judgment as seen earlier in Romans 8:1. We now "put to death the deeds of the body" by relating to God as our benevolent Father. In the battle against sin, we cry out to God in the most personal of ways, "Abba! Father!" Just how personal is this address? Consider that it is the same address Jesus used in Gethsemane on the eve of his crucifixion as he prayed, "Abba, Father, all things are possible for you. Remove this cup from me. Yet not what I will, but what you will" (Mark 14:36). As a child of God, the Christian has the privilege of approaching the Father in the same intimate way as the Son of God.

How does the Christian come to declare this? Paul explains something of the mystery of the inward testimony of the Holy Spirit in the believer: "The Spirit himself bears witness with our spirit that we are children of God" (v. 16). In the preceding verse, we're told that by the Spirit *we* cry "Abba! Father!" We cry out *as the Spirit bears witness to us* of our true identity as children of God. The Spirit testifies to us that we can approach God, knowing that when we do, we will find not a wrathful judge, but a gracious Father.

Fellow Heirs with Christ

To deepen our assurance, Paul draws out a profound implication of being children of God: "and if children, then heirs—heirs of God and fellow heirs with Christ" (v. 17). What does it mean to be a "fellow heir" with Christ? Or, to ask it differently, what is Christ's? In a word, everything. We see this clearly in the opening verses of the book of Hebrews: "Long ago, at many times and in many ways, God spoke to our fathers by the prophets, but in these last days he has spoken to us by his Son, whom he appointed the heir of all things, through whom also he created the world" (Heb 1:1–2; cf. Matt 28:18; Phil 2:9). In fulfillment of Psalm 2, the nations are his heritage, the ends of the earth his possession. Indeed, every beast of the forest is his, the cattle on a thousand hills (Ps 50:10).

As a fellow heir with Christ, everything that is Christ's is the Christian's. This is the argument Paul uses in 1 Corinthians 3, when he's chastising the church for the evident "jealously and strife" among them as they were lining up behind their favorite leader. Divisions were developing around Paul and Apollos (vv. 3–4). To this Paul reasons, "So let no one boast in men. For all things are yours, whether Paul or Apollos or Cephas or the world or life or death or the present or the future—all are yours, and you are Christ's, and Christ is God's" (1 Cor 3:21–23). Why, in other words, would you boast in men when everything that is Christ's is yours? Of course, this inheritance is of infinite worth because at its heart is God—it will be the glorious fulfillment of the new covenant promise, "You shall be my people and I will be your God" (Ezek 36:28; cf. Luke 12:32).

A Necessary Condition

Having explained the Christian's identity as a child of God and co-heir with Christ, the Apostle adds a necessary condition: "and if children, then heirs—heirs of God and fellow heirs with Christ, *provided* we suffer with him in order that we may also be glorified with him" (v. 17; emphasis added). The Greek word translated provided ("if indeed," NIV/NASB) is a conditional particle (ειπερ) indicating a real condition that must be fulfilled by anyone who would be an heir.[10] The condition that must be fulfilled is suffering.

The Greek word used in Romans 8:17, translated "we suffer with" is συμπασψηομεν (*sympaschomen*), means "to share in suffering." Moisés Silva glosses it, "to suffer the same as, suffer with."[11] William Mounce similarly glosses it, "to suffer as another," "endure corresponding sufferings."[12] This suffering is "to feel or endure distress."[13] And we do this in solidarity with Christ and his sufferings. It is, as Paul says in Philippians 3:10, a "fellowship in his sufferings." It is important to note that the word is a *present active indicative*, meaning that this suffering is not a one-time event, but an ongoing *condition* for the Christian this side of heaven.

The experience of suffering here is similar to the idea Paul develops later in Romans 8 when he speaks of our "groaning." After noting that "the whole creation has been groaning together in the pains of childbirth until now" (v. 22), the Apostle explains that God's people are likewise "groaning" under the curse of sin: "And not only the creation, but we ourselves, who have the firstfruits of the Spirit, groan inwardly as we wait eagerly for

---

10. For other uses of the conditional participle ειπερ, see Rom 3:30; 8:9; 1 Cor 8:5; 15:15; and 2 Thess 1:6.
11. Silva, *New International Dictionary of NT Theology*, 666.
12. Mounce, *Analytical Lexicon*, 430.
13. Silva, *New International Dictionary of NT Theology*, 666.

adoption as sons, the redemption of our bodies" (v. 23).[14] Mounce glosses "groan" (στεναζομεν) as "to groan, sigh."[15] Paul takes up this idea of groaning in 2 Corinthians 5:2–4 where he considers the ongoing burden of waiting for our final salvation: "For in this tent we groan (στεναζομεν), longing to put on our heavenly dwelling, if indeed by putting it on we may not be found naked. For while we are still in this tent, we groan (στεναζομεν), being burdened—not that we would be unclothed, but that we would be further clothed, so that what is mortal may be swallowed up by life." This groaning, this suffering, is the *normal, perpetual* condition of Christians as we live this pilgrim life on our way to the Celestial City. After all, Paul says, "while we are still in this tent"—that is, while we live in this body—"we groan, being burdened."[16]

The Design of God

What the prosperity preachers fail to see (or willfully neglect) is the design of God in the Christian's suffering. They do not sufficiently appreciate the all-important conjunction (ινα) in Romans 8:17: "*in order that* we may also be glorified with him" (emphasis added). The purpose or design behind our suffering is glory (a restatement of "inheritance"). In other words, *glory is the ultimate meaning of our suffering*; and glory will not come any other way. Jesus was resurrected, but not before his death. This is why in Mark's Gospel three times we see Jesus teaching his disciples about the necessary road to Calvary that would precede his resurrection.[17] There was an exaltation but not apart from the humiliation of the cross. This is Paul's point in Philippians 2:5–11:

> Have this mind among yourselves, which is yours in Christ Jesus, who, though he was in the form of God, did not count equality with God a thing to be grasped, but emptied himself, by taking the form of a servant, being born in the likeness of men. And being

---

14. Note the *already* and *not yet* of Paul's theology: we have *already* the "firstfruits of the Spirit" even as we "groan inwardly as we wait" for the *not yet* of our final salvation, the "redemption of our bodies."

15. Mounce, *Analytical Lexicon*, 422.

16. Cf. 1 Peter 4:12–13, "Beloved, do not be surprised at the fiery trial when it comes upon you to test you, as though something strange were happening to you. But rejoice insofar as you share Christ's sufferings, that you may also rejoice and be glad when his glory is revealed."

17. See Mark 8:31; 9:30–31; 10:33–34.

> found in human form, he humbled himself by becoming obedient to the point of death, even death on a cross. Therefore God has highly exalted him and bestowed on him the name that is above every name, so that at the name of Jesus every knee should bow, in heaven and on earth and under the earth, and every tongue confess that Jesus Christ is Lord, to the glory of God the Father.

Paul makes it clear that this pattern of humiliation to exaltation is the Christian's pattern when he exhorts, "Have this mind among yourselves" (v. 5). Paul knows that he must "share Christ's sufferings" if he would "attain the resurrection from the dead" (Phil 3:10). According to the design of God, "this light momentary affliction is preparing for us an eternal weight of glory beyond all comparison" (2 Cor 4:17). Murray Harris comments on this verse, "In the divine economy, affliction actually generates glory."[18] Disciples of Christ must "follow in his steps" (1 Pet 2:21). And those steps take the Christian "outside the camp" to "bear the reproach he endured" (Heb 13:13).

Of course, none of this should surprise the student of the Bible, for it was Jesus himself who explained the essence of discipleship when he said, "If anyone would come after me, let him deny himself and take up his cross and follow me" (Mark 8:34). The prosperity gospel knows nothing of denying self or of taking up a cross. After all, what is a cross but an emblem of suffering and shame? Prosperity preachers peddle a "gospel" of self-indulgence and ease, a message that misses the design of God in salvation. In one form or another, they teach that suffering and affliction are inconsistent with the victorious life Jesus wants them to have.

The Geneva Reformer, John Calvin, explains the design of God in the Christian's suffering when he comments on Romans 8:17: "Various are the interpretations of this passage, but I approve of the following in preference to any other, 'We are co-heirs with Christ, provided, in entering our inheritance, we follow him in the same way in which he has gone before.'" What is the way of Christ, according to Calvin? "Christ came to it [his inheritance] by the cross; then we must come to it in the same manner."[19] Likewise,

---

18. Harris, *Second Epistle to the Corinthians*, 362; see also Guthrie, who notes, "The verb κατεργαζομαι (katergazomai), which Paul uses extensively, has to do with accomplishing or producing something, or bringing something about." Guthrie, *2 Corinthians*, 271–72. Or, as Mark Seifrid explains, "Present suffering and affliction is not vain and pointless. To the contrary, in God's hand it works an 'eternal weight of glory' beyond all measure." *Second Letter to the Corinthians*, 218.

19. Calvin, *Commentaries on Romans*, 301–2.

Suffering

Charles Hodge, the nineteenth-century Princeton divine, saw the necessary connection between the Christian's suffering and final salvation:

> We suffer as Christ suffered, not only when we are subject to the contradiction of sinners, but in the ordinary sorrows of life in which he, the man of sorrows, so largely shared. We are said to suffer with Christ ινα, "in order that," we may be glorified together. That is, the design of God in the affliction of his people, is not to satisfy the demands of justice, but to prepare them to participate in his glory. To creatures in a state of sin, suffering is the necessary condition of exaltation.[20]

More recently, Leon Morris notes how the Christian's suffering on the way to glory is "not some perverse accident." He explains, "Neither Paul nor any other New Testament writer lets us forget that believers have no easy path. Their Master suffered, and they are called to suffer, too. This is not some perverse accident but an integral part of discipleship . . . our sufferings are not meaningless. We suffer *in order that we may also share in his glory*. The path of suffering is the path to glory."[21] Perhaps Douglas Moo summarizes this teaching best when he states,

> Because we are one with Christ, we are his fellow heirs, assured of being "glorified with him." But, at the same time, this oneness means that we must follow Christ's own road to glory, "suffering with him" . . . the suffering Paul speaks of here refers to the daily anxieties, tensions, and persecutions that are the lot of those who follow the one who was "reckoned with the transgressors" (Luke 22:37). Paul makes clear that this suffering is the condition for the inheritance; we will be "glorified with" Christ (only) *if* we "suffer with him." Participation in Christ's glory can come only through participation in his suffering. What Paul is doing is setting forth an unbreakable "law of the kingdom" according to which glory can come only by way of suffering.[22]

The great tragedy of the prosperity gospel is that it teaches a way to glory contrary to God's design. Like Formalist and Hypocrisy in *Pilgrim's Progress*, who thought they could bypass the Kingsway and blaze a trail of their

---

20. Hodge, *Romans*, 268.
21. Morris, *Epistle to the Romans*, 318.
22. Moo, *Epistle to the Romans*, 505–6; see also Murray, who argues, "There is no sharing in Christ's glory unless there is sharing in his sufferings." Murray, *Epistle to the Romans*, 299.

own, prosperity preachers announce a way to glory that, in the end, leads only to destruction.

Implications for Pastoral Ministry

The implications of this teaching for pastoral ministry are significant. A Pauline theology of suffering as outlined above means that churches need not prosperity pastors but pilgrim pastors. In contrast to the prosperity pastor, a pilgrim pastor assumes that pastors and their people will suffer. Indeed, because God has ordained suffering as the way to glory, a pastor *thinks* a particular way about ministry. In this section, I outline the hallmarks of a prosperity pastor and a pilgrim pastor, commending the latter for our churches today.

Prosperity Pastors

Prosperity pastors are not new. And they have their roots in soil much older than the ministry of E. W. Kenyon, the late nineteenth-century/early twentieth-century evangelist whose "positive confession" theology helped birth Word of Faith Pentecostalism.[23] In fact, prosperity pastors can be found in a passage of Scripture referenced in chapter 1, Ezekiel 34:1–6:

> The word of the LORD came to me: "Son of man, prophesy against the shepherds of Israel; prophesy, and say to them, even to the shepherds, Thus says the Lord GOD: Ah, shepherds of Israel who have been feeding yourselves! Should not shepherds feed the sheep? You eat the fat, you clothe yourselves with the wool, you slaughter the fat ones, but you do not feed the sheep. The weak you have not strengthened, the sick you have not healed, the injured you have not bound up, the strayed you have not brought back, the lost you have not sought, and with force and harshness you have ruled them. So they were scattered, because there was no shepherd, and they became food for all the wild beasts. My sheep were scattered; they wandered over all the mountains and on every high hill. My sheep were scattered over all the face of the earth, with none to search or seek for them.[24]

---

23. For a helpful discussion of Kenyon's ministry, and his role in the history of the prosperity gospel, see Bowler, *Blessed*, 15–20.

24. Cf. Jeremiah 23:1–4.

The metaphor of *shepherd* is being used to describe the leaders of Judah. Clearly, these shepherds are benefiting at great cost to the sheep. They are abusing their power by lording it over the people for their own selfish gain. Like contemporary prosperity pastors, these corrupt shepherds are using people to satisfy their own appetites for power and riches. The indictment is severe: "You eat the fat, you clothe yourselves with the wool, you slaughter the fat ones, but you do not feed the sheep" (v. 3). The consequences for the people are tragic. Those who remain under this tyranny are resigned to perish in gross neglect, while other sheep are scattered and lost, left to "become food for all the wild beasts" (v. 5).

Of course, God will not allow this to go on forever. After rehearsing his indictment on the faithless shepherds, God announces the judgement: "Thus says the Lord GOD, Behold, I am against the shepherds, and I will require my sheep at their hand and put a stop to their feeding the sheep. No longer shall the shepherds feed themselves. I will rescue my sheep from their mouths, that they may not be food for them" (34:10). The Lord declares that he is "against the shepherds," a posture he undoubtably has toward contemporary prosperity pastors.

Pilgrim Pastors

Pilgrim pastors, unlike prosperity pastors, take seriously the example of Jesus who "set his face to go to Jerusalem" (Luke 9:51; cf. Isa 50:7). Pilgrim pastors are theologians of the cross who seek to embody the sacrifice of Christ in the service of his people (Col 1:24). After all, it was Jesus who set himself apart from the faithless shepherds of Ezekiel 34 when he said, "I am the good shepherd. The good shepherd lays down his life for the sheep" (John 10:11). Our suffering, of course, is not at all redemptive or atoning like that of Jesus. As Michael Horton explains, "His suffering was redemptive, whereas our is a participation in that already accomplished victory. But our cross bearing is still real. It is not another cross that we bear, our own burden for sin and guilt, but sharing in his humiliation and shame as those who belong to him."[25] This is why ministry for pilgrim pastors is not about using people as a means to the end of their wealth or platform or influence or fame, but a laying down of their lives for the good of the churches they serve.

---

25. Horton, *A Place for Weakness*, 47.

Resolutions of a Pastor

In Mark's Gospel, we see two prosperity pastors in training—that is, until Jesus takes hold of the curriculum. This familiar story features James and John in the grip of a theology of glory as they approach Jesus with an audacious request: "And James and John, the sons of Zebedee, came up to him and said to him, 'Teacher, we want you to do for us whatever we ask of you.' And he said to them, 'What do you want me to do for you?' And they said to him, "Grant us to sit, one at your right hand and one at your left, in your glory'" (Mark 10:35–37). James and John *thought* they knew what Jesus's ministry was all about: a theology of glory that would have him sitting in the halls of power once his military and political kingdom was established in Jerusalem. And they wanted in. Sensing this, Jesus begins to set them straight about the heart of his mission and what would be the implications for them:

> Jesus said to them, "You do not know what you are asking. Are you able to drink the cup that I drink, or to be baptized with the baptism with which I am baptized?" And they said to him, "We are able." And Jesus said to them, "The cup that I drink you will drink, and with the baptism with which I am baptized, you will be baptized, but to sit at my right hand or at my left is not mine to grant, but it is for those for whom it has been prepared" (vv. 38–40).

What do the images of "cup" and "baptism" signify for Jesus? Jesus recognizes that his messianic mission is to drink the *cup* of God's wrath for sin and suffer under the *baptism* of God's judgment on sin (Cf. Mark 14:36; and Luke 12:50). How do these images of cup and baptism apply to the disciples? Not in a judicial sense, but in a moral sense. This imagery refers to the persecutions and sufferings that will inevitably fall upon those who follow Christ in salvation. In other words, this is a reminder that sacrifice and suffering is the way of Jesus, and therefore, the path of all who would follow him.

This story continues with particular application to those who would be leaders in the church. Jesus proceeds to give foundational training in being a pilgrim pastor:

> And when the ten heard it, they began to be indignant at James and John. And Jesus called them to him and said to them, "You know that those who are considered rulers of the Gentiles lord it over them, and their great ones exercise authority over them. But it shall not be so among you. But whoever would be great among you must be your servant, and whoever would be first among you

must be slave of all. For even the Son of Man came not to be served but to serve, and to give his life as a ransom for many" (vv. 41–45).

Servants and slaves. This is the outcome of those who understand that suffering is the way of Christ. After all, "*even* the Son of Man came not to be served but to serve, and to give his life as a ransom for many" (emphasis added). A pastor's leadership in the church is governed by his fellowship in the sufferings of Christ.

Rethinking Seminary Training

As a seminary professor, I am concerned with what I hear from some of my students about their desires for ministry. Too often the "vision" for ministry sounds more "prosperity" than "pilgrim." The causes for this, I imagine, are manifold, and the seminaries are not entirely to blame. But those of us entrusted with the vital work of theological education would do well to examine our curriculum and manner of teaching. A series of questions come to mind:

1. Does our *curriculum*, as evidenced in our lectures and syllabi (particularly in our systematic theology, pastoral theology, and leadership disciplines), emphasize a Pauline theology of suffering?

2. Does the *manner* of our teaching embody something of what it means to "take up our cross and follow him"? In other words, are we communicating with an urgency and soberness in accordance with what we know to be true about the way to glory?

3. Are we thinking critically and deeply about how a Pauline theology of suffering translates to *online education*? How should a robustly biblical anthropology inform our pedagogy in our digital age?

4. As more seminaries are partnering with other institutions to offer an MBA alongside an MDiv, what are we doing to ensure that we are training not corporate executives, but *pastor-theologians* for the church?

5. Are *we* pilgrim professors as evidenced by our life and doctrine?

How we answer these questions will help determine what kind of leaders our seminaries are producing. With secularization continuing to spread throughout the Western world, with the paradoxical rise in the challenge of

Islam, our seminaries must be vigorous training grounds in sound doctrine and true piety. Indeed, the greatest need of our churches is pilgrim pastors. Our seminaries have the human capital and physical resources to serve as the premier institutions for this vital work. The question is, do we have the vision and the will to do so?

In this chapter, I argued that the prosperity gospel is inconsistent with a Pauline theology of suffering and, therefore, what the prosperity gospel offers is no gospel at all. As demonstrated, suffering is the way to glory, and glory is the ultimate meaning of our suffering. Like Formalist and Hypocrisy in Bunyan's classic *Pilgrim's Progress*, the prosperity gospel seeks its own way to glory rather than obedience to the Kingsway. Tragically, the end of the path of prosperity teaching is destruction; nothing less than eternity is at stake. For this reason, and for the sake of pilgrim pastors in our day, a Pauline theology of suffering is essential to reclaim and embrace.

11

Eternity

"Besides this you know the time, that the hour has come for you to wake from sleep. For salvation is nearer to us now than when we first believed."

—Romans 13:11

"The end of all things is at hand."

—1 Peter 4:7

Resolution 11: Resolved to pastor in view of the end.

A PASTOR MUST MINISTER with a clear vision of where all human history is moving. That is, eschatology matters for the shepherd's work. As a pastor sees his ministry in the context of the second coming of Christ and the final judgement of all mankind, there will be an urgency to his labors and a clarity of focus that is lacking in evangelicalism today. This chapter is not merely a systematic theology of the end, but an argument for how eschatology must inform a pastor's present care of the church.

Michael Horton helpfully explains how eschatology (the study of "last things") is not exclusively about things *future*. Moreover, Horton is convinced that eschatology "must thoroughly inform a pastor's life and ministry":

> Eschatology is the study of "last things" (*ta eschata*), so it is natural that many Christians think its exclusive focus is on things to come. Yet with the incarnation, life, death, resurrection, and ascension of Christ, the new creation has already begun, the kingdom inaugurated, and the Spirit poured on all flesh. With Christ as the prototype and pioneer, the future has penetrated into the present. While awaiting the consummation, we have even now been "enlightened," "have tasted the heavenly gift, and have shared in the Holy Spirit, and have tasted the goodness of the word of God and the powers of the age to come" (Heb 6:4–5). This reality must thoroughly inform a pastor's life and ministry. The gospel minister must envision all his labors in relation to God's kingdom now come in Christ, as unfolded in Scripture, that he might exhibit its arrival in his proclamation and explain its significance for our present lives.[1]

In other words, given the events associated with Christ's first coming, the future has everything to do with today.

While Horton is helpful in explaining the end (or, as he says, *telos*) of our existence as it relates to our identity in Christ, and the "already" of the kingdom of God, the focus in this chapter is on what the apostle Peter calls "the end of all things" (1 Pet 4:7) and the implications of this great event in redemptive history for the shepherd's work.[2] That is, as we live in the "already" of the kingdom, our work as pastors must be greatly informed by the "not yet" of the kingdom. Indeed, this future hope and coming judgment is the necessary context of all pastoral ministry.

---

1. Edwards, Ferguson, and Van Dixhoorn, *Theology for Ministry*, 490.

2. Of his contribution in *Theology for Ministry*, Horton writes, "Although biblical eschatology has many implications for pastoral theology, I focus on its significance for personal identity as we minister to those created in the image of God, in relationship with him and others, as we either realize or resist the purpose for which we are made" (490). For my discussion of identity, the image of God, and pastoral theology, see chaps. 3 and 4. Whereas Horton in his discussion of eschatology for ministry focuses on the significance of the *already* of the kingdom of God, my focus in this chapter is on the significance of the *not yet* of the kingdom for pastoral ministry.

ETERNITY

The Eschatological Context of the Bible

The world works overtime, and I'm sure the devil is greatly behind this, to keep people fixated on the here and now—as if this present life is all there is. As Calvin observes, "We undertake everything as if we were establishing immortality for ourselves on earth."[3] The devil must relish seeing people go into that dark night of death having thought nothing of eternity, but only of maximizing pleasure and limiting pain in this fleeting life on earth. It's the philosophy of the man in the parable Jesus told as a warning about living only for this world:

> And he told them a parable, saying, "The land of a rich man produced plentifully, and he thought to himself, 'What shall I do, for I have nowhere to store my crops?' And he said, 'I will do this: I will tear down my barns and build larger ones, and there I will store all my grain and my goods. And I will say to my soul, "Soul, you have ample goods laid up for many years; relax, eat, drink, be merry."' But God said to him, 'Fool! This night your soul is required of you, and the things you have prepared, whose will they be?' So is the one who lays up treasure for himself and is not rich toward God." (Luke 12:16–21)

According to Jesus, to live exclusively for this world is to be a fool.

Jesus, of course, is not alone when it comes to keeping death and eternity before our eyes. The context of the whole Bible is "the age to come." Indeed, the biblical authors are relentless in their efforts to lift our eyes beyond the present that we might behold the landscape of eternity. The apostles, for example, often give exhortations in the context of eternity. Consider the following texts:

- [Peter preaching in the Temple square] "Repent therefore, and turn back, that your sins may be blotted out, that times of refreshing may come from the presence of the Lord, and that he may send the Christ appointed for you, Jesus, whom heaven must receive until the time for restoring all the things about which God spoke by the mouth of his holy prophets long ago" (Acts 3:19–21).

- [Paul preaching in Athens] "The times of ignorance God overlooked, but now he commands all people everywhere to repent, because he has fixed a day on which he will judge the world in righteousness by a

---

3. Calvin, *On the Christian Life*, 49.

- man whom he has appointed; and of this he has given assurance to all by raising him from the dead" (Acts 17:30–31).
- "He will render to each one according to his works: to those who by patience in well-doing seek for glory and honor and immortality, he will give eternal life; but for those who are self-seeking and do not obey the truth, but obey unrighteousness, there will be wrath and fury. There will be tribulation and distress for every human being who does evil, the Jew first and also the Greek, but glory and honor and peace for everyone who does good, the Jew first and also the Greek. For God shows no partiality" (Rom 2:6–11).
- "So whether we are at home or away, we make it our aim to please him. For we must all appear before the judgment seat of Christ, so that each one may receive what is due for what he has done in the body, whether good or evil" (2 Cor 5:9–10; cf. Rev 20:11–15).
- "And it is my prayer that your love may abound more and more, with knowledge and all discernment, so that you may approve what is excellent, and so be pure and blameless for the day of Christ, filled with the fruit of righteousness that comes through Jesus Christ, to the glory and praise of God" (Phil 1:9–11).
- "When Christ who is your life appears, then you also will appear with him in glory" (Col 3:4).
- "For you yourselves are fully aware that the day of the Lord will come like a thief in the night" (1 Thess 5:2; cf. 2 Pet 3:10).
- "And just as it is appointed for man to die once, and after that comes judgment, so Christ, having been offered once to bear the sins of many, will appear a second time, not to deal with sin but to save those who are eagerly waiting for him" (Heb 9:27–28).
- "And now, little children, abide in him, so that when he appears we may have confidence and not shrink from him in shame at his coming" (1 John 2:28; cf. 3:2).

As this short sample makes clear, the themes of Christ's second coming and judgement in perfect righteousness are not peripheral issues to the apostles, but are at the heart of their understanding of God's plan for history—and motivation for *present* faithfulness. On this point, article 32 (sec. 3) of the London Baptist Confession (1689) is representative of the rich Protestant history when it concludes:

> As Christ would have us to be certainly persuaded that there shall be a Day of Judgment, both to deter all men from sin, and for the greater consolation of the godly, in their adversity; so will he have that day unknown to Men, that they may shake off all carnal security, and be always watchful, because they know not at what hour, the Lord will come; and may ever be prepared to say, Come Lord Jesus, Come quickly, Amen.[4]

Living in the Light of the End

The biblical connection between the end of all things and pastoral ministry struck me anew when preaching through 1 Peter; over the course of that year, I found it remarkable how thoroughly eschatology influenced this one-time fisherman. Eternity is always on Peter's mind, and he longs for the "elect exiles of the Dispersion" (1 Pet 1:1), Christians scattered throughout the world, to embrace the pilgrim life as they journey toward their heavenly home. Peter is convinced these homesick sojourners need to see just how practical eternity is to their present sufferings. For example, Peter wastes no time as he opens the letter by pointing his readers to their future home in heaven: "Blessed be the God and Father of our Lord Jesus Christ! According to his great mercy, he has caused us to be born again to a living hope through the resurrection of Jesus Christ from the dead, to an inheritance that is imperishable, undefiled, and unfading, kept in heaven for you, who by God's power are being guarded through faith for a salvation ready to be revealed in the last time" (1 Pet 1:3–5). Weary, persecuted saints need to know that they have an inheritance in heaven kept secure by a sovereign God, a "salvation ready to be revealed in the *last* time." One can feel the apostle pleading with his readers to keep the end of all things in view. Indeed, the "last time" has everything to do with *this* time.

Peter makes this point still more clear when, just eight verses later, he exhorts Christians to ensure that their hope is rightly set on the future: "Therefore, preparing your minds for action, and being sober-minded, set your hope fully on the grace that will be brought to you at the revelation of Jesus Christ" (1 Pet 1:13). A sober-minded, prepared-for-action Christian has a hope "fully set on the grace that *will be* brought" to him or her at the end of time. I get no sense from reading Peter that he thinks meditating on

---

4. Van Dixhoorn, *Creeds, Confessions, and Catechisms*, 288.

the future is some kind of impractical, useless exercise. In fact, it's just the opposite.

Peter could not fathom any present faithfulness without also keeping eternity in sight, as evidenced by chapter 4 of his first epistle:

> The end of all things is at hand; therefore be self-controlled and sober-minded for the sake of your prayers. Above all, keep loving one another earnestly, since love covers a multitude of sins. Show hospitality to one another without grumbling. As each has received a gift, use it to serve one another, as good stewards of God's varied grace: whoever speaks, as one who speaks oracles of God; whoever serves, as one who serves by the strength that God supplies—in order that in everything God may be glorified through Jesus Christ. To him belong glory and dominion forever and ever. Amen. (1 Pet 4:7-11)

Notice the apostolic logic: because the end of all things is at hand, therefore be. In other words, the reason Peter gives for faithful living in the present is the impending "end of all things."

By proclaiming the end of history is "at hand," Peter did not mean the second coming of Christ was going to happen in a few days or weeks or even months. The actual timing of Christ's return is not Peter's point. He means that all the major events in redemptive history, as outlined in 3:18-22, have happened such that the next great event in history that is "at hand" is the return of Christ in glory. Christ's incarnation, earthly ministry to fulfill all righteousness, atoning death, resurrection from the grave, and ascension to glory with the corresponding giving of the Holy Spirit—all of this has happened. And so, the posture of the church in these last days is a longing for a Savior from heaven, the Lord Jesus Christ, who will come again to judge the living and the dead (cf. Phil 3:20-21). This is what is "at hand." Believers live in great anticipation of the consummation of all things.

This, of course, is not an anticipation unique to Peter. One might call this an "apostolic anticipation." Paul, for example, has the end in view when he exhorts the Roman Christians to "wake from sleep," to be alert to the consummation of all things: "Besides this you know the time, that the hour has come for you to wake from sleep. For salvation is nearer to us now than when we first believed" (Rom 13:11). The author of Hebrews instructs the church to persevere in "encouraging one another" because "the Day is drawing near" (Heb 10:24-25). James preaches patience and endurance, and the absence of grumbling among believers, given that "the Judge is standing at the door" (Jas 5:8–9). Finally, John explains how the presence of "antichrists" is evidence "that it is the last hour" (1 John 2:18), and that all who hear his prophecy should "keep what is written in it, for the time is near" (Rev 1:3). In concert with the other apostles, Peter is exhorting his readers to live in the light of eternity. So, with the end in view, according to Peter, what should uniquely mark the church? Very practical things like prayer, love, hospitality, and service.

The first mark of the church Peter outlines is prayer: "The end of all things is at hand; therefore be self-controlled and sober-minded for the sake of your prayers" (v. 7). In evangelical history, talk of the end has unfortunately promoted things like hysteria or paranoia or other forms of irrationality. This mentality is a prayer-killer, forgetful of God in the frantic, frenzied scramble to "prepare" for the end. In contrast to this, Peter calls the church to be "self-controlled" and "sober-minded." Christians are to "keep their heads" for the purpose of prayer. We need to be sober-minded, remembering what prayer demonstrates so clearly, namely, our dependence on God who stabilizes our hearts as we contemplate our future hope. This is Paul's logic in Philippians 4:4–7 when he considers the Lord being "at hand": "Rejoice in the Lord always; again I will say, rejoice. Let your reasonableness be known to everyone. The Lord is at hand; do not be anxious about anything, but in everything by prayer and supplication with thanksgiving let your requests be made known to God. And the peace of God, which surpasses all understanding, will guard your hearts and your minds in Christ Jesus."

With the end in view, a second practical mark of the church is love. "The end of all things is at hand; therefore . . . . Above all, keep loving one another earnestly, since love covers a multitude of sins" (vv. 7–8). This is not the first we've heard from Peter about love. Earlier, he exhorted Christians to "love one another earnestly from a pure heart" (1:22), and a little later, he encouraged, among other things, the virtue of "brotherly love" (3:8). In emphasizing love in the last days, Peter would recall hearing first-hand Jesus's warning about the tendency for love to grow cold in the last days: "Then they will deliver you up to tribulation and put you to death, and you will be hated by all nations for my name's sake. And then many will fall away and betray one another and hate one another. And many false prophets will arise and lead many astray. And because lawlessness will be increased, the love of many will grow cold" (Matt 24:9–12). But this cannot be the case with the church. Indeed, with the end in view, love must increase. And don't miss what love does: love "covers a multitude of sins." This is an allusion to Proverbs 10:12 where Solomon counsels: "Hatred stirs up strife, but love covers all offenses." The idea is to so love that we actually overlook the sins and offences of others. What an amazing (and practical), otherworldly reality this is. This kind of love—love that covers a multitude of sins—is motivated by a recognition that the end of all things is at hand.

With the end in view, a third practical mark of the church is hospitality. "The end of all things is at hand; therefore . . . . Show hospitality to one another without grumbling." In the ancient world, travelers (surely exiles like Peter's readers) would have to rely on relatives or friends or acquaintances to provide lodging for a night or more. Generally speaking, inns were unsafe or unsanitary (or both).[5] The practice of hospitality is no insignificant task. After all, faithfully showing hospitality is one requirement for being an elder (1 Tim 3:2; Titus 1:8); and by offering hospitality "some have entertained angels unawares" (Heb 13:2). As a spur to this most practical practice, Peter exhorts his readers to keep the end in view. Knowing that the end of all things in at hand, we can—without grumbling or complaining—show hospitality in the present. The reasoning seems to be something like this: a temporary inconvenience is more easily and sincerely embraced when seen against the backdrop of eternity.

With the end in view, a fourth practical mark of the church is service. "The end of all things is at hand; therefore . . . . As each has received a gift, use it to serve one another, as good stewards of God's varied grace." Peter says every Christian has received a gift, that is, a capability or skill resulting from God's grace, and Peter doesn't leave us to wonder why God has given us grace to steward. Indeed, the stewardship is "to serve one another." In this passage, Peter outlines some representative gifts that God has given his people. The list he offers is not exhaustive. The point is not to list all the gifts, but to make clear that spiritual gifts are not a privilege but a responsibility. Our gifts are not ultimately about us, but others. They are given by God "to equip the saints for the work of the ministry, for building up the body of Christ" (Eph 4:12). What a beautiful thing it is when Christians recognize their spiritual giftedness and how these gifts are given by God to serve others.

Do you see the picture Peter has painted? Do you see something of the glory of the church? With the end of all things in view, we should see God's people praying earnestly, loving fervently, hosting cheerfully, and serving

---

5. Kistemaker, *1 Peter*, 168.

one another as stewards of God's varied grace. This is the masterpiece Peter has painted as he considers what it means to live in the light of the end. Peter sees eschatology as utterly practical for today.

Pastoring in the Light of the End

To be sure, every pastor must labor to promote the very things Peter outlines in the passage above: love, prayer, hospitality, and service. The purpose of the previous exposition was to show from Peter's first epistle how practical the "end of all things" is to the church's present living. In this section I consider four specific pastoral duties that should be directly informed by the reality of the end of all things being at hand.

Preaching

In chapter 8, I outlined what preaching *is* and what it *does*. Here I want to consider the necessary eschatological context of all faithful Christian preaching. We see this eschatological context in the apostle Paul's charge to his young apprentice Timothy: "I charge you in the presence of God and of Christ Jesus, who is to judge the living and the dead, and by his appearing and his kingdom: preach the word; be ready in season and out of season; reprove, rebuke, and exhort, with complete patience and teaching" (2 Tim 4:1–2). The importance of preaching is impressed upon Timothy with what precedes the charge. In other words, Timothy is accountable to Jesus Christ, the Judge of all the earth, for how faithfully he fulfills the office of preacher. To arouse Timothy to diligence in preaching the Word, Paul reminds him of the certain "appearing" of Jesus Christ, when he returns to "judge the living and the dead." Paul seems to think that *current* faithfulness in preaching is motivated by a glorious *future* event: the second coming of Christ.

In a sermon on 2 Timothy 4:1–2, Calvin explains Paul's use of "God's judgment seat" in spurring Timothy on in his work of preaching:

> Paul ... summons Timothy before God's judgment seat to remind him of Ezekiel's words, that preachers of his word are like watchmen, and if they do not cry aloud when danger is near, men's souls will be required at their hand (Ezek. 3:17; 33:7–8). If, then, people perish through our indolence when God has made us his messengers, their blood will be required of us; we will be condemned before God as responsible for the loss of those we failed to teach.

> Such is the summons which Paul issues and which confirms Ezekiel's earlier prophecy. He makes it clear that those chosen to be teachers are more tightly bound, and will be liable for the death not of men's bodies but of their souls when they fail to turn sinners from the path of destruction.[6]

As Timothy keeps before his mind's eye the return of Christ to judge the living and the dead, he will be inspired to work diligently in the preaching of the Word, knowing that he, too, will stand before the Judge. In the same sermon, Calvin continues to draw out the implications of the return of Christ for present faithfulness in preaching:

> In describing Jesus Christ as the Judge of the world, Paul wants Timothy to know that any who forsake the flock, who do not protect it from wolves or who leave the sheep hungry for the food of life, must expect vengeance from our Lord Jesus Christ. Why? Because he claims for himself the office of Judge: it is before him that we must appear. He therefore honours us by making us his representatives, so that the man who goes into the pulpit to preach speaks with the authority of God's Son and in his name. Paul thus declares that God has appointed us his ambassadors, so that we may exhort the church in his name and proclaim the gospel on his authority (2 Cor. 5:20). Since he honours us who are mere earthworms by allowing us to represent him, to speak as through his lips and with such authority that he might seem to be present among us—since, then, our Lord Jesus Christ honours us this way, if we fail to do as he commands how can he be merciful to us? Do we not deserve awful retribution from him for our faithlessness and ingratitude?[7]

Calvin is surely right to understand Paul as warning Timothy about what the Judge will require from a "mere earthworm" who has been honored with such a lofty position as "ambassador for Christ," if he is faithless and ungrateful: nothing less than "vengeance from our Lord Jesus Christ." (It is the echo of Jesus in Luke 12:48, the climax of a parable given in the context of the return of Christ: "Everyone to whom much was given, of him much will be required, and from him to whom they entrusted much, they will demand the more.") By qualifying the charge to "preach the word" with a warning about the second coming of Christ in judgment, Paul is "sharply prodding Timothy so that he duly performs his office," according

---

6. Calvin, *Sermons on 2 Timothy*, 358–59.
7. Calvin, *Sermons on 2 Timothy*, 360–61.

Eternity

to Calvin.[8] Pastors will do well to heed this apostolic warning for present faithfulness in preaching the word.

Suffering

I have in mind, here, how a pastor helps God's people persevere through suffering. Even as Romans 12:15 says, "Rejoice with those who rejoice, weep with those who weep," it seems like a pastor spends a disproportionate amount of time weeping with those who weep. What does the "end of all things" have to do with a suffering church? Everything. Let me explain.

I remember well the day my beloved first wife Julia was diagnosed with stage 4 breast cancer. Just thirty-eight years old and the mother of four young children, Julia was determined to do everything she could to beat the cancer. One of the biblical texts that served as an anchor for our soul in those early, indescribably hard days as we absorbed the news was 2 Corinthians 12:9: "My grace is sufficient for you, for my power is made perfect in weakness." This was Jesus's promise to Paul after he had pleaded three times for the removal of his "thorn in the flesh" (2 Cor 12:7–8). Julia was able to endure for five years all of the treatments associated with her cancer—while still flourishing as a wife and mother—because God's grace was sufficient for the hour.

But there was also another key passage of Scripture that served as a bulwark against fear and despondency during this time, Psalm 103:1–5:

> Bless the LORD, O my soul, and all that is within me, bless his holy name! Bless the LORD, O my soul, and forget not all his benefits, who forgives all your iniquity, who heals all your diseases, who redeems your life from the pit, who crowns you with steadfast love and mercy, who satisfies you with good so that your youth is renewed like the eagle's.

The third verse was particularly comforting to us: "who heals all your diseases." One of the Lord's "benefits" David recounts is the healing of all diseases. Of course, as Julia and I prayed for the immediate healing of her cancer, we were comforted to know that ultimately her cancer was healed. If not in this life, Julia would be free from cancer in the next. It was this eschatological hope for healing that made a massive difference in our fight against cancer in the present. This is why I was able to say through tears at

---

8. Calvin, *Sermons on 2 Timothy*, 361.

Julia's funeral, "The gospel of Jesus Christ offers an unshakable hope for life beyond the grave—death, we trust, is not the final word for Julia, but life, everlasting life."

Pastors may be tempted to withhold talk of eternity when counseling someone going through deep suffering. Many ministers, it seems, have been conditioned to think that talk of heaven is somehow belittling the pain the person is going through in the present. But the hope of heaven is immensely practical for the suffering saint. Pastors must compassionately help those who are suffering see their trial in the light of eternity. That there is coming a day for the believer when God will "wipe away every tear from their eyes, and death shall be no more, neither shall there be mourning, nor crying, nor pain anymore" (Rev 21:4) redeems all present pain. This is why the words of Psalm 16:11 are etched on Julia's headstone: "You make known to me the path of life; in your presence there is fullness of joy; at your right hand are pleasures forevermore."

Lord's Supper

Given the realities of present suffering among God's people, it is necessary for a pastor to emphasize the eschatological context of the ordinances. One of the great privileges of a pastor is to preside over the Lord's Supper. The apostle Paul outlines this ordinance in 1 Corinthians 11:23–26:

> For I received from the Lord what I also delivered to you, that the Lord Jesus on the night when he was betrayed took bread, and when he had given thanks, he broke it, and said, "This is my body, which is for you. Do this in remembrance of me." In the same way also he took the cup, after supper, saying, "This cup is the new covenant in my blood. Do this, as often as you drink it, in remembrance of me." For as often as you eat this bread and drink the cup, you proclaim the Lord's death until he comes.

According to the apostle Paul, the Supper is a looking back (i.e., remembrance) and a looking forward (i.e., until he comes). Pastors must not only emphasize the past dimension of the Supper, but also the future dimension. It is essential, of course, that we "remember" the once for all sacrifice of Christ that secures our salvation (Heb 7:27). It is this sacrifice that enables us to sing, "Jesus paid it all, all to him I owe; sin had left a crimson stain, he washed it white as snow." But there is also a glorious future aspect to the Supper. We come to the table today by faith. This faith not only believes that God will strengthen us in the remembrance of Christ's sacrifice for sin—what he's done in the past—but also believes in the promise of a future meal we'll share with Christ in glory. The apostle John explains,

> Then I heard what seemed to be the voice of a great multitude, like the roar of many waters and like the sound of mighty peals of thunder, crying out, "Hallelujah! For the Lord our God the Almighty reigns. Let us rejoice and exult and give him the glory, for the marriage of the Lamb has come, and his Bride has made herself ready; it was granted her to clothe herself with fine linen, bright and pure"—for the fine linen is the righteous deeds of the saints. And the angel said to me, "Write this: Blessed are those who are invited to the marriage supper of the Lamb." And he said to me, "These are the true words of God." (Rev 19:6–9)

The church comes to the Lord's Table only "until he comes." It is a temporary ordinance pointing to "an inheritance that is imperishable, undefiled, and unfading, kept in heaven for you, who by God's power are being guarded through faith for a salvation ready to be revealed in the last time" (1 Pet 1:4–5). A pastor emphasizes the eschatological context of the Lord's Supper as a means of strengthening faith in the present.

Church Discipline

The grace of church discipline is one of the "keys of the kingdom" given to the church. As the Heidelberg Catechism asks and answers (Lord's Day 31): "What are the keys of the kingdom? The preaching of the holy gospel and Christian discipline toward repentance. Both of them open the kingdom of heaven to believers and close it to unbelievers."[9] Jesus outlines the process of church discipline in Matthew 18:15–18:

> If your brother sins against you, go and tell him his fault, between you and him alone. If he listens to you, you have gained your brother. But if he does not listen, take one or two others along with you, that every charge may be established by the evidence of two or three witnesses. If he refuses to listen to them, tell it to the church. And if he refuses to listen even to the church, let him be to you as a Gentile and a tax collector. Truly, I say to you, whatever you bind on earth shall be bound in heaven, and whatever you loose on earth shall be loosed in heaven.

---

9. Van Dixhoorn, *Creeds, Confessions, and Catechisms*, 316.

In this passage the church is given a clear, four-step way forward when a professing believer remains in unrepentant sin.

What is church discipline designed to do? First, church discipline is *remedial* in the sense that it seeks a remedy; and the remedy is restoration through repentance of the one caught in sin (Gal 6:1). Second, church discipline is *prophetic* in the sense that any temporal judgment made by the church is intended to point toward a greater judgment to come. In other words, *present* judgment by the church on sin is to awaken the sinner under discipline (and, in some cases, the church as a whole, if the process goes beyond step 2) to the final judgment of God in Christ. Church discipline is made effective in large part because of its prophetic role in warning of the return of Christ to "judge the living and the dead" (2 Tim 4:1). The logic of church discipline is this: *In the light of the return of Christ in glory when he will judge the world in righteousness, repent of your sin today. True repentance will ensure that you can stand in the judgment on the Day of Christ.* Pastors fail to bring all of the needed gospel pressure on the unrepentant person when church discipline is not seen in its eschatological context.

The Pastor's Crown

With his eyes riveted on the future, the apostle Peter exhorts his fellow pastors toward faithfulness:

> So I exhort the elders among you, as a fellow elder and a witness of the sufferings of Christ, as well as a partaker in the glory that is going to be revealed: shepherd the flock of God that is among you, exercising oversight, not under compulsion, but willingly, as God would have you; not for shameful gain, but eagerly; not domineering over those in your charge, but being examples to the flock. And when the chief Shepherd appears, you will receive the unfading crown of glory. (1 Pet 5:1–4)

Pastors must serve in the light of eternity. As Peter makes clear, we do not serve for a temporal crown. Our reward is not in this life. We labor for "the unfading crown of glory" that we'll receive "when the chief Shepherd appears." Present faithfulness is fueled by future glory. May God make us faithful shepherds, for the end of all things is at hand.

12

Slowness

"Walk slow."
—Mumford & Sons

"Be still, and know that I am God."
—Psalm 46:10

Resolution 12: Resolved to walk slow in a world of sprint.

The Tortoise wins.

I remember hearing Aesop's famous fable *The Hare and the Tortoise* as a little boy and thinking, "I'd still like to be a hare. After all, the tortoise may win, but who wants to be a tortoise? How boring." Many years later I've reconsidered, especially when it comes to pastoral ministry. If there ever was a vocation wherein "the race is not to the swift" (Eccl 9:11), it's the pastorate. A faithful shepherd will pace himself for the long haul given the nature of the work. Pastors, after all, are not pounding out "products," but doing heart work. And heart work can be messy, unpredictable, and slow.

Resolutions of a Pastor

When I was a child, our family took annual trips from our southern California home to the northwest corner of Iowa to visit my grandparents, aunt and uncle, and cousins. I come from a family of German immigrants who came to Iowa for its rich farmland. I recall the first time my grandfather pointed out the living room window of their home (a converted schoolhouse overlooking farmland as far as the eye could see), as he explained to me the way farmers rotated out the crops each year: corn, soybeans, corn, soybeans. This, I learned, was good for the soil. Patiently, and with the enthusiasm of a child, my grandfather would tell of how farmers needed to exert great effort and practice much patience as they waited for the crops to come in. To see the fruits of their labor farmers needed time: time to prepare the soil, time to plant, time to water, and, finally, time to bring in the harvest. Being a farmer is not work for those wanting instant gratification. The parallels to the pastorate are many. Much like the farmer, pastoral ministry demands patient toil.

This, of course, is not the world we live in. We live in the age of instant. We want our WiFi to fly, our coffee ready, our music streaming, our shopping at the speed of Prime, and our social media and news feeds constantly refreshed. As Cal Newport helpfully observes, our age mitigates against "deep work."[1] Pastoral ministry is the ultimate deep work. In 2009, David Gordon concluded that *Johnny Can't Preach* in large part because Johnny can't read and write.[2] The modern-day preacher seems increasingly unable to do the deep work required given how the media have shaped the messenger. Gordon was prophetic, writing before smart phones, Facebook, X, Instagram, TikTok, and texting became ubiquitous in the culture, making his thesis still more tenable. In the last decade, a steady stream of scholarship has focused on the impact of digital media on the mind. The literature is ominous regarding the effects of our technological age.[3] It seems that not only our minds, but our humanity itself, may be at stake.

Pastors must go counter to today's frenetic pace. Our digital world feels frenzied because, well, it is. There is a hyperactivity to our time that

---

1. Newport, *Deep Work*.
2. Gordon, *Why Johnny Can't Preach*.
3. See, for example, Haidt, *The Anxious Generation*; Twenge, *Generations*; *iGen*; Alter, *Irresistible*; Carr, *The Shallows*; Freitas, *The Happiness Effect*; Turkle, *Alone Together*; *Reclaiming Conversation*; and Vaidhyanathan, *Anti-Social Media*. Each of these scholars is building on the work of earlier philosophers and social scientists, such as Ellul, *The Technological Society*; McLuhan, *Understanding Media*; Postman, *Amusing Ourselves to Death*; and *Technopoly*.

works against pastoral ministry. What Nicholas Carr observes about the impact of the Internet on his life and thought can be applied to pastors today:

> The boons [of the Internet] are real. But they come at a price. As McLuhan suggested, media aren't just channels of information. They supply the stuff of thought, but they also shape the process of thought. And what the Net seems to be doing is chipping away my capacity for concentration and contemplation. Whether I'm online or not, my mind now expects to take in information the way the Net distributes it: in a swiftly moving stream of particles. Once I was a scuba diver in the sea of words. Now I zip along the surface like a guy on a Jet Ski.[4]

Pastoral work is not like riding a Jet Ski—zipping along the surface water of God's Word and people's hearts. Pastors are "stewards of the mysteries of God" (1 Cor 4:1) laboring for people's "progress and joy in the faith" (Phil 1:25). This is not work done in the shallows.

The apostles learned this vital lesson early on in the church. In Acts 6, we see the temptation for the church's leadership to be pulled away from the deep work required of an under-shepherd. Rather than be deterred from matters of first importance, the leadership provided for another way to satisfy a legitimate need that threatened to tear apart the young church. After all, widows being neglected in the daily distribution of food is no small thing. But their need couldn't be met at the expense of prayer and the ministry of the Word:

> Now in these days when the disciples were increasing in number, a complaint by the Hellenists arose against the Hebrews because their widows were being neglected in the daily distribution. And the twelve summoned the full number of the disciples and said, "It is not right that we should give up preaching the word of God to serve tables. Therefore, brothers, pick out from among you seven men of good repute, full of the Spirit and of wisdom, whom we will appoint to this duty. But we will devote ourselves to prayer and to the ministry of the word." (Acts 6:1–4)

The word translated *devote* means "to attend to, devote oneself to" with regularity and steadfastness.[5] Pastors must cultivate sustained, concen-

---

4. Carr, *The Shallows*, 6–7.
5. Mounce, *Complete Expository Dictionary*, 180.

trated focus on the ministries of the Word and prayer; and we need to be ruthless in keeping at bay distractions from this primary work.

The apostle Paul trained Timothy in this understanding of the pastorate when he reminded him of what every pastor should be dedicated to:

> Until I come, devote yourself to the public reading of Scripture, to exhortation, to teaching. Do not neglect the gift you have, which was given you by prophecy when the council of elders laid their hands on you. Practice these things, immerse yourself in them, so that all may see your progress. Keep a close watch on yourself and on the teaching. Persist in this, for by so doing you will save both yourself and your hearers. (1 Tim 4:13–16)

Note the verbs in this passage: *devote, practice, immerse, keep a close watch, persist*. To be sure, the current state of evangelicalism is not amenable to these disciplines. But this is no excuse for the pastor not to practice them.

Given this reality, a pastor needs to work hard to slow things down. More than ever, pastors need to cultivate thoughtfulness and reflection about matters of first importance, things like theology, ecclesiology, preaching, apologetics, and counseling. Pastors must set aside (and guard) time to absorb thoughtful writing in books, journals, and news outlets about topics relevant to their work. Some pastors are being buried under an avalanche of content each week such that sustained concentration for the sake of wise application cannot be attained.

Some years ago, I worked for a major media company doing editorial work. My boss had a phrase he loved to use when it came to the Internet: *daily addiction*. The idea was to have so much new, fresh content on a daily basis that people felt compelled to traffic our websites every day, throughout the day. And, believe me, this can work. Adam Alter is right.[6] But by feeding the frenzy, we were (unintentionally) undermining people's ability to think beyond the surface of any given issue because almost instantaneously, we were on to the next thing.

I recall an acquaintance of mine during my undergraduate years at the University of Washington. Brad and I attended the same campus ministry. The Inn, as it was called, met on Tuesday nights. Approximately 700 students gathered for the main event that included a "sermon" by one of the campus ministry leaders. Afterwards, the crowd would dissemble into smaller groups for deeper conversation and prayer over the theme of the message. One particular night, our group of guys was asked a question by

---

6. Alter, *Irresistible*.

our discussion leader about how we handled the hectic nature of our lives, how we carved out time (if we did at all) for thoughtful reflection on God and the Bible. What Brad said has stuck with me all these years. He said, "I walk slowly." Rather than move quickly from one class to the next, or from one meeting to another, Brad said, "I intentionally slow down my pace." Whether Brad was on time for things is beside the point. His effort to slow things down for the sake of contemplation seemed right in 1994, and seems all-the-more important in our time.[7]

Pastors, in one sense, need to become a manifestation of Neil Postman's "Loving Resistance Fighter."[8] In this resistance, we demand that this digital age serve us in our calling as pastors and teachers. We are not modern-day Luddites, longing for a past "golden age" before the Industrial Revolution gave birth to our wired world. That said, pastors must resolve that the Internet was made for man, not man for the Internet. We must serve just one Master.

Walking Like the Amish

A recent article caught my eye, having to do with the Amish and technology, wherein the author makes the provocative point that we can actually learn something from the Amish when it comes to technology use. Writing for *Psyche*, Alex Mayyasi outlines various Amish strategies for a more tech-savvy life. For example, picking up on Kevin Kelly's book *What Technology Wants*, he echoes Kelly's conclusion that the Amish offer an "honorable alternative" to the tech-addicted culture of our day:

> The foundation of this "honourable alternative" is to *not* adopt every single new technology, or use cars, phones and social media as soon as they become the norm. Instead, the Amish make slow and deliberate decisions as a collective. Rather than rushing optimistically or blindly into the future, they move forward cautiously, open but sceptical.[9]

The "caution" and "skepticism" with technology use is born out of a certain ethos the Amish work hard to cultivate: "The Amish ethos places prime value on family and neighbourly life. It also strives to maintain a separation

---

7. For help with your pace see, for example, Honore, *In Praise of Slowness*.
8. Postman, *Technopoly*, 181–200.
9. Mayyasi, "To Be More Tech-Savvy, Borrow Strategies from Amish."

from the world."[10] If there is a battle between technology and family/community, then tech loses. And being always connected to technology makes it hard to be separate from the world. With an ethos like this, it is easy to see how the Amish are not overrun with technology.

Perhaps the best strategy offered, however, is toward the end of the article when Mayyasi seems to step back and see that it's not really about some practical "how-to" that gives the Amish freedom from the tyranny of tech. It's something greater: "Above all, decide to be OK with seeming eccentric. The Amish's unusual approach has allowed them to survive for centuries, even while other cooperatives and intentional communities fall by the wayside."[11] Eccentricity as a way of survival. That's a bold claim, and one Christians would do well to embrace.

Eccentric (used as a noun) refers to a person who is unconventional while holding views that are, and exhibiting behavior that is, deemed slightly strange. When we say something like, "He's an engaging eccentric," we mean that he's something of a curiosity even if likable. Christians of all people should be seen as eccentric. After all, we are happily unconventional and, if we're honest, hold some strange (according to the world) beliefs and practices. Let's consider several of each.

Beliefs

- We believe in a holy Creator-God—a divine being who created the heavens and the earth. More strange: we believe this one God exists in three persons. Indeed, Christians are a Trinitarian people.

- We believe the whole human race fell into sin through the disobedience of our first parents, Adam and Eve. The fall makes the whole human race guilty before this holy God, and we are in need of forgiveness for our corporate rebellion against him.

- We believe the good news that God sent forth his Son, Jesus Christ, to fulfill God's perfect law on our behalf and to pay the penalty due our sin. We believe in the substitutionary sacrifice of Christ for sinners. We believe that after his death on the cross, he rose bodily from the grave and ascended into heaven, where he even now rules and reigns

---

10. Mayyasi, "To Be More Tech-Savvy, Borrow Strategies from Amish."
11. Mayyasi, "To Be More Tech-Savvy, Borrow Strategies from Amish."

as the victorious King of all the earth. We believe that Jesus is coming again to consummate his kingdom, judge the world in righteousness, and usher in the new heavens and new earth.

- We believe that this good news becomes good news for us through faith alone. Upon conversion, we believe we've been given the Holy Spirit as a deposit, guaranteeing our inheritance with Christ through a true spiritual union with him.
- We believe all of this (and much more) is included in the Bible, the inspired Word of God [read: God-breathed]. Because the Bible is ultimately a product of God's Spirit (i.e., inspired), we believe it is inerrant, authoritative, clear, and sufficient.

Practices

- We gather at least once a week on Sunday in local churches and worship this God corporately. These meetings always include singing and praying and the exposition of a passage from the Bible.
- We baptize people upon profession of faith by immersing them under water in the name of the Father and of the Son and of the Holy Spirit.
- We come to the Lord's Table often to eat bread and drink grape juice (or other fruit of the vine) in the grace-giving ordinance of remembering the Lord's body broken and blood shed for us.
- We set aside time in a day to read the Bible and pray alone and with our families.
- Some of us even join small groups of people from our local church that meet regularly to further encourage and equip one another for godly living—the practice of putting sin to death in our lives while putting on the virtues of Christ.

These are just some of the beliefs and practices that make us eccentric. Indeed, the world should look at Christians and see an unconventional people.

A stick-bug is an amazing insect. It has a natural camouflage allowing itself to go undetected by would-be predators or others. Like a leaf insect, stick-bugs blend into their surroundings such that they are almost unrecognizable from the stick or twig they're crawling along. Christians are not like stick-bugs. We are designed to stand out— not to blend in with our surroundings. We are to be detectible, remarkable, distinct like salt and explicit like light. Jesus intends for his followers to be obvious to a watching world:

> You are the salt of the earth, but if salt has lost its taste, how shall its saltiness be restored? It is no longer good for anything except to be thrown out and trampled under people's feet. You are the light of the world. A city set on a hill cannot be hidden. Nor do people light a lamp and put it under a basket, but on a stand, and it gives light to all in the house. In the same way, let your light shine before others, so that they may see your good works and give glory to your Father who is in heaven. (Matt 5:13-16)

The church is not called to a life of camouflage. Our natural instinct is to be known for Christ as we labor to bring the love of Christ to the world. The apostle Paul picked up on the image of light to encourage the Philippians in their calling to stand out: "Do all things without grumbling or disputing, that you may be blameless and innocent, children of God without blemish in the midst of a crooked and twisted generation, among whom you shine as lights in the world" (Phil 2:14-15). "Shining as lights" in "a crooked and twisted generation" will look eccentric. We will be out-of-step with the culture. We will be accused of having some very strange beliefs and practices. But could it be that our eccentricity will be our survival? And not only our survival, but the very means of the advance of the gospel in our day?

Pastors are called to be eccentrics even as they lead an eccentric people. Are you okay with being seen as eccentric? Are you okay moving at a pace that is out-of-step with the world? Or are you far too comfortable simply blending in, moving happily (and speedily) through life undetected, not knowing that assimilation is of the devil? Pastoral ministry does not require us to become Amish, but it does require an unconventional life. It requires us to walk slow.

Pastors are commissioned to "make the word of God fully known" (Col 1:25), and to "care for the church of God, which he obtained with his own blood" (Acts 20:28). Indeed, pastoral ministry is the ultimate deep work. Our churches desperately need pastors who can help them "walk slow" in this world of sprint. Our churches will follow our lead, and if we're caught up in the frenzy of this digital age, they will join us in the chaos. Tragically, they will come upon a beautiful promise like Psalm 46:10 where

God says to us, "Be still, and know that I am God," and potentially miss it given the deafening noise of our time.

I am aware that the world (and much of evangelicalism) doesn't prize the approach I've laid out in this chapter. It may seem too slow or too serious or not flashy enough. After all, the world doesn't revere turtles. But this book is written in the hope of enlisting thousands of turtles to join the ranks of pastors all over the world. Because the Tortoise wins.

Epilogue: The Courage to Be a Pastor

> Let goods and kindred go,
> this mortal life also;
> the body they may kill:
> God's truth abideth still;
> his kingdom is forever!
>
> — Martin Luther

> "Take courage; it is I. Do not be afraid."
>
> —Matthew 14:27

As the secularization of Western civilization shows no signs of slowing, this book closes with a call to courage. In generations past, pastors in America have experienced prominence in the culture. One thinks of clergy in colonial America and through the eighteenth century when Protestant ministers were among the most learned and influential leaders in the land. As the young nation grew into the nineteenth and twentieth centuries, clergy in America still had the ability to influence the culture given the general public support they received. However, a slow marginalization was taking place. God, and along with him pastors, were being moved to the margins of society, no longer operating from the center.

Today we find the church in America and her pastors not simply at the margins of society, but as David Wells has documented, in the wasteland.[1]

---

1. Wells, *God in the Wasteland*.

Epilogue: The Courage to Be a Pastor

No longer simply neutral to the church, today's culture is openly hostile. Given this, it is imperative that pastors "take courage" if they would be faithful in testifying to the gospel of Jesus Christ. Of course, this is a position pastors have been in before. The church, after all, was born in hostility. The book of Acts and the epistles all testify to the need for courage among the church's leaders given opposition from within and from without. It's not for no reason that Jesus said, "I will build my church, and the gates of hell shall not prevail against it" (Matt 16:18). Hell shall not prevail, but that doesn't mean it won't try.

What will courage require of pastors?

First, courage will require boldly standing for truth in a post-truth age. With militant progressivism on the march, biblical truth is seen not as one worldview among many that is allowed to coexist, but as an enemy to be destroyed. As we've seen throughout this book, biblical categories of creation, fall, redemption, and consummation (and their related doctrines) are viewed by the world as, among other things, hateful, bigoted, misogynistic, and imperialistic. The church is seen as an institution that needs to be shut down so that its influence in the culture is nullified. But regardless of the hostility of the world, the church is still called to be "a pillar and buttress of the truth" (1 Tim 3:15). In the face of open hostility toward the church, pastors will be tempted to muzzle themselves. But this is when we need to have a first century mindset and be prepared to respond like Peter and John in Acts 4:13–20:

> Now when they saw the boldness of Peter and John, and perceived that they were uneducated, common men, they were astonished. And they recognized that they had been with Jesus. But seeing the man who was healed standing beside them, they had nothing to say in opposition. But when they had commanded them to leave the council, they conferred with one another, saying, "What shall we do with these men? For that a notable sign has been performed through them is evident to all the inhabitants of Jerusalem, and we cannot deny it. But in order that it may spread no further among the people, let us warn them to speak no more to anyone in this name." So they called them and charged them not to speak or teach at all in the name of Jesus. But Peter and John answered them, "Whether it is right in the sight of God to listen to you rather than to God, you must judge, for we cannot but speak of what we have seen and heard."

Epilogue: The Courage to Be a Pastor

When threatened and warned to not speak or teach at all in the name of Jesus, may we have the courage to say with the apostles, "Whether it is right in the sight of God to listen to you rather than to God, you must judge, for we cannot but speak of what we have seen and heard."

Second, courage will require pastors to endure increased marginalization in the culture. It will take courage for men to go into the ministry knowing that the pastorate is quickly becoming one of the least respected vocational choices. While pastoral ministry has never been revered like careers in law or medicine or business, there was a time when it was at least seen as respectable. No longer. Solidarity with Christ in vocational ministry for the next generation of pastors will mean being reviled, mocked, and ridiculed in ways an older generation would have never thought possible in America. Moreover, I wouldn't be surprised if we saw the end of the "megachurch"—certainly for churches that are robustly biblical and theological in their orientation. As a result, bi-vocational pastorates may be even more common than what we've seen in contemporary evangelicalism. Will pastors have the courage to make less money, have less influence in the culture, and be scorned in ways akin to the age of the apostles?

Third, courage will require pastors to resist the AI revolution. Already we're seeing AI be peddled as a guide to sermon creation. The temptation for pastors to leverage Artificial Intelligence for content creation will prove disastrous to Spirit-empowered preaching as "efficiency" threatens to short circuit the necessary dependence on Word and Spirit a preacher must experience for power in the pulpit. Furthermore, pastors will find it even easier than it's been to preach sermons not their own. Plagiarism in the pulpit is already rampant. Virtual plagiarism is no less grievous.

Fourth, and finally, courage will require pastors to exercise faith. With a culture increasingly hostile to Christianity, vocational ministry further marginalized, the siren song of AI luring pastors into "fake" ministries, will pastors believe the promises of God are worth it? The courage of faith will look in the face of hostility and trust, "to live is Christ, and to die is gain" (Phil 1:21). The courage of faith will hear the world mocking the ministry and believe, "what does it profit a man to gain the whole world and forfeit his soul? (Mark 8:36). The courage of faith will recognize the seduction of AI and trust, "a day in your courts is better than a thousand elsewhere. I would rather be a doorkeeper in the house of my God than dwell in the tents of wickedness" (Psalm 84:10). The courage of faith will believe that all

Epilogue: The Courage to Be a Pastor

the promises of God find their Yes in Christ (2 Cor 1:20) and will, therefore, treasure him above all things.

You may recall what I wrote in the introduction about the glory of pastoral ministry. I adapted the words of Martyn Lloyd-Jones about preaching and applied them to the pastorate. They bear repeating at the close of this book:

> But, ultimately, my reason for being very ready to write this book is that to me the work of *pastoring* is the highest and greatest and the most glorious calling to which anyone can ever be called. If you want something in addition to that I would say without any hesitation that the most urgent need in the Christian Church today is true *pastors*; and as it is the greatest and most urgent need in the Church, it is obviously the greatest need of the world also.

"The greatest need of the world." This book was written because that statement is not hyperbole. My prayer is that these resolutions will be used not only to reform the pastorate in America, but also as one of the means of God calling an army of men to give their lives in the service of Christ and his church. His name and his bride are worth it. Amen.

Appendix A

Paul's Vision for Ministry and Us
An Exposition of Colossians 1:24–29
Delivered at Southern Seminary and Boyce College Chapel

September 13, 2016

Even as I preach the following message to you from God's Word, I want you to know I am preaching it to myself. We in this room, and those via livestream, are co-laborers in the cause of Christ, and equally in need of a biblical vision for ministry that gives direction to all of our unique callings. I'm very aware that in this room not all of you are, or will be, pastors. But all of us should have a great interest in an apostolic vision for ministry. What is our ministry to the church? Paul outlines it for us, and it is our responsibility for the glory of God and the good of his people, to keep Paul's understanding of ministry ever before us. Because Southern Seminary and Boyce College is a very dangerous place.

Do you feel that this morning? Do you feel what a dangerous place this is? Most of you are here to receive theological education. You will become masters in divinity. That's a dangerous thing. Most of you are here to do that, and Lord willing, you will earn an MA or an MDiv or a DMin or a PhD, and you're taught by men and women, most of whom already have their PhD. Indeed, we are the experts.

The temptations to pride through higher education are legion. Do you feel that this morning? I want you to feel that. After all, no one says the devil

Appendix A

isn't orthodox. We would do well to remember the awful warning of Proverbs 16:18: "Pride goes before destruction, and a haughty spirit before a fall." Some of you know that firsthand. I am convinced that if we see ministry the way the apostle Paul sees ministry, we will be saved from a multitude of sins, not least of which is pride. So my prayer for this sermon is that as we consider Paul's vision for ministry, we would be more determined than ever to see likewise so that we, in our respective ministries, are found faithful. So if you're not there already, would you turn with me to Colossians 1:24–29. And these verses will make up the remainder of our minutes together. Let me read them to get them out before us:

> Now I rejoice in my sufferings for your sake, and in my flesh, I'm filling up what is lacking in Christ's afflictions for the sake of his body, that is, the church, of which I became a minister according to the stewardship from God that was given to me for you, to make the Word of God fully known, the mystery hidden for ages and generations but now revealed to his saints. To them, God chose to make known how great among the Gentiles are the riches of the glory of this mystery, which is Christ in you, the hope of glory. Him we proclaim, warning everyone and teaching everyone with all wisdom, that we may present everyone mature in Christ. For this I toil, struggling with all his energy that He powerfully works within me.

There's a context to this passage, isn't there? The context of our passage, in one important sense, actually begins at the end of the creation narrative, with God looking at all he had created and declaring it "very good." Of course, this good creation would be radically tarnished with sin, given the rebellion of our first parents and the divine curse that ensued. But we know that while the whole creation was subjected by God to futility, it was subjected *in hope* that one day, this whole creation will be set free from its bondage to corruption and obtain the freedom of the glory of the children of God. That's the hope, for we know that the whole creation has been groaning together in the pains of childbirth until now. And not only the creation, but we ourselves, all of us in this room who have the first fruits of the Spirit, we groan inwardly, as we wait eagerly for adoption as sons, the redemption of our bodies, for in this hope we were saved.

Paul is ministering in this hope. That is, this time between the advents of Christ, when God is reconciling the world to himself. And Paul is really taken by the glory of being a part of this ministry. Do you feel that in this letter to the Colossians, how taken he is by how he gets to participate in

Paul's Vision for Ministry and Us

this ministry of reconciliation? Let me help you feel how Paul feels. Look at Colossians 1:19–23, just before our passage. Paul writes,

> For in him all the fullness of God was pleased to dwell, and through him to reconcile to himself all things, whether on earth or in heaven, making peace by the blood of the cross. And you, who once were alienated and hostile in mind, doing evil deeds, he has now reconciled in his body of flesh by his death, in order to present you holy and blameless and above reproach before Him, if indeed you continue in the faith, stable and steadfast, not shifting from the hope of the Gospel that you heard, which has been proclaimed in all creation under heaven, and of which I, Paul, became a servant, became a minister.

Paul is really taken by this. He can't believe he gets to be a part of this redemptive work. It's as if Paul were saying, and I paraphrase, "Indeed, I became a minister of *that* gospel, what I just described to you, the one that takes alienated, hostile, evil-loving sinners and reconciles them to God by the blood of the cross, such that one day, one glorious day, those very sinners are presented to God, holy and blameless and above reproach. That is, made fit for heaven where there is nothing for God's people except fullness of joy, pleasures forevermore at his right hand. I get to be a part of that? Are you kidding me?" No, not kidding. And you too get to be a part of that ministry, that gospel, and its advance around the world.

Now, Paul's going to move from that glorious realization that, "I've been made a minister of this, I get to give all my vital energies to the advance of this gospel that reconciles God to man and man to God," to show us what that looks like. What does that ministry look like, Paul? What we see in this text is that Paul has a radically gospel-driven vision for ministry made up of four distinct convictions. Let's take each one in turn.

First conviction I see from Paul: ministry is suffering. Look with me at verse 24: "Now I rejoice in my sufferings for your sake. And in my flesh, I am filling up what is lacking in Christ's afflictions for the sake of his body, that is, the church."

Now, this is crazy. Who talks like this? Paul is realizing what Jesus said to Ananias. Remember in Acts 9:15–16? Remember the context there? Ananias didn't want to go to this guy, Paul. He kills people, and Jesus said, "You go to him." And he says this to him, "Go, for he is a chosen instrument of mine to carry my name before the Gentiles and kings and the children of Israel, for I will show him how much he must suffer for the sake of my name." Paul is living that out. Jesus said it was going to happen: "I'm going to show him how much he must suffer for the sake of my name." Paul did not see his sufferings, his trials, his afflictions as abnormal, as if something strange were happening to him. On the contrary, Paul understood his sufferings as a means of filling up what is lacking in Christ's afflictions.

But what does that mean, Paul? What is lacking in Christ's afflictions? We bristle at that word "lacking" with respect to Christ's afflictions. Are you saying that Christ's afflictions are deficient in some way, Paul? It almost sounds blasphemous. So what does it mean? In what sense are Christ's afflictions lacking? Because that's what it says. So we have to deal with this. Let me first tell you what it doesn't mean.

Sometimes to get at what something *does* mean, you have to first plow away what it *doesn't* mean. Let me be clear. Paul does not mean that the sufferings of Christ are, in any way, lacking in terms of the atonement. There is no expiatory deficiency in Christ's afflictions. This would undermine the whole message of Colossians and the rest of the Bible, with its emphasis on the sufficiency of Christ's person and work for salvation. Consider right here in our letter, Colossians 2:13–14. Listen to the sufficiency of Christ's person and work for salvation: "And you, who were dead in your trespasses, God made alive together with him, having forgiven us all our trespasses, by canceling the record of debt that stood against us with its legal demands. This he set aside, nailing it to the cross." The cross is sufficient for atonement, for forgiveness of sins, for putting them away. And consider Hebrews 9:26, "But as it is, Christ appeared once for all at the end of the ages to put away sin by the sacrifice of himself." Nothing lacking in the cross of Christ for salvation, for atonement, for the putting away of sin. Indeed, Christ himself declared, with dying breath, "It is finished." Nothing left to do.

So if there is nothing lacking in the cross, what's lacking in Christ's afflictions? Because, again, that's what Paul says: "I'm filling up what is lacking in Christ's afflictions." I'm helped here by New Testament scholar James Dunn. I'm helped here because he points to the way Paul uses this very phrase in Philippians 2:30, in reference to Epaphroditus. Do you remember Epaphroditus? Paul's commending him to the Philippians, saying, "I'm going to send him back to you. So receive him in the Lord with all joy, and honor such men." Here's verse 30: "For he nearly died for the work of Christ, risking his life to complete what was lacking in your service to me." (Same phrase, "complete what is lacking in your service to me.") What does he mean?

The Philippians loved Paul, and wanted to help him with a tangible gift of support. There was nothing lacking in their love for Paul, except the expression of it in the giving of a gift. Enter Epaphroditus, as the "suffering to the point of death" expression of the Philippians' love for Paul. Nothing lacking in the Philippian church's love for Paul except the *expression* of that love. "We're going to give you a gift, Paul. We want to help you in a very tangible way. So we're going to send Epaphroditus." And Epaphroditus nearly died in filling up what was lacking in the love of the Philippian church for Paul.

This, I believe, is exactly how Paul saw his sufferings: as the display of the saving sufferings of Christ for his people. That's what is lacking in Christ's afflictions, the display of them to the world and the expression of them to the Colossians. This interpretation helps us understand passages where Paul talks so otherworldly, so radically, like 2 Corinthians 4:7–10. Listen to the connection between his sufferings and the gospel of Jesus Christ advancing:

> But we have this treasure in jars of clay, to show that the surpassing power belongs to God and not to us. We are afflicted in every way, but not crushed; perplexed, but not driven to despair; persecuted, but not forsaken; struck down, but not destroyed; always carrying in the body the death of Jesus, so that the life of Jesus may also be manifested in our bodies. For we who live are always being given over to death for Jesus's sake, so that the life of Jesus also may be manifested in our mortal flesh. So death is at work in us, but life in you.

"Our suffering lives," Paul in essence says, "are the expression of the saving sufferings of Christ on the cross for all those who would believe. See his life in me, in my suffering. My hope is in this Christ, the one who suffered for me and for all those who would believe." It's Romans 8:36, isn't it, where Paul says, "As it is written, 'For your sake we are being killed all the day long. We are regarded as sheep to be slaughtered.'" Why? So that you can see the suffering, saving work of Jesus in us for you.

Paul sees ministry as suffering for the sake of Christ and his redemptive purpose for the world, a suffering to be shared by all of God's people. Now, I'm going to draw this out for us. This is a suffering that we don't leave for Paul, but it is for all of God's people, this side of heaven. Isn't this the call of discipleship by our Lord in Mark 8:34? He calls to the crowd and says,

Appendix A

"If anyone will come after me, let him deny himself, take up his cross, and follow me."

That's what it means to be a Christian. Take up your cross. What's a cross? An emblem of suffering and shame. That's what you're called to, Christian. It's Philippians 1:29–30, where Paul writes, "For it has been granted to you that for the sake of Christ, you not only believe in him, but also suffer for his namesake, experiencing the same conflict you saw I had and now hear I still have." It is a grace for us not only to believe in Jesus, but to suffer for the advance of his gospel around the world. It's 2 Timothy 1:8: "Therefore, do not be ashamed of the testimony about our Lord, nor of me his prisoner, but share, Timothy, in suffering for the Gospel by the power of God." Do this, Timothy. Share in it. Embrace it. It's the call of a Christian.

Later in that same epistle, he says again to Timothy: "Share in suffering as a good soldier of Jesus Christ." This is a call to God's people. God has ordained that his gospel will advance around the world through his triumphant, yes, and suffering church. It is a triumphant and suffering church. And in the infinite wisdom of God, that's what he has ordained. That's how it's going to be. It's not optional.

Now, friends, I could take a minute or two or more and try to rehearse for you the suffering of God's people all around the world and the advance of the gospel coinciding with it. But let me bring it closer to home. I've seen the power of this truth in my own life. I've witnessed it firsthand. My late wife Julia ministered in Bellingham, Washington, as a pastor's wife with stage 4 breast cancer, faithfully, winsomely, powerfully, until the last two months of her life when she couldn't minister any more. I don't have time to rehearse for you the ministries she began, the countless hours of fellowship with people after the service, praying with people, knowing that the next day, she'll spend six hours hooked up to a chemo drip. But I saw a church rise up. I saw people recalibrate their lives around the gospel. I saw them look at my wife and hear her testimony of, "My hope is built on nothing less than Jesus' blood and righteousness." And I saw people say, "Come, Jesus, be more real in my life." I saw marriages strengthened. I saw people come back to church because they heard of this testimony of one who was suffering, carrying about in her body the death of Jesus, so that the life of Jesus would be made manifest. I've seen this reality in my own life, and it's true, based on the authority of God's Word and what I have seen as a result of it.

Oh, brothers and sisters, take heart that your suffering for the sake of Christ and his church is not in vain, but is designed by God for the advance of the gospel among you. He has great redemptive purposes for your suffering. That's conviction number one, and I have four.

Conviction number two: ministry is a stewardship. It's not only suffering, it's a stewardship. Look with me at verse 25: "I became a minister according to the stewardship from God that was given to me for you, to make the Word of God fully known." Stop right there. It's a stewardship. I'm a minister of this gospel according to, by virtue of, a stewardship God Almighty has given to me. We need to make much of this word *stewardship*.

Paul knew he was called to be an apostle to the Gentiles, to fulfill a unique role in salvation history. "A mystery," Paul says, had been "hidden for ages and generations, but now has been revealed, Christ in you, the hope of glory." Union with the living God by grace alone, through faith alone, in Christ alone, that has now been revealed to the world, and Paul saw himself as a steward of this great reality. In 1 Corinthians 4:1, he says, similarly, "This is how one should regard us, as servants of Christ and stewards of the mysteries of God." We're stewarding something glorious, the mysteries of God. In other words, Paul saw himself as a caretaker of this glorious gospel. Unlike Paul, now we do not fulfill the office of apostle, but like Paul, we are stewards of the grace of God in Christ. Our ministry to the church is a stewardship from God, to make the Word of God fully known.

Do you feel that this morning, as you're training to be a pastor perhaps or a preacher, any kind of vocational minister? Do you realize you've been given a stewardship, and we're to care for it? Well, now, there are at least two important, very important, implications of seeing ministry as a stewardship. Let me try to set them out for your consideration.

First, understanding our ministry as a stewardship of God's grace is a great motivator in our work and will move us to strive for excellence in all we do. We are not peddlers of wares. Do you realize this? Do you have an idea of what you're stewarding? Not peddlers of wares, but stewards of the glories of God in Christ. Nothing less, nothing greater. Therefore, we ought to work harder than all the rest and set standards for our ministry that are so lofty, so unbelievably high that, apart from Christ, we'll never reach them. Do you have standards that high for yourself and for your ministry? All this is is 1 Corinthians 10:31, right? "So whether you eat or drink or write book reviews or research papers or parse verbs or preach, or whatever you do, do everything to the glory of God." In other words, do everything consistent with his majesty, with his glory, with his perfections.

That's the call, everything. Even the things that the world might say are mundane, do it that God might be shown to be great in your life. Standards of excellence, brother. Do not coast at seminary. Do not wake up late. Do not skirt your reading. Do not bang out a research paper in one night. You're stewarding the glories of God in Christ with that fifteen-page paper. God help us to not be mediocre for the glory of your great Name.

Second, if we understand our ministry as stewards, this will keep us out of the spotlight, won't it? Oh, and it needs to! If I'm a steward of the glories of God in Christ, then it's not about *me*. It's not about *you*. We are caretakers, not of our reputation or image or fame or platform (a word I hate). No. We are stewards of the glories of God in Christ. So we agree with Paul in 2 Corinthians 4:5 when he says, "For we proclaim not ourselves, but Jesus Christ as Lord, with ourselves as your servants for Jesus' sake." Too many professing believers proclaim self in this digital age. We need to see our ministries as a stewardship of God's reputation, his fame.

Conviction number three: ministry is proclamation. Look with me at verse 28: "Him we proclaim, warning everyone and teaching everyone with all wisdom, that we may present everyone mature in Christ." As ministers, we engage in a great work of proclamation. The word literally means "to announce" or "herald" or "proclaim." Therefore, more than conversationalists, we are heralds of good news.

Isn't this how Jesus talked? He was commissioning his disciple in Matthew 10:7, and he says, "And proclaim as you go." He doesn't say, "Talk as you go" or "share as you go" or "converse as you go." No. That's not what he says. "Proclaim as you go, saying, 'The kingdom of heaven is at hand.'" That's news worth declaring. Later in Matthew 10, [he] says it again, "What I tell you in the dark, say in the light, and what you hear whispered, proclaim on the housetops." Get up on that roof and proclaim, "Jesus is Lord and Savior. Why should you perish?" That's news worth heralding. The very nature of the gospel calls for more than mere talk.

Yesterday in the mail, as God would have it, I received a big flyer, a brochure-type thing. New church plant coming out to the suburbs, going to be meeting in a movie theater. Isn't that great? Popcorn and Christ. I don't know how it's going to work. But meeting out there in a movie theater, and it lists the things on the flyer one should expect. We do that on our websites. We do that at church. What to expect when you come. First thing listed was "a casual environment."

Paul's Vision for Ministry and Us

Second, "Our band will play a couple songs." Now the third bullet point really got my attention. I was going to throw it away, and then I got interested, because I read this: "Easy-to-understand talk based on the Bible." I roll this over in my mind—"An easy-to-understand talk based on the Bible." (I'm preparing for this morning, so I'm reading that, going, "Are you kidding me?") And then I thought, "Okay. Most charitable reading on that is, 'Look, they're just saying 'talk,' but what they really mean is preaching." But if that's true, it's actually worse. That doesn't help the problem because now they're just being deceptive.

This is the gospel of Jesus Christ, and it demands, by its very nature, more than mere talk. We proclaim Christ because he is the fulfillment of God's promised Messiah. He is the Lamb of God who takes away the sin of the world, the one to whom the whole Old Testament points. Jesus is the end of the law for righteousness, so we proclaim him. He is the perfect sacrifice for sin, so we proclaim him. In Jesus are hidden all the treasures of wisdom and knowledge, so we proclaim him. In him, all the fullness of deity dwells bodily, so we proclaim him. Jesus is the radiance of the glory of God and the exact imprint of his nature. Through him, all things were created and are, even now as I preach, upheld by the Word of his power in Christ. And through his blood, God and man are reconciled. We proclaim Jesus because there's salvation in no one else, for there's no other name under heaven given among men by which we must be saved. The gospel of Jesus Christ is of infinite worth. Therefore, him we proclaim.

Now, notice, as we stay here with this third conviction, I'm a preaching professor, so I have to linger here and show you the purpose of our proclamation. Do you see it? This should blow your minds pastors, Christians. What's the purpose of our proclamation? In this text, what is Paul saying happens as a result of our proclaiming Christ? "That we may present everyone mature in Christ." Wow. Really? Through preaching? Through proclamation? People are going to be built up in Christ? Wait, I thought preaching was just for conversions? Not according to Paul. We proclaim Jesus so that we may present everyone mature in Christ. This proclamation by God's grace has transforming power.

Proclaiming Christ is not only the means of awakening the unconverted, but also the means of getting the converted to glory. You see that here in the text. Contrary to what some pastors might argue, one of the great means of discipleship in the church is proclamation. You want a program for making disciples? So did Timothy. He said, "Paul, I need a

Appendix A

program. They're killing me here in Ephesus. They want me to have some kind of program. I don't have one. They want to be discipled. What do I do?" You know what he said to him? "Preach the Word. Preach the Word. You be ready, Timothy, in season and out of season to preach the Word of God, and as you do that you're going to build them up in the faith." You want a program for making disciples? You preach the Word. Now, that's not the only thing we do, but it's the main thing. Preach the Word. Oh God, would you reform our pulpits around the world today so that our time will be written about as a golden age of preaching, when your church was strengthened through expository pulpits! Perhaps more than ever, we need to privilege proclamation in the church. We need to privilege it. Not apologize for it, not devalue it, but privilege it. Privilege proclamation.

One of our forefathers here at this school, John Broadus, believed this. I'm gripped by the opening pages of his excellent work *On the Preparation and Delivery of Sermons*, his lecture notes put in book form, first published in 1870. Listen to what he says about preaching compared to the written Word:

> The great appointed means of spreading the good tidings of salvation through Christ is preaching, words spoken, whether to the individual or to the assembly. And this, nothing can supersede. Nothing. Printing has become a mighty agency for good and for evil, and Christians should employ it with the utmost diligence and in every possible way for the spread of the truth. But printing can never take the place of the living word. When a man who is apt in teaching, whose soul is on fire with the truth which he trusts has saved him and hopes will save others, when that man speaks to his fellow men, face to face, eye to eye, and electric sympathies flash to and fro between him and his hearers, till they lift each other up, higher and higher, into the most intense thought and the most impassioned emotion, higher and higher, till they are borne as on chariots of fire above the world, when that happens through preaching and the power of the Holy Spirit, there is a power to move men, to influence character, life, destiny, such as no printed page can ever possess.

I stand with Broadus. By God's ordination, there is a peculiar glory to the proclamation of the gospel, a glory that the printed word does not possess. That said, work hard to be better writers. Strive for more clear, winsome prose, but not as an end in itself, but for the better proclamation of the gospel. To turn a phrase from the German Reformer Martin Luther, "Oh, if

Paul's Vision for Ministry and Us

I could today become the author of 10,000 books, I would not give up my office of preacher!"

Fourth conviction: not only does Paul see ministry as suffering, as a stewardship, and as proclamation, but Paul sees ministry as dependence. Look with me at verse 29: "For this I toil, struggling with all his energy that He powerfully works within me." This is gospel hope for us that should inspire us to be the kind of ministers Paul describes!

Paul doesn't take anything away. He says, "That's the vision. That's what you're to do, but you don't do it in your own strength." The word translated toil, do you see that? "For this I *toil*." You might have "for this I labor." This word literally means "to labor to the point of exhaustion." Paul is saying, "I spend myself. I'm so tired at the end of the day. I've got nothing left. I've just laid my life down this day for the gospel, and I'm done. I'm done." He wasn't craving leisure or quiet time. Paul has no patience for a lazy minister. He calls us to spend ourselves for Christ and his church. Elsewhere he'll say stuff like, "I worked harder than all of them." Right? He's boasting in the Lord, saying, "I've worked harder. No one outworks me." Can that be said of you? Is that your aim? "No one's going to outwork me here on this campus." Make that your goal. No one's going to outwork you. You're going to work harder than all of them.

But then finish the verse in 1 Corinthians 15:10: "Yet not I, but the grace of God within me." The vision Paul has for ministry is impossible to fulfill in the flesh. That's right. He sets something before us—a vision for ministry—that is absolutely impossible to attain apart from Christ. But here's the good news. This is gospel hope. What God calls us to, he equips us for.

We toil and struggle for the sake of Christ and his people, but we do it with his energy that he powerfully works within us. Now, why did God set it up this way? Why did he create, by definition, a ministry of dependence, not on self, but on him? Why would God do this? God, I believe, set it up this way so that we get all the help we need, and he gets all the glory. He will get all the glory in our ministries. And if we bring any of our own energy to the table as if it's doing something, we get some glory. "Oh, I worked hard." Paul's really quick to guard himself against that kind of thinking by saying, "Yet not I, not I, but the grace of God within me. Oh, yeah, I worked harder than all of them, but no glory to me. All glory to God. It's *his* energy that's working so powerfully within me, that allows me to spend everything I've got for the gospel."

Appendix A

This helps makes sense of 2 Corinthians 4:7: "But we have this treasure in jars of clay." Why are we these jars of clay, these broken, weak vessels? Why is ministry happening through us? To show that the surpassing power belongs to God and not to us. Not to us, oh Lord, but to your name. It's 1 Peter 4:11, "Whoever serves, as one who serves by the strength that God supplies, in order that in everything God may be glorified through Jesus Christ." It is a ministry of dependence.

What a blessing to serve you during your time at Southern Seminary and Boyce College as you train to become more faithful ministers of the glorious gospel of Jesus Christ. There is no greater calling. So my prayer for you (and myself) is that in these days, months, and years to come, you would *suffer well* for the gospel, that you would *steward faithfully* the gospel, that you would *boldly proclaim* the gospel, and that you would do it all in the very *strength of God* so that you get all the help you need and God gets all the glory due his matchless name.

Appendix B

An Excerpt from the Second Helvetic Confession (1566)

The Duties of Ministers

THE DUTIES OF MINISTERS are various; yet for the most part they are restricted to two, in which all the rest are comprehended: to the teaching of the Gospel of Christ, and to the proper administration of the sacraments. For it is the duty of the ministers to gather together an assembly for worship in which to expound God's Word and to apply the whole doctrine to the care and use of the Church, so that what is taught may benefit the hearers and edify the faithful. It falls to ministers, I say, to teach the ignorant, and to exhort; and to urge the idlers and lingerers to make progress in the way of the Lord. Moreover, they are to comfort and to strengthen the fainthearted, and to arm them against the manifold temptations of Satan; to rebuke offenders; to recall the erring into the way; to raise the fallen; to convince the gainsayers; to drive the wolf away from the sheepfold of the Lord; to rebuke wickedness and wicked men wisely and severely; not to wink at nor to pass over great wickedness. And, besides, they are to administer the sacraments, and to commend the right use of them, and to prepare all men by wholesome doctrine to receive them; to preserve the faithful in a holy unity; and to check schisms; to catechize the unlearned, to commend the needs of the poor to the Church, to visit, instruct, and keep in the way of life the sick

Appendix B

and those afflicted with various temptations. In addition, they are to attend to public prayers of supplications in times of need, together with common fasting, that is, a holy abstinence; and as diligently as possible to see to everything that pertains to the tranquility, peace and welfare of the churches.

But in order that the minister may perform all these things better and more easily, it is especially required of him that he fear God, be constant in prayer, attend to spiritual reading, and in all things and at all times be watchful, and by a purity of life to let his light to shine before all men.[1]

---

1. In chap. 18, "Of the Ministers of the Church, Their Institution and Duties."

Appendix C

A Minister's Prayer

O MY LORD,

Let not my ministry be approved only by men,
    or merely win the esteem and affections
      of people;
But do the work of grace in their hearts,
  call in thy elect,
  seal and edify the regenerate ones,
  and command eternal blessings on their souls.
Save me from self-opinion and self-seeking;
Water the hearts of those who hear thy Word,
  that seed sown in weakness may be raised
    in power;
Cause me and those that hear me
  to behold thee here in the light of special faith,
  and hereafter in the blaze of endless glory;
Make my every sermon a means of grace to myself,
  and help me to experience the power
    of thy dying love,
  for thy blood is balm,
    thy presence bliss,
    thy smile heaven,
    thy cross the place where truth
      and mercy meet.
Look upon the doubts and discouragements
  of my ministry

Appendix C

and keep me from self-importance;
I beg pardon for my many sins, omissions,
   infirmities,
   as a man, as a minister;
Command thy blessing on my weak,
   unworthy labours,
   and on the message of salvation given;
Stay with thy people,
   and may thy presence be their portion
   and mine.
   When I preach to others let not my words
   be merely elegant and masterly,
   my reasoning polished and refined,
   my performance powerless and tasteless,
   but may I exalt thee and humble sinners.
O Lord of power and grace,
   all hearts are in thy hands,
   all events at thy disposal,
Set the seal of thy almighty will
   upon my ministry.[1]

---

1. *The Valley of Vision*, 338–39.

Bibliography

Adam, Peter. *Speaking God's Words: A Practical Theology of Preaching*. Vancouver, BC: Regent College, 2004.
Allen, Lewis. *The Preacher's Catechism*. Wheaton, IL: Crossway, 2018.
Alter, Adam. *Irresistible: The Rise of Addictive Technology and the Business of Keeping Us Hooked*. New York: Penguin, 2018.
Augustine. *Confessions*. Translated by Sarah Ruden. New York: Modern Library, 2017.
———. *On Christian Teaching*. Translated by R. P. H. Green. Oxford: Oxford University Press, 2008.
Bavinck, Herman. *Guidebook for Instruction in the Christian Religion*. Edited by Cameron Clausing. Translated by Gregory Parker. Peabody, MA: Hendrickson Academic, 2022.
———. *Reformed Dogmatics*. Vol. 4, *Holy Spirit, Church, and New Creation*. Edited by John Bolt. Translated by John Vriend. Grand Rapids: Baker Academic, 2003.
———. *The Wonderful Works of God: Instruction in the Christian Religion According to the Reformed Confession*. Translated by Henry Zylstra. Glenside, PA: Westminster Seminary Press, 2019.
Baxter, Richard. *The Reformed Pastor*. Puritan Paperbacks. Carlisle, PA: Banner of Truth, 1974.
———. *The Reformed Pastor: Updated and Abridged*. Edited by Tim Cooper. Wheaton, IL: Crossway, 2021.
Beeke, Joel R. *Living for God's Glory: An Introduction to Calvinism*. Lake Mary, FL: Reformation Trust, 2008.
Beeke, Joel R., and Sinclair B. Ferguson, eds. *Reformed Confessions Harmonized*. Grand Rapids: Baker, 1999.
Bennett, Arthur, ed. *The Valley of Vision: A Collection of Puritan Prayers & Devotions*. Edinburgh: Banner of Truth, 1975.
Bolsinger, Tod E. *Canoeing the Mountains: Christian Leadership in Uncharted Territory*. Exp. ed. Downers Grove, IL: InterVarsity, 2018.
Bonar, Andrew. *Memoir and Remains of Robert Murray M'Cheyne*. Edinburgh: Banner of Truth, 1973.
Bowler, Kate. *Blessed: A History of the American Prosperity Gospel*. New York: Oxford University Press, 2018.
Brakel, Wilhelmus à. *The Christian's Reasonable Service: In Which Divine Truths Concerning the Covenant of Grace Are Expounded, Defended against Opposing Parties, and Their Practice Advocated, as Well as the Administration of This Covenant in the Old and New Testaments*. Edited by Bartel Elshout and Joel R. Beeke. Vol. 2. Grand Rapids: Reformation Heritage, 1992.

Bibliography

Brenneman, Todd M. *Homespun Gospel: The Triumph of Sentimentality in Contemporary American Evangelicalism*. New York: Oxford, 2014.

Bridges, Charles. *The Christian Ministry: With an Inquiry into the Causes of Its Inefficiency*. Edinburgh: Banner of Truth, 1976.

Bullinger, Henry. *The Decades of Henry Bullinger*. 2 vols. Grand Rapids: Reformation Heritage, 2021.

Bunyan, John. *Prayer*. Puritan Paperbacks. Carlisle, PA: Banner of Truth, 1965.

Calvin, John. *Calvin's Commentaries*. Edited by Henry Beveridge. Translated by William Pringle. Grand Rapids: Baker, 2009.

———. *Calvin's Institutes: A New Compend*. Edited by Hugh T. Kerr. Louisville: Westminster/John Knox, 1989.

———. *Institutes of the Christian Religion*. Edited by John T. McNeill. Translated by Ford Lewis Battles. 2 vols. Library of Christian Classics. Philadelphia: Westminster Press, 1960.

———. *Institutes of the Christian Religion*. Edited by A. N. S. Lane and Hilary Osborne. Grand Rapids: Baker, 1987.

———. *On the Christian Life: A New Translation*. Edited by A. N. S. Lane. Translated by Raymond Andrew Blacketer. Wheaton, IL: Crossway, 2024.

———. *Sermons on Second Timothy*. Translated by Robert White. Carlisle, PA: Banner of Truth, 2018.

Carr, Nicholas G. *The Shallows: What the Internet Is Doing to Our Brains*. New York: W. W. Norton, 2020.

Chapell, Bryan. *Christ-Centered Preaching: Redeeming the Expository Sermon*. 3rd ed. Grand Rapids: Baker Academic, 2018.

Clowney, Edmund P. *The Church*. Contours of Christian Theology. Downers Grove, IL: InterVarsity, 1995.

Comer, John Mark. *The Ruthless Elimination of Hurry*. Colorado Springs: WaterBrook, 2019.

Dawn, Marva J. *In the Beginning, GOD: Creation, Culture, and the Spiritual Life*. Downers Grove, IL: IVP, 2009.

Dever, Mark. *Nine Marks of a Healthy Church*. 4th ed. Wheaton, IL: Crossway, 2021.

Edwards, William R., John C. A. Ferguson, and Chad B. Van Dixhoorn, eds. *Theology for Ministry: How Doctrine Affects Pastoral Life and Practice*. Phillipsburg, NJ: P&R, 2022.

Ellul, Jacques. *The Technological Society: A Penetrating Analysis of Our Technical Civilization and of the Effect of an Increasingly Standardized Culture on the Future of Man*. Translated by John Wilkinson. New York: Vintage, 2011.

Feinberg, John S. *Light in a Dark Place: The Doctrine of Scripture*. Wheaton, IL: Crossway, 2018.

Ferguson, Sinclair B. *Children of the Living God*. Carlisle, PA: Banner of Truth, 1989.

———. *Some Pastors and Teachers: Reflecting a Biblical Vision of What Every Minister Is Called to Be*. Edinburgh: Banner of Truth, 2017.

Frame, John M. *Concise Systematic Theology: An Introduction to Christian Belief*. Edited by John J. Hughes. Phillipsburg, NJ: P&R, 2023.

———. *The Doctrine of the Word of God*. Theology of Lordship 4. Phillipsburg, NJ: P&R, 2010.

———. *Systematic Theology: An Introduction to Christian Belief*. Phillipsburg, NJ: P&R, 2013.

Bibliography

Freitas, Donna. *The Happiness Effect: How Social Media Is Driving a Generation to Appear Perfect at Any Cost*. New York: Oxford University Press, 2019.

George, Timothy. *Theology of the Reformers*. Nashville: B&H, 1988.

Gibson, David, and Jonathan Gibson, eds. *Ruined Sinners to Reclaim: Sin and Depravity in Historical, Biblical, Theological, and Pastoral Perspective*. Wheaton, IL: Crossway, 2024.

Gordon, T. David. *Why Johnny Can't Preach: The Media Have Shaped the Messengers*. Phillipsburg, NJ: P&R, 2009.

Groeschel, Craig. *It: How Churches and Leaders Can Get It and Keep It*. Grand Rapids: Zondervan, 2008.

Grudem, Wayne A. *Bible Doctrine: Essential Teachings of the Christian Faith*. Edited by Jeff Purswell. Grand Rapids: Zondervan, 1999.

———. *Bible Doctrine: Essential Teachings of the Christian Faith*. Edited by Alexander Grudem. 2nd ed. Grand Rapids: Zondervan, 2022.

———. *Systematic Theology: An Introduction to Biblical Doctrine*. 2nd ed. Grand Rapids: Zondervan Academic, 2020.

Guthrie, George H. *2 Corinthians*. Baker Exegetical Commentary on the New Testament. Grand Rapids: Baker, 2015.

Haidt, Jonathan. *The Anxious Generation: How the Great Rewiring of Childhood Is Causing an Epidemic of Mental Illness*. New York: Penguin, 2024.

Harris, Murray J. *The Second Epistle to the Corinthians: A Commentary on the Greek Text*. New International Greek Testament Commentary. Grand Rapids: Eerdmans, 2005.

Harvey, David T. *Am I Called? The Summons to Pastoral Ministry*. Wheaton, IL: Crossway, 2012.

Hatch, Nathan O. *The Democratization of American Christianity*. New Haven, CT: Yale, 1989.

Hedges, Brian G. *Christ Formed in You: The Power of the Gospel for Personal Change*. Wapwallopen, PA: Shepherd, 2010.

Hendriksen, William. *Exposition of the Gospel According to Luke*. Grand Rapids: Baker, 1983.

Hiestand, Gerald, and Todd Wilson. *The Pastor Theologian: Resurrecting an Ancient Vision*. Grand Rapids: Zondervan, 2015.

Hodge, Charles. *A Commentary on Romans*. Carlisle, PA: Banner of Truth, 1986.

———. *Systematic Theology*. Peabody, MA: Hendrickson, 2003.

Hoekema, Anthony A. *Created in God's Image*. Grand Rapids: Eerdmans, 1986.

Holifield, E. Brooks. *God's Ambassadors: A History of the Christian Clergy in America*. Grand Rapids: Eerdmans, 2007.

Honoré, Carl. *In Praise of Slowness: Challenging the Cult of Speed*. New York: Harper One, 2005.

Horton, Michael Scott. *Christless Christianity: The Alternative Gospel of the American Church*. Grand Rapids: Baker, 2012.

———. *The Christian Faith: A Systematic Theology for Pilgrims on the Way*. Grand Rapids: Zondervan, 2011.

———, ed. *A Confessing Theology for Postmodern Times*. Wheaton, IL: Crossway, 2000.

———. *The Gospel Commission: Recovering God's Strategy for Making Disciples*. Grand Rapids: Baker, 2011.

———. *The Gospel-Driven Life: Being Good News People in a Bad News World*. Grand Rapids: Baker, 2012.

Bibliography

———. *Pilgrim Theology: Core Doctrines for Christian Disciples*. Grand Rapids: Zondervan, 2011.

———. *A Place for Weakness: Preparing Yourself for Suffering*. Grand Rapids: Zondervan, 2006.

Jamieson, Bobby. *The Path to Being a Pastor: A Guide for the Aspiring*. Wheaton, IL: Crossway, 2021.

Kauflin, Jordan. "All I Have Is Christ," © 2008 Sovereign Grace Praise/BMI (adm. by Integrity Music).

Kistemaker, Simon J. *Exposition of James, Epistles of John, Peter, and Jude*. New Testament Commentary. Grand Rapids: Baker Academic, 1987.

Leeman, Jonathan. *Church Discipline: How the Church Protects the Name of Jesus*. Wheaton, IL: Crossway, 2012.

Lindberg, Carter, ed. *The European Reformations Sourcebook*. 2nd ed. Malden, MA: Wiley Blackwell, 2014.

Lloyd-Jones, David Martyn. *Preaching and Preachers*. Grand Rapids: Zondervan, 1972.

———. *Preaching and Preachers*. 40th anniversary ed. Grand Rapids: Zondervan, 2011.

Logan, Samuel T., ed. *The Preacher and Preaching: Reviving the Art in the Twentieth Century*. Phillipsburg, NJ: P&R, 2011.

Luther, Martin. *Luther's Works*. Vol. 51, *Sermons 1*. Edited by John W. Doberstein and Helmut T. Lehmann. Translated by John W. Doberstein. American ed. St. Louis: Concordia, 1959.

———. *What Luther Says*. Edited by Ewald M. Plass. St. Louis: Concordia, 2006.

Marshall, Colin, and Tony Payne. *The Trellis and the Vine: The Ministry Mind-Shift That Changes Everything*. Kingsford, Australia: Matthias Media, 2009.

Martin, Albert N. *The Man of God: His Calling and Godly Life*. Pastoral Theology. Montville, NJ: Trinity Pulpit, 2018.

Master, Jonathan L. *Reformed Theology*. Phillipsburg, NJ: P&R, 2023.

Mastricht, Peter van. *Theoretical-Practical Theology*. Vol. 3, *The Works of God and the Fall of Man*. Grand Rapids: Reformation Heritage, 2018.

McLuhan, Marshall. *Understanding Media: The Extensions of Man*. Cambridge: Massachusetts Institute of Technology Press, 1994.

Mohler, R. Albert, Jr. *The Gathering Storm: Secularism, Culture, and the Church*. Nashville: Thomas Nelson, 2020.

Moo, Douglas J. *The Letter to the Romans*. 2nd ed. New International Commentary on the New Testament. Grand Rapids: Eerdmans, 2018.

Morris, Leon. *The Epistle to the Romans*. Grand Rapids: Eerdmans, 1994.

Mounce, William D. *The Analytical Lexicon to the Greek New Testament*. Grand Rapids: Zondervan, 1993.

———, ed. *Mounce's Complete Expository Dictionary of Old and New Testament Words*. Grand Rapids: Zondervan, 2006.

Murray, John. *The Epistle to the Romans*. Glenside, PA: Westminster Seminary Press, 2022.

Newport, Cal. *Deep Work: Rules for Focused Success in a Distracted World*. New York: Grand Central, 2016.

Ortlund, Gavin. *Theological Retrieval for Evangelicals: Why We Need Our Past to Have a Future*. Wheaton, IL: Crossway, 2019.

Owen, John. *Complete Works of John Owen*. Vol. 15, *Sin and Temptation*. Edited by Kelly M. Kapic, Justin Taylor, and Shawn D. Wright. Wheaton, IL: Crossway, 2023.

Bibliography

———. *Sin and Temptation: The Challenge to Personal Godliness*. Edited by J. M. Houston. Vancouver, BC: Regent College, 1983.

———. *Works of John Owen*. Vol. 3, *The Holy Spirit*. Carlisle, PA: Banner of Truth, 2000.

———. *Works of John Owen*. Vol. 6, *Temptation and Sin*. Carlisle, PA: Banner of Truth, 2004.

Packer, J. I. *Concise Theology: A Guide to Historic Christian Beliefs*. Wheaton, IL: Tyndale House, 1993.

———. *Concise Theology*. Wheaton, IL: Crossway, 2020.

———. *A Quest for Godliness: The Puritan Vision of the Christian Life*. Wheaton, IL: Crossway, 1994.

Parker, T. H. L. *Calvin's Preaching*. Louisville: Westminster/John Knox, 1992.

Piper, John. *Let the Nations Be Glad! The Supremacy of God in Missions*. Grand Rapids: Baker, 1993.

———. *This Momentary Marriage: A Parable of Permanence*. Wheaton, IL: Crossway, 2012.

———. *The Supremacy of God in Preaching*. Rev. and exp. ed. Grand Rapids: Baker, 2015.

Pohlman, Michael E. *Broadcasting the Faith: Protestant Religious Radio and Theology in America, 1920–50*. Eugene, OR: Wipf and Stock, 2021.

Postman, Neil. *Amusing Ourselves to Death: Public Discourse in the Age of Show Business*. New York: Penguin, 2006.

———. *Technopoly: The Surrender of Culture to Technology*. New York: Vintage, 1993.

Powell, Kara Eckmann. *Growing Young: Six Essential Strategies to Help Young People Discover and Love Your Church*. Grand Rapids: Baker, 2016.

Prime, Derek, and Alistair Begg. *On Being a Pastor: Understanding Our Calling and Work*. Chicago: Moody, 2013.

Rainer, Thom S. *Autopsy of a Deceased Church: Twelve Ways to Keep Yours Alive*. Nashville: B&H, 2014.

Rainer, Thom S., and Jess W. Rainer. *The Millennials: Connecting to America's Largest Generation*. Nashville: B&H, 2011.

Renn, Aaron M. *Life in the Negative World: Confronting Challenges in an Anti-Christian Culture*. Grand Rapids: Zondervan, 2024.

Robinson, Haddon W. *Biblical Preaching: The Development and Delivery of Expository Messages*. Grand Rapids: Baker Academic, 2014.

Ryle, J. C. *Practical Religion: Being Plain Papers on the Daily Duties, Experience, Dangers, and Privileges of Professing Christians*. Edinburgh: Banner of Truth, 2013.

Sayers, Mark. *Facing Leviathan: Leadership, Influence, and Creating in a Cultural Storm*. Chicago: Moody, 2014.

Scroggins, Clay. *How to Lead in a World of Distraction: Four Simple Habits for Turning Down the Noise*. Nashville: Zondervan, 2019.

Scruton, Roger. *The Meaning of Conservatism*. Rev. 3rd ed. South Bend, IN: St. Augustine's Press, 2013.

Seifrid, Mark A. *The Second Letter to the Corinthians*. Pillar New Testament Commentary. Grand Rapids: Eerdmans, 2014.

Silva, Moisés, ed. *New International Dictionary of New Testament Theology and Exegesis*. 2nd ed. Grand Rapids: Zondervan, 2014.

Sproul, R. C. *Chosen by God*. Carol Stream, IL: Tyndale House, 2010.

———. *Essential Truths of the Christian Faith*. Carol Stream, IL: Tyndale House, 1992.

———. *The Holiness of God*. 2nd ed. Carol Stream, IL: Tyndale House, 2006.

Bibliography

Spurgeon, C. H. *Lectures to My Students*. Fearn, Scotland: Christian Heritage, 1998.

Stanley, Andy. *Deep and Wide: Creating Churches Unchurched People Love to Attend*. Grand Rapids: Zondervan, 2016.

Stewart, James S. *Heralds of God: A Practical Book on Preaching*. Vancouver, BC: Regent College Press, 2001.

Stott, John R. W. *Between Two Worlds: The Challenge of Preaching Today*. Grand Rapids: Eerdmans, 2017.

Trueman, Carl R. *Crisis of Confidence: Reclaiming the Historic Faith in a Culture Consumed with Individualism and Identity*. Wheaton, IL: Crossway, 2024.

———. *The Rise and Triumph of the Modern Self: Cultural Amnesia, Expressive Individualism, and the Road to Sexual Revolution*. Wheaton, IL: Crossway, 2020.

Turkle, Sherry. *Alone Together: Why We Expect More from Technology and Less from Each Other*. New York: Basic Books, 2017.

———. *Reclaiming Conversation: The Power of Talk in a Digital Age*. New York: Penguin, 2015.

Twenge, Jean M. *Generations: The Real Differences between Gen Z, Millennials, Gen X, Boomers, and Silents—and What They Mean for America's Future*. New York: Atria Books, 2023.

———. *IGen: Why Today's Super-Connected Kids Are Growing up Less Rebellious, More Tolerant, Less Happy and Completely Unprepared for Adulthood: And What That Means for the Rest of Us*. New York: Atria Books, 2018.

Vaidhyanathan, Siva. *Antisocial Media: How Facebook Disconnects Us and Undermines Democracy*. New York: Oxford University Press, 2021.

Van Dixhoorn, Chad B., ed. *Creeds, Confessions, and Catechisms: A Reader's Ed*. Wheaton, IL: Crossway, 2022.

Vanhoozer, Kevin J., and Owen Strachan. *The Pastor as Public Theologian: Reclaiming a Lost Vision*. Grand Rapids: Baker Academic, 2015.

Warfield, Benjamin B. *The Religious Life of Theological Students*. Phillipsburg, NJ: P&R, 1983.

Warren, Rick. *The Purpose Driven Church: Growth Without Compromising Your Message and Mission*. Grand Rapids: Zondervan, 1995.

Watson, Thomas. *The Godly Man's Picture*. Puritan Paperbacks. Edinburgh: Banner of Truth, 1992.

Wells, David F. *God in the Wasteland: The Reality of Truth in a World of Fading Dreams*. Grand Rapids: Eerdmans, 1994.

———. *God in the Whirlwind: How the Holy-Love of God Reorients Our World*. Wheaton, IL: Crossway, 2014.

———. *The Courage to Be Protestant: Reformation Faith in Today's World*. 2nd ed. Grand Rapids: Eerdmans, 2017.

———. *Losing Our Virtue: Why the Church Must Recover Its Moral Vision*. Grand Rapids: Eerdmans, 1998.

———. *No Place for Truth, or, Whatever Happened to Evangelical Theology?* Grand Rapids: Eerdmans, 1993.

Wilson, Todd A., and Gerald Hiestand, eds. *Becoming a Pastor Theologian: New Possibilities for Church Leadership*. Downers Grove, IL: InterVarsity, 2016.

Witmer, Timothy Z. *The Shepherd Leader: Achieving Effective Shepherding in Your Church*. Phillipsburg, NJ: P&R, 2010.

Index

Adam, 49–50
adversity, 37–38
agriculture, 170
Allen, Lewis, 113
already and not yet concept, 156
Amish, 173–74
Ananias, 185
antichrists, 161
apostles, 78
Arand, Charles, 84–85, 86
artificial intelligence (AI), 54–56, 180
Athens, 14
Atsinger, Ed, 7
Augustine of Hippo, 9–10, 92–94, 109
Augustinian tradition, 9–10

Bavinck, Herman, 21, 48, 69–70
Baxter, Richard, xvii, 9, 67–68, 122, 123, 138, 139
Beeke, Joel, 7–8
Belgic Confession of Faith, 26–27, 32, 70
Billy Graham Rule, 135
Bon Jovi, 70–71
Bowler, Kate, 141–42
Brakel, Wilhelmus à, 65–66
Bridges, Charles, xvii, 62, 63–64
Broadus, John, 192
Brooks, Thomas, 9
Bullinger, Henry, 26
Bunyan, John, 99–103, 143
busy evangelicalism, 66

calling, xviii–xx, 38–45, 190

Calvin, John
  on eternity, 157
  on the gospel, 1
  on the Holy Spirit, 29–30
  on image of God, 49n2
  Institutes of the Christian Religion of, 82, 131
  on prayer, 91, 92, 99
  on preaching, 112–13, 163–64
  on self-denial, 6–7, 131–32
  on suffering, 148
Canons of Dort, 116–17
Carr, Nicholas, 171
Chapell, Bryan, 110n7
Christians/Christianity
  Americanization of, 142
  characteristics of, 8, 176, 188
  as children of God, 144–45
  defined, 117
  as fellow heirs with Christ, 145–46
  freedom of, 144
  self-denial of, 188
  as Spirit-led, 144
  suffering as condition of, 146–47
  as text-driven religion, 23
Christless Christianity, 33–34
church
  as a-theological, 83–84
  as beloved of God, 66–67
  as called out, 64, 69
  characteristics of, 69, 176
  as community, 136
  confessional, 84
  courage in, 179
  defined, 63–64, 65n4

205

Index

church (continued)
  description of, 65
  devotion in, 171–72
  disappearance of theology in, 76–77
  discipline in, 69–74, 167–68
  feeding of, 68
  gospel in, 33–34, 36–37
  health of, 71–72, 73
  holiness of, 69–70, 72, 73
  Holy Spirit's role in, 30
  hospitality of, 162
  hostility toward, 179
  as light, 176
  love of, 161–62
  mission creep and, 63
  mission of, 63–67
  negative world and, 60
  pastor as member of, 136
  pastor's love for, 74
  as people of God, 64–66
  as pillar and buttress of truth, 179
  posture of, 160
  prayer for, 102, 161
  protection of, 68–70
  radiance of, 73
  resolution regarding, 62–63
  servant-leadership in, 68, 162
  shepherding of, 67–74
  as sign of grace, 63
  slowness in, 171
  sober-mindedness of, 161
  training in glory of preaching in, 120–21
  worship as goal of, 11
  worth of, 67–68
clergy/pastorate
  as ambassadors, 34
  as calling, xviii–xx
  calling of, xviii–xx, 38–45, 190
  characteristics of, 119
  character of, 80
  commission of, 176
  courage for, 178–81
  duties of, 195–96
  eccentricity of, 176
  before the face of God, 1–3
  failures of, 124, 138
  glory of, xvii–xx
  as God's envoy, 113
  as God's instrument, 123
  as "incarnational," 57
  influences to, xvi
  marginalization of, 180
  Minister's Prayer of, 197–98
  mortification of, 127–37
  public opinion of, xviii, 105
  reformation of, xvii
  reward for, 168
  sanctification of, 29, 125–26
  significance of, xv
  trellis work of, 97
  as in the wasteland, 178–79
Clowney, Edmund, 62–63
community, staying in, 136
Confessions (Augustine), 92, 93–94
conversion, preaching for, 116–19
Copeland, Kenneth, 141
coram Deo (before the face of God), 1–3, 5–8, 9–16, 17
Council of Nicaea, 69
courage, for pastoring, 90, 178–81
Cowper, William, 13
creation, 57–61, 184
crisis of identity, 41
cross of Jesus, 136, 186. *See also* Jesus

daily addiction, 172
Davies, Dave, 96–98
Dawn, Marva, 14
death, 134
definitive sanctification, 125. *See also* sanctification
dependence, ministry as, 193–94
Dever, Mark, 71–72
devil, 3, 134, 157, 183–84
devotion, 171–72
discipleship, 119–20, 131–32, 148
discipline, 70–74, 167–68
doctrine
  Apostolic center of, 78–82
  courage to be Protestant and, 90
  delighting in dogma and, 82–86
  disappearance of theology and, 76–77
  as healthy/sound, 80
  map metaphor regarding, 84–85

Index

Reformation faith and, 86–90
resolution regarding, 75
Dollar, Creflo, 141
Driscoll, Mark, 4
Dunn, James, 186

eccentricity, 174, 176
Edwards, Jonathan, 115
Edwards, William, 43
effectual call, 39–40
elders, 79–81
eloquent nonsense, 109
Epaphroditus, 186–87
Ephesian church, 79, xviii
eschatology, 155–56
eternal destruction, 130–31
eternity
  anticipation for, 160
  church discipline and, 167–68
  eschatological concept of the Bible
    and, 157–63
  eschatology and, 155–56
  future glory in, 168
  hope in, 159–60
  ignorance of, 157
  living in the light of the end and,
    159–63
  Lord's Supper and, 166–67
  pastoring in light of, 163–68
  pastor's crown and, 168
  preaching in light of, 163–65
  resolution regarding, 155–56
  suffering and, 165–66
evangelicalism, 66, 87
Eve, 49
evil, as sanctification enemy, 126–27
exaltation, 147–48

faith, 89, 92, 180–81
faithfulness, 160, 164, 168
the fall, 54, 184
farmers, slowness of, 170
Feinberg, John, 23, 27
Feinberg, Paul, 20
flattery, 4–5
flesh, 3, 134–35
Frame, John, 21, 22–23, 24, 51
freedom, 144

future glory, 168

gender, 51–52
George, Timothy, 5–6
God
  anger of, 11
  Augustine and, 92–94
  as calling to himself, 39
  centrality of, 14
  corporate culture of, 7–8
  dependence on, 95, 193–94
  devotion to, 6
  displacement of, 33
  excellency of, 137
  faithfulness of, 115
  genius of, 114
  glory of, 11–12, 113–16
  holiness of, 115
  judgment of, 15–16, 151, 163–64
  justice of, 115
  as living *coram Deo*, 10–15
  missionary zeal of, 117–18
  pastoring before the face of, 1–3
  power of, 114
  rebellion against, 54
  relationship with, 54–56
  sovereignty of, 115
  spirit from, 5
  submission to, 102–3
  as sufficient, 23–25
  as taking lightly, 3–5
  will of, 102–3
  wisdom of, 115
  wrath of, 128
God-centered life, 7–8, 10, 11, 12–13
godliness
  battling until life ends for, 132–33
  deceitfulness of sin and, 133–34
  dependence on the Holy Spirit in,
    137
  eternal destruction warning and,
    130–31
  excellency of God and, 137
  looking to the cross in, 136
  making no provision for the flesh in,
    134–35
  mortification of the pastor in,
    127–37

Index

godliness (continued)
  practicing self-denial and, 131–32
  resolution regarding, 122–24
  sanctification of the pastor and, 125–26
  sanctification's great enemy in, 126–27
  spiritual sword in, 135
  staying in community in, 136
  surprise attacks in, 133
  taking heed in, 138–39
  universal obedience and, 129–30
  victories in, 133
  See also holiness
"God Moves in a Mysterious Way" (Cowper), 13
Godward leadership, 16–18
Gordon, David, 170
gospel
  centrality of, 35, 36–37
  as for Christians, 34–37
  decline of, in the church, 33–34
  defined, 32
  as marginalized, 35
  necessity of, 34
  for pastors, 37–45
  prosperity, 105, 141–43, 148, 149–51, 154
  resolution regarding, 32–33
  as setting agenda for pastoral ministry, 43–44
grace, 29, 89, 134, 135–36
Graham, Billy, 135
gratitude, 58–61
groaning, 146–47
Grudem, Wayne, 23, 39, 49, 65n4
Gurnall, William, 9
Guthrie, William, 9

Habakkuk, 137
Hagee, John, 141
Hagen, Kenneth, 141
Haidt, Jonathan, 71
Harris, Murray, 148
Harvey, Dave, 39
healing, 165–66
heaven, 128
Heidelberg Catechism, 8, 35–36, 167

hell, 128
Hendriksen, William, 95
Hodge, Charles, 20, 21, 49n2, 149
Hoekema, Anthony, 46, 50–51
Holifield, E. Brooks, xv
holiness, 69–70, 115. *See also* godliness
"Holy Club," 139
Holy Spirit, 20–21, 29, 30, 101–2, 137, 144–45
homeless community, 46–47
hope, 159–60, 184–85
Horton, Michael, 32, 33–35, 84, 88, 125, 151, 155–56
hospitality, 162
Houser, Meghan, 56
humanity
  in age of AI, 54–56
  creation of, 48–50
  dominion of, 48–49
  gratitude and, 58–61
  in image of God, 48–57
  "incarnational" pastors for, 57
  modern self of, 51
  relational aspect of, 56
  relationship with God and, 54–56
  resolution regarding, 46–48
  as revelation of God, 48
  sexual differentiation of, 51, 58
  sin and, 53–54
  vision of, 47–48
  wonder of, 50, 57–61
humiliation, 147–48

identity crisis, 41
idolatry, 14
image of God
  confidence and consolation in, 60
  head and crown of entire creation and, 48–51
  "incarnational" pastors and, 57
  in Jesus, 50–51
  modern self and, 51–54
  overview of, 48
  relational aspect of, 54–56
  sin and, 50, 53–54
The Inn, 172–73
Institutes of Christian Religion (Calvin), 82, 131

Index

isolation, 56

Jakes, T. D., 141
James, 152, 160–61
Jesus
  baptism of, 55, 152
  calling and, 40
  Christians as fellow heirs with, 145–46
  on church discipline, 167
  crucifixion of, 136, 186
  cup of, 152
  death of, 66
  on eternity, 157
  as example, 151
  freedom in, 144
  as fulfillment, 22
  glory of, 149
  on hell, 128
  image of God and, 50–51
  incarnation of, 55–56, 95, 106–7
  ministry of, 95, 107, 118, 152
  prayer and, 94–99, 100, 103
  preaching and, 106–8
  proclamation of, 190–92
  sacrifice of, 151, 166–67
  on sanctification, 125
  as Savior, 34
  on servant-leadership, 152–53
  sola Christus (Christ alone) and, 89–90
  suffering of, 147–48, 149, 185–86
  on temptation, 133
  victory of, 136
Job, 137
John (apostle), 152, 179
John the Baptist, 44
judgment, 15–16, 151, 163–64

Kelly, Kevin, 173
Kenyon, E. W., 150
Kuyper, Abraham, 21

Lakewood Church (Houston), 141
law, 126–27
Let the Nations Be Glad (Piper), 10–11
lion metaphor, 28

Lloyd-Jones, D. Martyn, xix–xx, 92–93, 98, 104, 105–6, 119, 181
The Loft, 4–5
London Baptist Confession, 19, 158–59
Lord's Supper, 56, 166–67
love, 161–62
Luther, Martin, 5–6, 25, 28, 35, 112, 178, 192–93

map metaphor, 84–85
marriage, 72–73
Marshall, Colin, 97
Martha, 43
Martin, Albert, 122n1
Master, Jonathan, 87–88
Mayyasi, Alex, 173–74
M'Cheyne, Robert Murray, 123
Methodism, 139
Meyer, Joyce, 141
Minister's Prayer, 197–98
ministry
  adequacy for, 42
  calling to, xviii–xx
  as dependence, 193–94
  gravity of, 103
  increase of Christ in, 44
  of Jesus, 95, 107, 118, 152
  as life, xviii–xix
  Paul's vision for, 183–94
  prayer as, 98–99
  as proclamation, 190–92
  as stewardship, 189–90
  as suffering, 185–86, 187–88
  theologically driven, 43
mission creep, 43, 63, 67
modern self, image of God and, 51–54
Moo, Douglas, 149
Morris, Leon, 149
mortification, 127–37
Mounce, William, 146, 147

Neuhaus, Richard John, 2n2
new birth, 125–26
Newport, Cal, 170
9Marks Ministries, 71–72

obedience, 129–30
Old Testament, 22. *See also* Scripture

Index

operational principle, 126–27
Oral Roberts University, 141
organic inspiration, 21
Osteen, Joel, 141
Owen, John, 127, 128, 129–31, 132–34, 137

Packer, J. I., 9, 65n4, 110–11, 125–26, 127
Parker, T. H. L., 112–13
pastoral epistles, 79–80
Paul
  on devotion, 172
  to Ephesian pastors, xviii
  on eternity, 157–58, 160
  on the gospel, 12, 36–37, 79
  on idolatry, 14–15
  ministry of, 183–94
  on obedience, 130
  preaching and, 106–8, 163–64
  as preeminent pastor-theologian, 78–82
  on sanctification, 125
  on Scripture, 24
  on sin, 128
  on stewardship, 189
  on suffering, 143–50, 187
Payne, Tony, 97
Pentecostalism, 142
personal holiness. *See* godliness; holiness
Peter, 16, 27, 56, 78, 157, 159–60, 161, 162, 168, 179
Pharisees, 100
Philippian church, 186–87
Pietism, 138
pilgrim pastors, 151–53
The Pilgrim's Progress (Bunyan), 83, 99, 143, 149–50, 154
Piper, John, 10–11, 37–38, 115–16, 140
plagiarism, 180
Plantinga, Cornelius, Jr., 71
plenary inspiration, 22–23
positive confession theology, 150
Post-It Note metaphor, 114
Postman, Neil, 173
postmodernism, 84
praise, 4–5

prayer
  as affectionate, 101
  of Augustine of Hippo, 92–94
  characteristics of, 100
  cry for help in, 103
  faith and, 92
  as for the good of the church, 102
  Holy Spirit in, 101–2
  of Jesus, 94–99
  as mark of the church, 161
  as ministry, 98–99
  necessity of, 91, 95–96
  process of, 92–93
  resolution regarding, 91–92
  Scripture as content of, 102
  as sensible, 100
  sincerity in, 100
  sober-mindedness in, 161
  as submitting to will of God, 102–3
  toward a definition of, 99–103
  as Trinitarian, 99–100
preaching
  centrality of, 104
  for conversions, 116–19
  for discipleship, 119–20
  as displaying glories of God, 113–16
  as eloquent nonsense, 109
  expository, 110
  glory of what it does, 113–20
  glory of what it is, 109–13
  God-centered, 114
  importance of, 163
  Jesus and, 106–8
  in light of eternity, 163–65
  missionary heart of God in, 118–19
  as monologue from Heaven, 111–13
  Paul and, 106–8
  Post-It Note metaphor regarding, 114
  priority of, 105–8
  as proclaiming, 190–92
  resolution regarding, 104
  sanctification and, 120
  training churches in glory of, 120–21
Price, Frederick, 141
pride, 183–84
principle, 126–27
proclamation, ministry as, 190–92

Index

progressive sanctification, 120
prosperity gospel, 105, 141–43, 148, 149–51, 154. *See also* gospel
protection, of the church, 68–70
Protestant, courage to be, 90
Puritans, 9, 138

reconciliation, 185
Reformation theology, 5–8, 86–90
regeneration, 125–26
Renn, Aaron, 60
resolutions, defined, xx. *See also specific topics*
retirement, 41
Rhema Bible Training Center, 141
Roberts, Oral, 141
Robinson, Haddon, 110
Roman Christians, 36
Ryle, J. C., 17

Salem Media Group, 7
salvation, 34, 39–40
sanctification, 29, 120, 125–27
Satan, 3, 134, 157, 183–84
Scripture
    apostles' understanding of, 78
    centrality of, 28
    as content of prayer, 102
    doctrine of inspiration and, 20–23
    eschatological concept of, 157–63
    feeding on, 68
    God-centeredness of, 14
    historic sufficiency of, 25–27
    increase from, 28–29
    as infallible, 21
    map for reading of, 84–85
    Old Testament as, 22
    organic inspiration of, 21
    pastoral epistles in, 79–80
    pastoring according to sufficiency of, 19–20
    as plenary inspiration, 22–23
    power of, 28
    preaching as exposition of, 110
    shepherding in sufficient word of, 27–31
    sola Scriptura (Scripture alone) and, 89
    as spiritual sword, 135
    in spiritual warfare, 117
    sufficiency of, 23–31
    verbal character of, 23
Scruton, Roger, xvin3
second coming of Christ, 155, 160. *See also* eschatology; eternity
Second Helvetic Confession, 195–96
secularization, 2, 53
self-denial, 131–32, 188
seminary training, on suffering, 153–54
servanthood, 152–53, 162
sexual revolution, 51–52, 58
sheep and, 67–74
shepherding/shepherd metaphor, 15, 27–31, 46–48, 68, 151
Shrier, Abigail, 71
Silva, Moisés, 146
sin
    battling against until life ends, 132–33, 145
    Billy Graham Rule regarding, 135
    deceitfulness of, 133–34
    as enemy, 3
    grace and, 135–36
    image of God and, 50
    mortification and, 127–28, 130
    in postmodern thinking, 53–54
    as sanctification enemy, 126–27
    spiritual sword against, 135
    surprise attacks of, 133
    victory against, 133
    vigilance against, 132–33
slavery, 152–53
slowness, 169–77
Smith, Christian, 71
sober-mindedness, 161
sola fide (faith alone), 89
sola gratia (grace alone), 89
sola Scriptura (Scripture alone), 89
soli Deo gloria (to the Glory of God Alone), 90
solus Christus (Christ alone), 89–90
Spener, Philip, 138
spiritual warfare, 117
Sproul, R. C., 65n4, 76
Spurgeon, Charles, 28, 38–39, 109–10, 124

stewardship, 162, 189–90
Stewart, James, 110n5
stick-bug, 175–76
Stott, John, 111n7
submission, 102–3
suffering
    as design of God, 147–50, 188–89
    eternity and, 165–66
    glory as meaning of, 147, 149
    groaning and, 146–47
    hope in, 187
    imagery regarding, 152
    implications for pastoral ministry and, 150–54
    ministry as, 185–86, 187–88
    as necessary condition, 146–47
    Pauline theology of, 143–50
    perseverance in, 165–66
    pilgrim pastors and, 151–53
    prosperity gospel and, 141–43
    prosperity pastors and, 150–51
    resolution regarding, 140–41
    rethinking seminary training regarding, 153–54

taking heed, 138–39
technological revolution, 54–56, 173
Theckston, Jerry, 3–4, 46–47, 61
theology, 76–77, 83–86, 87–88
thoughtfulness, 172
Timothy, 24, 79–80, 81, 139, 163–65, 172, 188

Titus, 79–80
tongue, 47
Treat, Casey, 140–41
Trinity, 55, 99–100. *See also specific persons*
Trueman, Carl, 33, 51–52, 60, 80–81, 85n14
truth, deceit *versus*, 134

ungodliness, 81
universal obedience, 129–30

van Mastricht, Petrus, 58–61

Warfield, Benjamin, 103
Watson, Thomas, 9, 91, 123–24
Wells, David, 1–2, 53, 71, 77, 78, 178
Wesley, Charles, 138–39
Wesley, John, 138–39
Westminster Confession of Faith, 27
Westminster Shorter Catechism, 126
Whitefield, George, 138–39
Witmer, Timothy, 68–69
Word of Faith Pentecostalism, 150
worship, 11
wrath, 128
Wynne, R. Carlton, 24–25, 29

Young, Julius, 141

Zacchaeus, 118

www.ingramcontent.com/pod-product-compliance
Lightning Source LLC
Chambersburg PA
CBHW062023220426
43662CB00010B/1442